green dragon, sombre warrior

green dragon, sombre warrior

A JOURNEY AROUND CHINA'S SYMBOLIC FRONTIERS

LIAM·D'ARCY BROWN

JOHN MURRAY
Albemarle Street, London

First published in 2003
by John Murray (Publishers) Ltd,
50 Albemarle Street, London W1S 4BD

The moral right of the author has been asserted

A catalogue record for this book is available from the British Library

ISBN 0–7195–6038 1

Typeset in 11.5 pt Bembo by Servis Filmsetting Ltd, Manchester

Printed and bound in Great Britain by
Butler & Tanner Ltd, Frome and London

To Alice Tyrrell of Dundalk

Contents

Illustrations

The illustrations opposite are examples of *wadang*, decorative eave-end tiles from the Western Han dynasty unearthed in Chang'an (present-day Xi'an). They portray the animals of the four cardinal compass points, from which the four sections of *Green Dragon, Sombre Warrior* take their names. The last, the Sombre Warrior, was depicted as a black tortoise – the prime example of the carapaced creatures symbolic of the north – in an embrace with a snake. Tortoises, as products of *yin*, were believed to be exclusively female, only able to reproduce by union with the *yang* serpent.

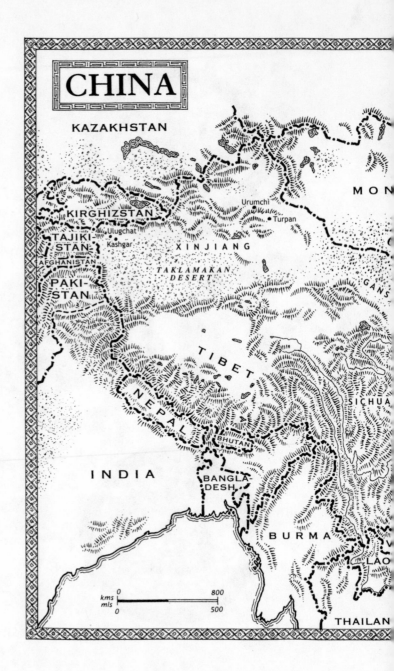

Prologue

IN THE CENTURIES before the despotic first emperor Qin Shihuang conquered the last of the Warring States and absorbed their territories into what we now think of as the Chinese nation, the Chinese mind conceived of a creation engendered by the interaction of two opposing principles, *yin* and *yang*. On their dichotomy was constructed a framework of opposites – female and male; dark and light; passive and active. Their modern written characters retain echoes of their earliest forms, depictions of the clouded, northern face and the sunlit, southern face of a hill. But just as the *yang* rays of the sun would occasionally warm the northern slopes of the northernmost hill, so the southern slopes of the southernmost would sometimes be veiled in cold, *yin* shadow. In the most extreme *yin* was seen to reside a germ of its polar opposite *yang*, and vice versa.

The ancient Chinese mind also divided the zodiac into twenty-eight lunar mansions and grouped these into four celestial quadrants, each with its symbolic animal – the Green Dragon of the East, the Scarlet Phoenix of the South, the White Tiger of the West and the Sombre Warrior or Black Tortoise of the North.

As each day began with the rising of the sun in the east, so each year began with the appearance above the eastern horizon of the first star of the mansion *jiao*, the Dragon's Horns. With the annual reappearance of *jiao* came the rebirth of trees. Thus the element of 'wood' governed the verdant season of spring and renewal. The south was intuitively associated with the heat of the sun and with 'fire', redness and summer. The civilized, Chinese dominions were ruled by 'earth', whose totemic yellow derived from the distinctive colour of central China's soil. The west, wherein the sun set each day, was the direction of death and misery. There, 'metal' – from which the Chinese of antiquity cast their spears and halberds – held sway, the white of the desert's gypsum and snowy mountain peaks its symbolic colour. Finally the north was the wintry seat of 'water', the rain-drenched realm of *yin* in its black opposition to the *yang* of the bright south.

These five – wood, fire, earth, metal and water – were elemental forces, manifesting themselves as they underwent their cycles of change, constantly in flux, both producing and conquering one another. Wood as it burned produced fire; fire produced earth in the form of ash; earth gave rise to metal ores; metal produced water in the form of the morning dew that gathered on polished divinatory mirrors; and water gave rise to wood in the form of sap. By producing its successor, each contributed to the turning of the seasons: wood ruled over spring and produced the fire which was to rule over summer, and so the cycle progressed. Conversely, trees were felled by metal axes; bronze was melted by the white heat of a foundry fire that in turn could be quenched by water; water was held back by earthen dams; and earth was displaced by the wooden plough or by the growing roots of trees. Their eternal cycle controlled the affairs of All under Heaven. Individuals were born and died by their ethereal machinations; political activity or passivity were divined by courtiers versed in their movements. Dynasties rose and fell in accordance with their mutual conquest.

The Five Elements Theory enabled the Chinese to categorize

and so explain the natural world. There were clearly five cardinal directions – including that of China in the centre – the five physical senses we still talk of, and five observable planets moving across the heavens. Other phenomena were to be less gracefully shoehorned into its five-fold divisions: each direction was allotted an emotion – anger, joy, yearning, sadness or fear – and there were argued to be five bodily organs, five varieties of edible grain and five kinds of animal life – scaly, feathered, naked, fur-covered and carapaced. Everything in creation could be linked to an element, a colour, a direction and so on. The theory was far from being a modern scientific methodology, and from the outset it had its detractors: earth would not always dam a river; and, if fire was meant to conquer metal, how was it that a bronze spade could be used to beat out a fire? Yet by the end of the first millennium AD, the five elements and their layers of correlation and portent had become a fundamental of Chinese thought. Only from the seventeenth century did the knowledge brought to China by the West slowly begin to undermine China's native natural sciences, and not until the twentieth century did the Mandate of Heaven by which dynasties ruled finally cease to apply. Since then the five elements have retreated into the nooks and crannies of popular imagination.

The early Chinese world covered just a fraction of the People's Republic. Spreading out from what are now the provinces of Shaanxi, Shanxi and Henan, it jutted north-east into the woods and grassland beyond what is now Beijing, extended westward into the Ordos – that great upward swing of the Yellow River through the loess plateau – eastward to the sea, and south to the pestilential forests of central China and the Yangtze. To its inhabitants, the distant peripheries of All under Heaven were possessed of an elemental clarity, tangible manifestations of *yin* and *yang* and of the five elements. Together they demonstrated a unity in multiplicity, a harmony in divergence.

Prologue

In the closing decades of the twentieth century, however, China let its impassive mask slip to reveal a rapidly changing nation. The strain of holding itself together could be seen on the face of what had until recently seemed to outsiders a textureless, monolithic state. Cracks had started to open up along economic, geographical and ethnic fault lines. Perhaps, I thought, taking the same frame of reference as the ancient Chinese themselves had taken, I would find in China's remote modern peripheries the same harmony in divergence, the same unity in multiplicity. Perhaps I might begin to reconcile China's seemingly irreconcilable extremes.

Spreading out a map of China, I began to circle four destinations at the very extremities of China's cardinal points, from a three o'clock starting-point off the bulge of her eastern coast right through to a Siberian midnight.

The first – the farthest dominion of the Green Dragon of the East – was a miniscule blue speck in the East China Sea. It had no name attached to it and was so insubstantial as to conceivably have been a printing error. A tiny wishbone of a headland – a forked cluster of pixels where Hainan Island grazed at the map's flowered border – marked the southern boundary of the Scarlet Phoenix's realm. The town of Ulugchat, a dot on the blue line of an unnamed river, lay closer to the mountain folds of Kirghizstan than to the nearest Chinese city, at the edge of the desert wastes where the White Tiger of the West held sway. And my ultimate destination, the point at which the sepia thread-vein of a road finally died out in the northernmost tip of Manchuria, was Mohe. Its name floated amidst an ocean of taiga, the northernmost sphere of the Sombre Warrior.

Green Dragon

'In the east there is a star, its season that of spring. Its vital force begets wood. In its season, the tasks for the ruler to decree are the regulation and cleaning of the shrines of the spirits and the attentive saying of prayers; the maintenance of dykes, fords and bridges, and the repair of irrigation channels and buildings.'

Guanzi or *The Writings of Master Guan*,
a collection of treatises dating from the
Warring States period

But for the unhurried mutation of north China's arid browns into the moist greens of the Yangtze delta, the scenery outside my railway carriage gave little indication of the passage of each day. From dawn to dusk the sun remained obscured by a featureless blanket of cloud, seeming to a casual observer hardly to vary in intensity or position and so offering little by way of a heavenly cue as to the hour. I was heading for the Zhoushan archipelago in the East China Sea.

In the absence of natural changes in our surroundings, time was marked with monastic regularity by the rasp of the attendants and by the purr of the lipsticked girl who flirted with passers-by from her cramped broadcasting room. The day dragged on, its middle reaches punctuated by the seamless intonation that welled up in the carriages of the Beijing-to-Shanghai slow train like distant plainsong. Each time, it would begin hesitantly: a diaphragmatic rumble that rose in assurance and pitch as it reverberated through the chest. Then the final knot of vowels would be barked out on a husky lungful of cheap smoke: *'Pijiubaijiukuangquanshuichayebabaozhoufangbianmianxiangchangrousongyuganlai'a!'* 'Beersorghumspiritmineralwaterteaeighttreasurericeporridgeconveniencenoodlesfragrantsausagedriedmeatflossdriedfish*comeandget'em!*'

Then, as dusk fell unexpectedly from a sky that still looked much the same as it had at noon, there came the chanting of vespers: *'Weishengzhiyashuayagaomianjintuoxielai'a!'* A roll of Moon Rabbit toilet paper, a toothbrush, a tube of snake's bile toothpaste, a face-cloth, a pair of slippers. Arms were stretched lazily into the gangway to signal a need for the items hawked from the trolley.

Compline began with a polite warning to take care nobody left the train with our luggage in the darkness, '. . . and we wish all our dear passengers *wan'an* – a peaceful night'. Presently the ceiling lights died, and the few who remained awake either took to the juddering gaps between the carriages to continue reading or else filed themselves away in their pigeonhole bunks. Then, throughout the night, the tick-tock of the tracks was broken only by the silences of anonymous station halts.

At seven sharp an artificial chorus of birds twittered matins through what proved to be a resolutely tamperproof speaker by my head, and by nine the train was pulling alongside the platform at Suzhou.

The city, I soon discovered, was busily being demolished and rebuilt. Bright red banners, strung taut across the streets, declared that the local Party chiefs intended to 'Beautify the tourist environment!' and 'Cordially welcome guests from beyond the four seas!'

'*Jiu buqu, xin bulai!*' a wall slogan added in self-assured strokes – 'If the old doesn't go, the new won't come.' It was the political catchphrase of the moment, having struck a chord in China's rich coastal cities where the mindset was now one of dizzying reconstruction. In the days since my arrival in China I had seen and heard it repeated many times – in newspaper headlines, in advertising slogans, on the radio – but most notably from the pimp who had latched on to me outside Beijing railway station. I told him I was attached, and the phrase had sprung ready-made to his lips. England was a long way away, and *jiu buqu, xin bulai* . . .

'Forget your old girlfriend, we're entrepreneurs now! This is Miss Ling. Comrade Deng Xiaoping would have been proud of us!' I suspect the conservative Deng would have turned in his cinerary urn at the thought of Miss Ling's leather miniskirt, her near transparent blouse that barely hid two small breasts, and her age: she could not have been more than fourteen.

At one time Suzhou ranked amongst the largest cities on earth. From the dawn of the seventh century it spanned the

Grand Canal, that great artery along whose 1,000-mile length barges brought rice from the fertile plain of the Yangtze to the imperial capitals of the north. The houses that opened on to each and every street and waterway were for centuries built in the characteristic *jiangnan*, or 'south of the Yangtze', style of this region. The whitewashed plaster walls, the granite corbels and the jumble of black, lichen-encrusted tiles that shrugged off the East China rains would all have been as familiar to a traveller in the Tang dynasty as they were to a tourist in the 1980s. But in Suzhou's headlong tumble towards modernization, its ancient vernacular buildings had to make way for the new. As I walked, I watched them being eaten away courtyard by courtyard, street by street, neighbourhood by neighbourhood.

Locals called it *canshi* – nibbling away like a silkworm – and just as the plump silkworms were nibbling away at their mulberry leaves in countless factories across this flat, wet portion of southern Jiangsu, so soulless pastiches of its *jiangnan* style were slowly supplanting the city's rambling medieval streets. Most of the narrow roads of the crowded old centre, shaded by their avenues of planes, had been widened and improved. Trees had been felled, flagstones worn smooth by centuries of footfalls replaced by pink marble, slouching shacks torn down to make way for the spry uniformity demanded by ferro-concrete.

The replacements stood smartly to attention, a parade-ground of frontages straightening their shoulders for inspection. Regimented rows of extruded aluminium and plate glass had supplanted the clutter of shuttered shop-fronts. Only Suzhou's gardens, cultivated by the urbane scholar-officials who made the medieval city their home, were spared. They remained as islands surrounded by a heaving sea of construction work. Suzhou's newly affluent Chinese tourists do not come to the city to be reminded of the tumbledown houses in which they, their parents and generations of ancestors before them grew up. As for myself, I had seen the gardens years before, had tried despite the crowds to appreciate the extravagant soaring of their eaves, had glimpsed through forests of torsos the painstakingly engineered distillations of China's mountain wilderness. My reason now for stopping at Suzhou on my way east lay not here but a few miles west, close by the Grand Canal.

During the reign of Emperor Xuanzong of the Tang, at the height of Suzhou's fame, a scholar named Zhang Ji passed through the city on his way back from the imperial examinations in the capital Chang'an. Overcome by the beauty of a bridge beside which he tied up his boat, and intoxicated by the sound of the bell from Hanshan Temple, Zhang Ji reached for his brush, paper, ink-block and grinding stone, and composed 'Mooring by Night at Maple Bridge'.

> The moon sets, crows caw and a frost pervades the air.
> I lie sleepless amongst the shadows of maples and the
>   glow of the fishing lamps.
> Outside Suzhou's city wall, the tolling of the midnight
>   bell reaches my boat from Cold Mountain Temple.

A handwritten scroll of the poem hung beside my bed in England, a souvenir of my first, brief visit to China, and each morning for close on a decade its blurred barcode of black ink on white silk had been the first thing I would see on waking. It was not the best poetry to be written under the highly cultured Tang dynasty, but I had grown fond of it and would often catch myself reciting it in a half-sleep. The temple's name evoked an image of serene, contemplative retreat that I had often longed for but had never found in the cut-throat bustle of modern China. A journey of at least ten thousand miles stretched out ahead of me. As we slid through Suzhou's corolla of industrial estates, I decided I would leave the train early to fulfil a small ambition.

The battered taxi I flagged down on People's Road crawled through an urban sprawl of coachworks and roadside restaurants before finally pulling up beside the mustard-coloured wall of a Buddhist temple. Behind it, the crowns of the courtyard pines swayed in a spring breeze, but there was no sign of a mountain-side temple shrouded in swirling mists. We were still in the suburbs.

The gateway to Hanshan Temple was set back somewhat from a branch of the Grand Canal. The alluvial plain on which Suzhou grew up is traversed by countless man-made branches watered by this main canal, and by the many tributaries of the nearby Yangtze. Some of these waterways are little more than irrigation channels for Jiangsu's patchwork of paddy and market gardens. Others are a dozen or more yards wide and stretch for tens of miles in elegant straight lines. This particular channel, on the small side at fifteen feet across, had once transported the rich produce of low-lying farmland that had since been subsumed by the city's post-war expansion. Now it served as both the mooring stage for a flotilla of rusty sightseeing boats and as the sewer for the tumbledown shacks of Maple Village on its opposite bank. The value the villagers attached to the canal's literary significance was all too apparent from the black water that moved sluggishly southwards, carrying with it a film of oil and a heavy cargo of household rubbish that gathered in its eddies: polystyrene packaging, discarded plastic drinks bottles, polythene carrier bags lively with brand names. Where the stream's original stone facing had been plundered for building material, the eroded earth of the banks had become a multicoloured refuse tip which tumbled down into the water in a mess of mouldering peelings, toilet paper and sludge.

Maple Bridge itself strained its back fastidiously skyward as if to keep as great a distance as it could between itself and its putrid neighbour. It was of typical *jiangnan* design: a graceful semi-circle arching high over the water to allow a junk to pass comfortably underneath. The day had turned out warm and clear, and Maple Bridge's close-fitting stones, of fine-grained granite from the hills to the west, sparkled in the sun. Reflected in the China ink surface below, its half moon became an effortlessly beautiful full circle. I bought a ticket and a guidebook and stepped over the vermilion doorsill into the first courtyard of the temple.

Inside the doorway a shaven-headed monk in saffron robes and white puttees was shovelling the collection from the offertory box into a cloth sack. 'Widely sow the fields of happiness' had been stencilled on its side. Small change clinked cheerfully – the chunky aluminium of 1 *jiao* coins with their grubby chrysanthemums mingling with the brassy plum blossoms of the 5 *jiao*. Then the monk replaced the wooden chest on its stool, locked the lid and shuffled away clutching the takings.

Japanese tour groups milled about as worshippers stood before a bronze incense-burner alive with coiling dragons. Feet planted firmly together, their heads bowed, arms bent upwards in supplication, they clutched bouquets of incense-sticks that gushed clouds of steel-blue smoke. Three rapid obeisances, a bending of arthritic waists, mumbled prayers rising on the perfume, and then the petitioners tossed the unburnt remainder into the flames where they were consumed to white ash.

At a signal from their guides' bright pennants the groups continued their tour. *En masse* each heaved across the courtyard's herringbone-tiled floor, a sea of yellow baseball caps momentarily swamping its bonsai pines and dwarf fruit trees before disappearing through a wooden doorway.

For a short while I had the smoke-filled space almost to myself, and I took my camera from my bag. The calm was broken by pop music spurting from a radio on the Fujifilm stand next to the censer. There a tracksuited girl sat, her chin resting on her left hand while her right abstractedly turned the dial in search of the next station. She watched me dispassionately as I tried to frame a shot of the main hall free from her white and green awning and her teetering pyramid of films. She found another station and turned the volume up.

'Ooh, baby, woke up and found you'd gone . . .'

An inner courtyard beyond was dominated at its far end by a further hall, scarlet-pillared and lined with statues of grimacing Buddhist disciples in glass cases – the skeletal Pindola, said to have lived in the west, surviving on stones for food; the aged Ashita the Invincible, his long eyebrows tumbling to the floor. Behind this hall rose the temple pagoda, five crimson storeys of ponderous timbers and weightless flying eaves. A portly Buddha sat facing me on his dais inside, convulsed with laughter. Devotees had offered him steamed buns and boiled sweets earlier in the day, and their propitiatory joss-sticks had trailed lines of ash across them. He didn't seem to mind.

The pagoda's airy structure filtered out the noise of the crowds below and, by the time I had shuffled to the top, the only sounds to reach me were the gentle sigh of the breeze in the pines and the insistent chug-chug of the two-strokes that powered the barges on the canal. Relishing the tranquillity of being fifteen yards away from the rest of China, I fished out my *Pocket Atlas of Jiangsu Province* and oriented myself to my sur-roundings.

A range of low, jade-forested mountains in the west marked the shore of Lake Tai, a shallow expanse of fresh water bigger than Greater London. Invisible forty miles to the north of the pagoda, the Yangtze flowed eastward a hundred miles to meet the sea beyond the tip of Shanghai. Eighty miles to the south, the Qiantang River widened to become Hangzhou Bay. The broad triangle of land between the two great waterways lay spread out like a tablecloth to my north, east and south. Here the verticals were all artificial: construction-site cranes, factory chimneys and cooling towers, straggling pylons and files of poplars. Water-towers and apartment blocks receded into the haze of a darkening horizon, even the tallest of them dwarfed by the vast canopy of the sky, their miniscule presence serving only to accentuate the claustrophobic flatness of this alluvial landscape. One hundred and forty miles beyond lay my first destination.

The Grand Canal itself was hidden behind the vigorous spring growth on its banks. Zhang Ji would have recognized nothing beyond the shape of the crumpled hills in one quadrant and the unremitting featurelessness of the other three. Under the Tang Hanshan Temple had been isolated save for the canal, though the poet might have made out Suzhou's great, squat city walls in the distance. They have been bulldozed only within living memory. He would not, however, have recognized the fabric of the temple. The one he visited had first been consecrated under the Liang dynasty in the early sixth century. Destroyed at the bloody fall of the Mongol Yuan dynasty in the late fourteenth, it was quickly rebuilt under the first emperor of the conquering Ming. The temple as I now saw it did not even date from then but was a twentieth-century structure completed during the brief reign of Aisin Goro Puyi, Bertolucci's Last Emperor, after the Ming complex had accidentally been burned to the ground in 1859. This final incarnation had itself been restored after the violent excesses of the Cultural Revolution. The temple bell tolled languidly on cue.

The bell hung in its wooden campanile in a shaded precinct close by the pagoda. The single note I had heard had been struck not by a shaven-headed acolyte as I had fancied but by a Japanese tourist. His wife's turn came, and she swung the oak beam slung from a rafter above. Its face, distended outwards with use to the size and shape of an elephant's foot, struck the bronze rim and a long, low note enveloped us. She was silent, held for a few seconds spellbound by the sound as it echoed and died, then with a broad grin she turned to her husband, who had videoed the ceremony, and began to chatter.

'Are you going to ring it?' asked a monk seated at a makeshift counter nearby. I shook my head.

'It's very quiet today. You'd be better off coming at New Year,' he continued. In their New Year ceremony, Buddhists strike a bell one hundred and eight times, in the belief that each note dispels a portion of the old year's torment from each of the believers who hears it and so gives them a fresh start in the coming year. 'There are lots more people then – really crowded it gets. Lots of locals from Suzhou, and lots of tourists.' He glanced at the two Japanese who were still discussing the video camera and gesticulating at the oak beam. A mercenary smile flickered over his plump face.

'And reporters!' he enthused, holding his own imaginary camera to his eye. 'They show it on television!'

I asked my taxi driver whether he had ever been to the temple at New Year.

'Me?' He shook one hand in front of him and laughed. 'I don't believe in Buddhism. My wife does, though. She normally prays in the local temple, but she's been to Hanshan at New Year a few times with her mother. They started doing all those cere-monies in the seventies, after Mao died, and her old mother relishes going.'

'In the seventies? I thought they'd held the ceremony there for centuries.'

My driver puffed his cheeks out and shrugged. 'Maybe, before Liberation, who knows? The monks there are rich,' he said, rubbing his thumb against his forefingers. 'Japanese Zen Buddhists – now, *they've* got money to burn. They come to see the temple because of that legend, the one about the two monks. One of them sailed to Japan to found a temple there. Have you heard it?' I hadn't, and he didn't know enough to relate it to me. 'That's why, when the Japanese departed after the War of Resistance, they stole the bell and took it back to Japan with them.'

'You mean the one in the bell tower isn't the original?'

'No. I suppose the monks replaced the one that got stolen with some other bell. I'll ask my wife.'

I slumped back in my seat. I had interrupted my journey to see a reconstructed temple with a newly cast bell that an affluent band of monks tolled to welcome the New Year in a ceremony dating from at least the seventies. I resolved to press on to Shanghai and the sea the next day.

The concierge assigned to my landing at the hotel had been a schoolchild in Suzhou and knew the legend of the two monks in full. As we walked the length of the corridor, depositing fresh Thermos flasks of boiled water in each of the occupied rooms, she began to recount it.

'Now, Han Shan — the monk the temple's named after — originally lived in the north. He had a wife and a young apprentice named Shi De. He treated Shi De like a son, as he had no son of his own.

'I've opened this door for you — change the used glasses and give them a full flask and new teabags.' The couple in the room were both asleep fully clothed on their beds and never knew that the Westerner whom they had commented on at reception was also their chambermaid.

'One morning, Han Shan set out for the city, but after a while realized he had left his bag of cash at home and turned back. When he reached his house, he peered in through a window and saw Shi De and his wife in bed together asleep. What he didn't know was that his wife had put an extra quilt on Shi De's bed while he slept, as it was a cold day. Seeing how cosy he was, she had climbed in too and had dozed off. You swap the water in number 233; I'll do next door . . .

'So, Han Shan assumed that his wife and Shi De were lovers, and rather than confront them he ran away, leaving his wife a note in which he told her that his heart was broken. When they awoke, the two discovered what had happened and Shi De set out to look for Han Shan. Years passed. At last Shi De turned up late at night and in a rainstorm at the temple at Maple Bridge.

He banged on the door and begged to be let in. The gate was opened by Han Shan. He too had travelled as an itinerant before discovering that the life of a monk suited him. He scolded Shi De for having left his wife alone back home, and in return Shi De scolded Han Shan for having jumped to such an unfair conclusion, but the truth soon came out.' We stopped outside the door to my room.

'The two grew fond of each other again, and then one year there was a terrible storm that caused Lake Tai to overflow and flood the whole area. A big bronze bell floated up against the gates. Han Shan told the monks to lift it inside but it refused to leave the water. The monks said Buddha must have sent the bell, because despite the rain it was dry inside. Shi De climbed into the bell to take a closer look, but immediately it set off across the water with him still inside. It didn't stop until it reached Japan, where Shi De founded a Buddhist temple.

'Han Shan pined for his friend, and every day he stood calling for him. The monks couldn't bear to see this and had a craftsman cast a bell exactly like the one in which Shi De had been carried away. Every day Han Shan tolled it, and eventually the sound reached Japan. Shi De heard it and tolled his bell in response. The sound travelled back to Suzhou. Even though they were apart, each knew the other was well.'

'So the bell the monks cast is the same bell that Zhang Ji heard, and the same one the Japanese stole?'

'The legend of the monks is just a story,' she said, looking at me in mild surprise, 'but the Japanese bandits did steal the temple bell, this I learned at school.'

I picked up a fresh Thermos and swapped it for the one in my own room. 'You should pay me for doing your job for you,' I joked.

'Storytelling has to pay better than changing the flasks in this dump. I reckon you owe me.'

PUDONG

IT WOULD HAVE been hard to choose four more wildly varying places within China had I sat down with that intention.

The first, Shengshan, was an island barely two miles long in the rich fishing grounds of the East China Sea, 120 miles' sailing from boomtown Shanghai. The easternmost point along China's sweeping belly, it was not, however, the most easterly point of all China: visiting this would have meant travelling to the intriguingly named Black Blind Man's Island that faces the Siberian city of Khabarovsk across the Amur River, accessible from the nearest hamlet on the Chinese side only by tackling twenty miles of impassable swamp. A dotted line encompassing the island on one map I studied indicated that it was disputed territory. Since my ultimate northern destination was Mohe, upriver from Black Blind Man's Island, I would gain little by risking a lonely death in a remote Manchurian bog of uncertain sovereignty. Besides, the lower Amur, like Mohe, lay for the ancient Chinese well within the northern realm of the Sombre Warrior, despite now being at the eastern cusp of the nation.

My southerly destination of Jinmujiao, or Brocaded Mother's Point, was a headland on the tropical island of Hainan. Hainan has a land area a little larger than that of Belgium, but a claim on the seas to its south has resulted in the anomaly that Hainan is, at roughly twice the size of Egypt, technically the largest province of the People's Republic. The official line from Beijing is that the reefs and islets (not forgetting the oilfields) to its south have since the Han dynasty come under Chinese sovereignty. Its cartographers have therefore sketched in a 200-mile exclusive economic zone around each, thereby claiming that practically the whole of the South China Sea belongs to China. With remarkable serendipity recent government-sponsored archaeological digs have also turned up evidence that Chinese fishermen have inhabited the largest of the 260 islets of the Pratas Reefs, the Paracels and the Spratly Islands since the Ming dynasty. In recent years, disagreements with the other nations bordering them – Taiwan, the Philippines, Malaysia, Brunei and Vietnam – have led to little-publicized military clashes, the most violent occurring in 1988 when China sank three Vietnamese ships and drowned seventy-two sailors. A short boat ride from the coast of Malaysia and just four degrees above the Equator, the Zengmu Shoals would, if China's territorial claim were accepted, be her southernmost point, but the headland at Jinmujiao is indisputably so.

Ulugchat is the westernmost town in China, deep inside the Kizilsu Kirghiz Autonomous Prefecture in the restive Islamic province of Xinjiang. Before leaving England, I had decided that Ulugchat would mark my western terminus. My other three destinations were neatly defined on paper: each was where land met water. However, reaching that final intangible watershed where western China ended and Tajikistan began would add nothing to my understanding of the region. I would leave the last fifty mountainous miles beyond the town to their hardy goats and shivering border patrols.

Finally, I would follow the road that traces a lonely path through the larch forests of northern Heilongjiang to the riverside village of Mohe. There, across the mighty Amur River, lies the Russian settlement of Ignashino and beyond that the blank expanse of Siberia.

Next morning the express train from Suzhou devoured the flat miles to Shanghai. I sat with my head lolling against the glass, now and again lifting the border of the lace curtains to look at the passing countryside and to put a barrier between myself and the garrulous occupants of the carriage.

At close quarters, the indistinct pall I had seen spread out beyond the pagoda of Hanshan Temple resolved itself into a dense parquetry of cultivation: yellow rectangles of rape, squares of purple beans, dark swathes of cabbage and Chinese broccoli. Emerald patchwork quilts of rice paddy had been stitched together with the white blooms of onion and the purple threads of ginger. It was a landscape shaped by water. From the railway line there seemed to be barely a single road, all life and commerce relying for transport on a capillary matting of canals and irrigation ducts. The farmers paddled themselves in untidy coracles to and fro between their monochrome canalside houses and their waterbound fields, and three-plank sampans were moored by reedbeds or on artificial fishponds dotted with snow flurries of duck and geese.

Signs of prosperity were everywhere in Shanghai's fertile market garden, from the flotsam of plastic Sprite bottles on the ponds, each one marking the position of a pearl oyster creel, to the drifts of cash-crop polytunnels and the blue glass in the windows of the richer farmers' houses.

We passed close by an isolated hill named Horse Saddle Mountain. Its steep slopes were pleasantly wooded in cool contrast to our ocean of shadeless farmland. For tens of thousands of years, while the Yangtze worked silently to entrap it in a matrix of silt, it had been the last isolated peak of the mountains west of Suzhou, floating in the vast estuary of a prehistoric river. It was the only natural feature to break the horizontal monotony of the journey, and it held my attention from the moment I caught sight of it until the point came when I could press my face no further into the glass and watched it slide behind the tail of the last carriage. Stranded like a beached ship it possessed the same magical attraction as Glastonbury Tor seen from the Somerset Levels. I longed to explore it but instead I found myself being tapped on the shoulder and obliged to answer the usual litany of well-meaning questions. Where was I from? How much did I earn? *That* much? No, we're *not* all rich. *Really*, it's simply not enough to live on in London. No, some people *do* sleep on the streets. As usual, I might as well have been speaking to myself for all I managed to unburden anybody of a single misconception.

I awoke early the next morning and squeezed out through a window on to the rooftop. The men's dormitory of the Pujiang Hotel had an enviable view, looking out over the tricolour flying from Shanghai's Russian Consulate and beyond it to the curve of the Bund. The warm spring weather of the past few days had been replaced overnight by a front of beaten pewter. Leaning against the low granite wall, I decided to endure the drizzle rather than miss the dawn as it slowly unmasked the city. The banks and hotels on the waterfront hunched their massive shoulders against the damp and leaned into each other for warmth. Most were now well into their seventies and they showed their age in the cold half-light, their façades all ragged canvas awnings and rusted fittings that had been cosmetically concealed by the previous night's spotlighting. They seemed like so many elderly dowagers who had sparkled at the ball but who now awoke bleary-eyed, their foundation smudged and cracked. Later that same morning, at the ferry terminal at their feet, I joined eight other passengers on a coach headed for a wharf that lies on the tip of the Shanghai peninsula.

As the immense wedge of land between the Yangtze in the north and Hangzhou Bay in the south tapers to a point, it becomes known as Shanghai. On maps it resembles a rosebud, cupped between the protective calyxes of Jiangsu and Zhejiang. Its main river is the Huangpu which flows into the Yangtze twelve miles from its famous riverfront, the Bund. On the opposite bank lies the new district of Pudong, and beyond this Nanhui County merges into the mud of the East China Sea.

When Shanghai expanded after the arrival of the British in the nineteenth century, the great breadth of the Huangpu to its east forced it to do so to its west, while the land across the river in Pudong remained almost entirely agricultural save for a smattering of factories, warehouses and wharves associated with its riparian fringe of docks. Imagine a London that had expanded north of the Thames only, Southwark and Lambeth remaining as undeveloped fields and villages, or a New York that had failed to bridge the East River into Brooklyn and Queens, and you have an idea of the vacuum that existed within a few hundred yards of downtown Shanghai only two decades ago.

In 1990, however, things changed. Historically, the Yangtze had been likened to the arrow in the bow of China's coastline, with Shanghai as its arrowhead. Now, benefiting from a sweeping away of the state monopoly on land and an array of tax breaks and investment perks, Pudong became the tip of that arrow, pointing out across the Pacific to its rivals Japan and America. When China's paramount leader Deng Xiaoping gave the Pudong policies his personal and invaluable blessing by visiting the area two years later, he saw what had been achieved and regretted not having loosened the reins a decade earlier.

After the failure of the Great Leap Forward, the famines it brought about, and the decade of insanity that had preceded Mao's death, the Party followed comrade Deng to the library, dusted off Marx and Engels, and came to the consensus that the prime task of socialism was to create wealth for the people. Deng's maxim, that 'it doesn't matter whether a cat is black or white so long as it catches mice', summed up the Party's position over Pudong: the steel and glass of China's Manhattan were a staging-post on the road to true socialism, not a destination in themselves.

'*Wo jide, wo xiao de shihou zheli quanbu dou shi tian!*' His face was heavily scarred by some skin disorder, his red, pockmarked ears covered in small blood-specked squares of white sticking-plaster. Each was raised slightly in its centre, where a steel ball sat hard against an acupuncture point. Though he could not have been more than forty, he was not exaggerating. Pudong had shot up almost overnight, as its raw ugliness testified. The road skirted the New York skyline of the Lujiazui Financial and Trade Zone and ran straight through a history-book hotchpotch of Qing dynasty fields, pre-revolution villages, communist-era factories, post-reform light industry and brand-new housing estates. The mute concrete corpses of failed speculative ventures stood out amongst the bustle. Their construction had been halted at varying stages when it had become clear that they would remain untenanted and the banks had withdrawn funding. They squatted in embarrassment behind makeshift walls in their plots of bare earth and weeds, rust-stained and streaked with rain, any glass that had not cracked now looted, and with mouldy patches where their tiles had worked loose and fallen off. Here and there, migrants, who might otherwise be homeless, were visible in shanty towns of salvaged brick.

A tinny rendition of 'Jingle Bells' made me turn round. One of the women on the bus – middle-aged, heavily made-up and with dangling gold earrings – answered her mobile phone and launched into a conversation on a forthcoming trip to London that lasted until we arrived at the wharf. Her half of the dialogue was unselfconsciously peppered with the names of expensive hotels and details of visa arrangements.

Our tyres hissed on the wet road. Bridges crossed canals, each one momentarily revealing a vista that stretched like a silver ribbon between stone-lined banks to an indefinite horizon, before the impatient press of buildings on the opposite bank ushered us on. Small, isolated remnants of agricultural land had survived. They lay clamped between horizontals of grey cement and verticals of red brick. Some were green with ripening crops, a sign that some residents were still tending and harvesting what remained of their fields. Only the rapeseed refused to be cowed. It poked its yellow flowerheads through the rubble-strewn patches of soil on the verges and forecourts and in the untrodden corners of petrol stations and workshops that had escaped the attentions of the excavator's bucket. To the rapeseed at least, this was still all fields.

Urbanized Pudong thinned out and we passed into Nanhui County. The eight-lane highway that had been built to open up the peninsula's far villages now became a modest four-lane road that traversed fields of rice and rape. The land was imperceptibly dipping to the sea, and the banks of the drainage ditches were now barely a foot above the water they held.

Just as in the countryside I had seen from the Suzhou–Shanghai train, the farmers here had become wealthy overnight as their land had become desirable and they had splashed out on brash extravaganzas in colourful tiles and stucco, the result of having a hefty sample book from the local builders' merchant, too much disposable income and no experience of aesthetic restraint. For a full hour, and for as far as I could see through the rain-streaked glass, we lumbered past a garish funfair of buildings: Georgian balconies, classical porticoes, Tudor half-timbering, a pink-tiled garage topped with a weatherboarded New England church spire, a Greek pediment in plaster perched on a line of Corinthian columns, here a row of medieval battlements, there a set of immobile red windmill vanes. Everywhere the tawdry details of rural Chinese conspicuous consumption. The lexicon was European, with a comical disregard for period or provenance, but the execution was gaudily Asian.

'Yes, we'll be flying into Heathrow . . . Okay, book me a room . . . No, £200 isn't too much . . .'

Surrounding the farmers' nightmarish palaces and Barbie doll mansions was the same detritus of boomtown China that I had seen lapping the canal bank in Suzhou. The oily ditches and piles of rubble, the rotting garbage and sewage outfalls were identical. After two hours of this cultural dissonance, Nanhui County in its natural state of brackish reedbeds and water meadows re-asserted itself for a bare third of a mile before a final flourish of poplars marked the very fringe of coastal East China and the land melted into the Yangtze estuary. A sign in English welcomed us to Luchaogang Pass—g-r -erry W-arf. The tide was out, leaving a stretch of flat mud that we crossed on a barnacle-encrusted pier to reach deeper water. A school of fishing junks had been beached at anchor and had settled into the brown sludge. Muddy water pooled around them and ran away in brown rivulets. The rake of the shore was so shallow that it was hard to distinguish the mud from the sea.

Our coach stopped at the end of the pier and I got off with the other passengers. We caught each other's eyes and began to giggle nervously. We had been abandoned half a mile from land, and save for a bobbing seagull we were the only signs of life between the fingers of trees marking the water margin to our west and the slate horizon to the east. It was still drizzling. A collection of brick huts housed the toilets – designated male and female, but needlessly so, since both emptied through the same hole straight into the sea – and a single room where a guard lived. Some wag had chalked 'Nightclub' on his door.

'We're at Luchaogang . . . *Luchaogang* . . . *Lu*, as in reeds . . . yes . . . *Chao*, as in tidewater . . . That's the place! We're going to Putuoshan, didn't I tell you?'

Presently, the man with the pock-marked ears squinted through the mist and pointed to a silvery dot in the distance. Shortly afterwards the *Free Flying*, a catamaran built in Western Australia that had seen better and sunnier days, hove to alongside the tyres that lined the pier.

ZHOUSHAN

I HAD PAID an extra few *renminbi* to make the three-hour crossing on the upper deck. As it turned out, this allowed me the privilege of looking down on the ochrous surface of the Yangtze estuary through eight feet of mist rather than three. The boat was nearly empty. TV screens on both decks played a mixture of action films and advertisements for hotels on the island of Putuoshan. They resembled the cheaper kind still to be found in rural cinemas in Britain – scratchy voiceovers and a succession of blurred Polaroids – and included all the must-have facilities for a successful Chinese vacation: restaurants, a disco, karaoke, lewd cabaret, more restaurants. Combined with mood shots of Buddhist temples and pilgrims, they made the island look like a downmarket cross between Holy Island and Havana. A well-dressed tout stalked the boat, handing out leaflets for his own hotel to a captive audience, and yellow sun-visors to those who agreed to check it out. I took a leaflet but declined the visor.

The catamaran's picture windows had not been cleaned since Perth, and we were nearly on top of the outlying islets of the Zhoushan archipelago before I spotted them. Silhouetted dark green against the pale sky, they floated on the choppy water of Grey Turtle Ocean, as that portion of the East China Sea is known. Their names reflected the poetic imagination with which the Chinese have always viewed their surroundings: Gourd Mountain, Cat Islet, Golden Embankment, Pierced Nose Island, Ant Island. One, Peng Mountain, took its name from a mythical bird mentioned by the ancient Daoist philosopher Zhuangzi. He told of how the *peng*'s back was countless thousands of *li* broad, how the water beneath its wings was stirred up for three thousand *li* all around when it rose into the air, and how it needed to soar to a height of ninety thousand *li* before it had enough sky beneath it to begin its six-month glide to the Southern Ocean. Local legend has it that here the *peng* finally landed, though a host of other island communities make the same claim.

The largest island of the archipelago is the eponymous Zhoushan, Boat Mountain, named after its supposedly junk-like outline. As the *Free Flying* rounded one of its southern headlands I could distinguish the wharves and cranes of Zhoushan City. Its harbour was being transformed into a major deep-water terminal, Zhoushan City having been designated an Economic Development Zone in 1992 under Deng's reforms. The irony of the local government's drive to attract foreign investment is that Zhoushan, or Chusan as it was then known, was for a short time another little patch of red on maps of the British Empire, and the Union Jack once flew from its peak. If history had been different it might have been Zhoushan and not Hong Kong which Britain returned to China in 1997 as an economic miracle. Instead, it was almost unknown to the outside world.

Zhoushan's near-complete obscurity – the keen gardener might know of it as the island which gave *Trachycarpus fortunei*, the Chusan palm, its English name – belies its importance in the early history of Sino-British relations. At twenty-eight miles long it is the fourth largest of China's islands. Its excellent natural anchorages, access to the ports of Ningbo and Shanghai, and its proximity to the Yangtze with all the promise of China's rich hinterland made it a natural stopping-off place for Britain's first official embassy to the Chinese court, undertaken in 1793 by George Macartney in search of commercial opportunities for British merchants.

In the collection of watercolours published after his return, the embassy's official artist William Alexander several times depicted Ting-hae, now Zhoushan City. To an eighteenth-century public fascinated by chinoiserie, Chusan became a colourful island of walled towns, temples and wooded hills, at a time when Hong Kong was still just a dull trading outpost in the Pearl River delta. And as servicemen who took part in the coming clashes with the Chinese returned to embellish and publish their experiences, Chusan entered the British imagination as the site of daring naval engagements and hand-to-hand skirmishes with pigtailed Chinese pirates and cowardly imperial soldiers.

Macartney thought Chusan so desirable from a commercial point of view that he asked for trading rights there when he arrived in Beijing for his imperial audience. He went away empty-handed – China at that stage viewed Britain as nothing more than yet another vassal nation petitioning to present tribute at the court of the Son of Heaven – but within half a century Chusan was to become intimately linked with the story of the Manchus' decline and British muscular colonialism.

When, in 1839, China's Commissioner of the Campaign against Opium seized and burned British merchants' stockpiles of the drug in Canton (now Guangzhou), the incident was eagerly seized by the British as the pretext to strong-arm China into acceding to long-standing demands for commercial treaties. After half-hearted Chinese attempts at blockading the British merchants in Canton into submission, the First Opium War broke out in January of 1840, and in June a British naval detachment sailed north from Canton's Pearl River to Chusan where it demanded that the local Mandarin surrender his island to the Crown. When he refused, the British pulverized Ting-hae's hastily constructed defences with their ships' batteries before landing without resistance from the thoroughly bewildered survivors. The occupation of Chusan was made good and the detachment sailed on to the mouth of the Peiho River near Tianjin, within carrot-and-stick negotiating distance of Beijing. What followed was characteristic of the remaining decades of the Qing: Chinese bureaucratic intransigence and a punch-drunk inability to recognize their predicament, and British frustration at not being granted the trading rights they saw as perfectly natural by the norms of nineteenth-century international relations.

In January of the following year Captain Charles Elliot, Britain's plenipotentiary in China, graciously agreed that Britain would accept a vast indemnity of 6,000,000 silver dollars, the opening of Canton to trade, direct official dealings and governance in perpetuity of an island called Hong Kong. In return he gave back Chusan, a detail with which Queen Victoria, Prince

Albert and the Foreign Secretary Lord Palmerston were far from pleased – Elliot's orders had been to take and hold Chusan. He had squandered its value as a bargaining chip for little practical gain and was dismissed and replaced by Henry Pottinger, the man destined to become Hong Kong's first Governor.

Pottinger arrived in the newly British colony in August 1841 and straightaway dispatched a force northwards to the Chusan archipelago. In the interim, the island of Chusan had been strongly fortified and heavily garrisoned by the Chinese, and the new British commander, General Gough, required a full day to recapture it, at the cost of two English dead and a musket ball to his own shoulder.

Chusan was at last a part of the Empire, but despite being seemingly ideal for the British – a defensible island near the Yangtze, with deep harbours, on the trading routes to Japan and Korea, and abounding in a near-legendary amount of game and fish – it had a reputation during its spell under British rule as the unhealthiest posting in China. Cameronian Hill, as it was known to the troops on Chusan and to Shanghai's expatriates who flocked to the 'worshipping island' of Putuoshan next door, took its name from the cemetery where great numbers of Her Majesty's 26th, 'the Cameronians', who died of fever were buried.

As well as the Cameronians, and the Irish Rifles who went on from Chusan's capture to play 'God Save the Queen' from Ningbo's city walls, there were the sepoys of the Madras Native Infantry. The early holidaymakers who glimpsed Chusan often wrote of the smart red uniforms of the thousand or so troops garrisoned in barracks next to the beach. They also commented on the heaps of salt to be seen drying on the waterfront. Salt production – as well as the distilling of *samshoo* liquor from surplus rice – was a mainstay of the island's economy before Britannia arrived, but it was of poor quality, made gritty by the estuary's heavy load of silt. From salt and alcohol, economic life quickly gravitated towards the British army. The islanders, reacting quite differently to their Manchu rulers in their dealings with the foreigners, welcomed the chance to deprive them of their wages.

The Chinese flair for moneymaking, which was to make Hong Kong so successful under British patronage, was apparent from the outset in Chusan. Travellers who passed through in the 1840s noted how the inhabitants learned to provide the soldiers with exactly the home comforts they craved. They built brick ovens to bake bread, which was far more to the troops' liking than the locals' tasteless *mantou*, or steamed buns. They addressed all privates by the name 'A-say', which they had picked up from the opening words of the soldiers' conversations – 'I say!' – and which they had taken to be a title of rank. And, just like any Chinese street today, a shop sign in English was *de rigueur*, native shopkeepers erecting such imaginative signs as 'Squire Sam, Porcelain Merchant', 'Dominie Dobbs the Grocer' and 'Tailor to Her Most Graceful Majesty Queen Victoria and His Royal Highness Prince Albert, by appointment'.

Unlike Elliot, Pottinger extracted a high price for Chusan. Landing at Wusong, on the confluence of the Huangpu and the Yangtze, the British established control over Shanghai before sailing upriver to take the Grand Canal. This done, they advanced to wrest control of Nanjing, the largest city in the delta. The Chinese standing army was shown up for what it was – a poorly disciplined, badly armed and underpaid ragtag of men – and the Qing were forced back to the negotiating table. In the Treaty of Nanjing of August 1842, Pottinger agreed to withdraw Her Majesty's forces from Nanjing and the Grand Canal on the payment of the first instalment of China's indemnity to Britain, which – now that Pottinger had demonstrated how devastating Britain's forces could be – had been renegotiated to the sum of 21,000,000 silver dollars. Britain's military post on Chusan was to remain until the full sum had been paid and the arrangements completed for the opening up of five ports, including Shanghai, to British merchants. Once Shanghai became the focus of British interests in the Yangtze estuary, Chusan became surplus to requirements. In 1846 it was duly and without ceremony returned to China, and slipped into obscurity.

Had the Qing refused to open Shanghai or Ningbo to the British, Chusan's future would have been more uncertain. As a bargaining chip and staging-post it would in all probability have retained its garrison, perhaps even becoming an important centre for trade in its own right and eclipsing Shanghai. Shanghai might have remained a wholly Chinese city, and Ningbo might under Deng Xiaoping's reforms have become a second Shenzhen, facing not Hong Kong but the economic power-house of the British Crown Colony of Chusan.

PUTUOSHAN

A HONEYED SUN broke the cloud, and the drizzle abated as the *Free Flying* slipped through the channel separating Zhoushan and the island of Zhu Jia Jiao – Zhu Clan Point. Standing on the narrow gangway I saw Putuoshan spotlit by a sunburst that breathed welcome colour into the monochrome seascape. The low eminence now shimmered like a diadem set with opals and jade on a golden cushion. A giant burnished bronze statue of Avalokitesvara or Guanyin, the Buddhist embodiment of compassion, held out a glittering hand in benediction as we pulled alongside and each paid our 50 *renminbi* arrivals tax.

The hotel tout, Mr Liu, shepherded us through the marble and chrome arrivals hall and on to a minibus, past the hapless hoteliers who, unwilling to buy a ticket for the boat, had preferred to try their luck at the terminal. His girlfriend was waiting, her feet propped up on the dashboard, and she was clearly impressed by his haul which, at nine people, amounted to a good half of the ferry's complement.

Putuoshan was not a difficult place to get around. The only route was an unbeautiful cement-slab roadway which started at the wharf at the southern tip of the island and, hugging its eastern side, ended at a cable car that led to the island's highest peak. As we wheezed past restaurants and trinket shops and struggled up a low ridge in first gear, Mr Liu launched cheerily into a well-rehearsed introduction.

Putuoshan was one of China's four sacred Buddhist mountains. Did anyone know the other three? A mumbling of names above the desperate whine of the engine told me I was the only one who did not know the other three, not having been required to learn them at school as they had. Putuoshan was just one of 1,339 islands in the archipelago, he continued, which was first raised to county status in AD 738. Did anyone know why it was called Putuoshan? This time there was a satisfyingly unanimous silence.

'Under the Tang, an Indian monk came to the island and the bodhisattva Avalokitesvara appeared before him to expound the teachings of Buddha. The monk named the place "the sacred land where Avalokitesvara took form". Avalokitesvara was said to have come from a mountain in southern India called Potalaka, and so the island came to be seen as a second Potalaka Mountain. We Chinese pronounced the name as Putuoluojia Shan, which later got shortened to Putuoshan.' The rest of the minibus murmured appreciatively, while I ruminated on how the first Indian to land on the archipelago came to seek a bodhisattva – a saintly embodiment of Buddhist compassion – while those who followed him a millennium later were heavily armed Hindu soldiers in the pay of the British Empire.

Mr Liu's hotel was hidden from the road in a thicket of yew and camphor, on a low rise overlooking Thousand Pace Beach. It was almost noon, and the leaden clouds had by now faded to a powdery white sheen against a blue sky. A few brave cicadas and crickets had been warmed back to life by the sun, and with loud chirrups betrayed themselves to a flock of jays that swooped from the trees into the stubbly grass. The Pacific lapped the shore. In the sunshine it had taken on the patina of antique gold, and the statue of the Guanyin of the Southern Ocean that had blessed our arrival sparkled in its reflected light on her distant promontory.

In my hotel room, while the diminutive bath slowly filled with lukewarm, rusty water, I examined what appeared to be complimentary sachets of shampoo. They turned out to be something else: sachets of 'Yirenbao Lotion for Genital', in either blue or red, marked respectively 'man' and 'woman'. That they had been placed in the room at all, and that the attached notice warned of a charge of 10 *renminbi* for their use, was a clear indicator that Putuoshan was becoming as much a secular holiday resort as a place of earnest pilgrimage. On the back of each was printed:

> Yirenbao Dew for cleaning private parts. The traditional Chinese product is prepared from natural herb essence, developed for wash of men's or women's private parts. It can quickly kill latent bacterium and virus and form protection on private parts. It's suitable for family or travel use before or after sexual intercourse or when taking a bath. Efficacious to prevent venereal disease from spreading.

Family use? The obvious humour value aside, it was sad to think that the faith of the Chinese in traditional medicine, combined with their predilection for sex pills and potions, meant that credulous people were going to be needlessly infected with sexually transmitted diseases.

That syphilis and gonorrhoea were common had been obvious from the moment I had first stepped outside my hotel in Shanghai: almost every other lamp-post bore a photocopied fly-poster advertising confidential treatment, along with an unpleasantly detailed description of symptoms and a promise of 'no cure – no fee'. And where you find syphilis and gonorrhoea you will sooner or later find AIDS. Unfortunately the uncontrolled anonymity of a backstreet clinic is, to many Chinese, preferable to a visit to a state-run hospital, where their treatment is recorded and where they run the risk of being prevented from having children in the future.

It was late March, and Putuoshan's summer season had barely begun. By one o'clock the scant lunchtime rush was long finished, and shop-owners and taxi-drivers dozed the afternoon away. The shops outside my hotel formed two sides of a triangle, the roadway forming the third and the space in between serving as the drop-off point for a stream of minibuses ferrying pilgrims to the Fayu Temple nearby. A young couple heaved plastic washing-up bowls of seawater from the roadside to the shade of their restaurant's awning. After each was set down it was fed a plastic tube from a tangle that led to an electric pump. The pump hummed quietly, and air bubbled soporifically through the warm water. I was soon spotted and cajoled into sitting down with promises of cheap food. The young woman optimistically pointed out a nice carp in one of the bowls. It looked healthy, if a little short on space to move around in, but it was the length of my forearm and the width of my calf.

'Have you got anything a bit smaller?' I ventured.

'How about that *jiayu*?' She pointed at a beautiful horseshoe crab in a bowl much too small for it. The poor thing sat motionless, a relic from the Cretaceous era, its smoothly curved carapace a vivid green, with tiny black eyes and a rigid, pointed tail that provided little defence against a Chinese restaurateuse.

'Isn't it an endangered species?' I was unsure whether it was or not, but it looked as though it ought to be. She looked at me baffled and dismissed the idea with a wave. Then she picked the crab up by its tail, and its back curled to reveal a set of jointed legs wriggling uselessly.

'It's very fragrant. It's got green blood – you can drink it.'

'I'm really not that thirsty,' I lied. 'I'll just have fried noodles with vegetables, and a beer.'

Every Chinese town has its own-label beer – the Germans in their northerly Qingdao concession had taught the Chinese how to brew lager – and Putuoshan was no exception, though its beer was brewed on Zhoushan since there was not enough room for a brewery on the island itself. I sat in the sun drinking it and watched the menu trying to escape. There were translucent prawns, brown crayfish, cockles squirting streams of water into the air, sea snails, sea slugs and sea cucumbers, clams, carp and crabs, flatfish I did not recognize, *jiayu* and lobsters whose claws had been decommissioned by elastic bands. Every so often a crab would make a break for it by climbing over its cellmates, and the owner would run after it and throw it back, and then it would try again. If a trawler had come back with a mermaid I had no doubt she would have been incarcerated in a barrel of saltwater prior to being boiled alive.

A mountain of oily *chao mian* arrived, capped by a fried egg. It burst as I prodded it with my chopsticks and an avalanche of yolk slowly engulfed a mangetout village on the lower slopes. When I had finished eating under the unwavering gaze of the owner, I signed my palm with an imaginary pen. She shouted back into the kitchen.

'Hey! Did you tell the *laowai* how much the noodles and beer were?'

'They usually come to 8 *kuai*, don't they? Tell the foreigner it's ten!' The owner turned to me and paused for a second.

'Twelve.'

'He just said it was eight – I heard him!' She realized her mistake with a start and put her hand to her mouth to hide an embarrassed laugh.

'Business isn't good at the moment, it's the low season, and you're a *waiguoren*, from abroad, you can afford it.'

Amituofo, the Amita Buddha, sat cross-legged inside the Temple of the Universal Waters of the Buddha's Teaching. He smiled contentedly at the day's takings – chrysanthemum flowers, a bottle of vegetable oil, squares of gold leaf pasted on to crude paper that did service for ingots, and his favourite steamed buns and sweets. A service was taking place, as it would several times each day, a cohort of crimson-robed monks intoning from scriptures pressed close to their faces in the gloom. One acolyte rapped time on a wooden block carved in the shape of a cowry. It was an instrument which the most accomplished of musicians could not hope to make sound serious, and its cheerful staccato, far from conjuring an atmosphere of solemnity, reminded me of a primary school assembly.

Behind the monks, a gaggle of elderly women were resting on benches in a shadowy corner of the hall. Their outdated clothes marked them out as belonging to a certain generation of rural peasant: blue cotton padded jackets wrapped across flat chests and held fast by toggles, black cotton trousers and white ankle-length socks peeping out beneath cotton sandals. Their hair was uniformly salt-and-pepper grey, held back with kirby-grips from sun-tanned walnut faces. They chatted away in bevies, ignoring the best efforts of the monks to beg Guanyin's compassion on their behalf, while the monks for their part plodded through the order of service oblivious to the background noise.

'Thump, thump.' A few seconds' delay, then again 'thump, thump.' A deeper note had been added to the service. One of the pilgrims detached herself from the knot and hobbled to where I stood beside the deep crimson doorsill. She was so stooped she barely reached the height of my elbow.

'*Nagonin?*' She spoke in an almost unrecognizable dialect, her thin, near-colourless lips parting to reveal a mouth full of gold-capped stumps. I guessed it to be the standard opening gambit of '*Naguoren?*' – which country are you from? – and was touched by her innocent assumption that, whatever the answer, my national language would be the same as that of her home village. It was a heart-warming contrast to the restaurant owner's attitude.

'England,' I replied. She looked at me in quiet wonder.

'*Ingo* . . . Do you have all this in *Ingo*?' she asked, nodding towards the chanting monks and the Amita Buddha. I tried to explain that yes, there were some Buddhists in *Ingo*, but that it was a different kind of Buddhism, often followed by rich celebrities, and that we certainly did not have charming, Buddha-invoking old ladies like her. She understood hardly a word of my standard Mandarin. I conceded and abridged it all to a simple: 'No, we don't have all this . . .'

'You don't have Amita Buddha in *Ingo*?' She stared through me into the middle distance, her face screwed up in thought, and muttered his name for my salvation.

'Amituofo . . .' She looked full of pity for me and for the people of *Ingo*, wherever that was, then, turning back to her friends, she told them where I was from and that we hadn't heard the Buddha's teachings. A gentle chorus of Amituofos followed her announcement.

The acolyte upped the tempo on the cowry and the monks rose as one from their benches. The pilgrims did the same, the nearest ones shuffling to the long hassocks in front of Amituofo, the Buddha of Boundless Light, where they first knelt and then rocked back and forth in obeisance. 'Thump, thump . . . thump, thump . . . thump, thump . . .' Now the deep note was out of time with the monks' intonations, and I followed it to discover its source.

An elderly man, wearing spectacles and dressed in lay clothing instead of monkish saffron, stood bent forward over a long, low desk in one corner of the prayer hall, his thin shoulders rigid with concentration. His right hand gripped a square woodcut stamp by the handle on its back. A short line of pilgrims were placing silk shoulder bags on the desk in front of him. As each one did so his arm mechanically banged the stamp flat on to a large inkpad – thump! – and in the same swift movement impressed its vermilion characters – thump! – on to the silk, its spidery, stylized characters now proof that the owner had visited the Fayu Temple. One more step on the road to paradise, like a cockleshell from Santiago de Compostela or a palm branch from the Holy Land. Then each old woman – there were no male pilgrims – shouldered her precious bag and moved on to the next hall.

I followed them into the intervening courtyard, where a swarm of schoolchildren was buzzing around an incense-burner. A trio of smart young women dressed in designer clothes and with Gucci handbags over their slight shoulders stood facing it, their arms raised in prayer, heads bowed. A breeze sprang up, sending thick clouds of sandalwood smoke billowing from the embers and engulfing them. They backed away, coughing and spluttering but still clutching their burning joss-sticks.

Inside the hall beyond, devotional banners proclaimed the name of Sakhyamuni, the historical founder of Buddhism, in vertical lines of silken characters. Beneath were listed donors who had contributed to the restoration of the temple. Some were from China, but most were overseas Chinese devotees from Hong Kong, Singapore, Indonesia, even Canada. I leaned on the door jamb to watch two of the schoolchildren perform their kowtows.

They both wore identical purple and white tracksuits, the same meaningless 'Lifehealthyenergy, For Ethletic Use Only' stencilled in peeling vinyl on their backs, all four wrists a jumble of sandalwood beads. A sign on the door strictly prohibited the burning of incense inside the hall, and so they stood before Sakhyamuni with empty hands held, palms touching, in front of their nervous young faces. They knelt down on the long hassock, their hands now gripping its far edge, and once, twice, three times their foreheads touched the faded cloth before they straightened up, bowed and turned to walk away. A monk walked over and smiled at me. I greeted him and together we watched an elderly woman as she followed the children on the hassock.

This time the prayers were offered with the smoothness of an action honed over decades – the maximum number of prostrations achieved with the smallest amount of effort. Her every cycle of kneeling and bowing was pared down to the merest movement of the legs and the head, so that she barely left the kneeler when standing and hardly moved her head when kowtowing. Over and over and over she repeated the Buddha's many honorific names and prayed to him to look after her family. For all the strength of her commitment – and this I could not doubt – she looked to me a child pestering a parent it hoped would eventually give in, an uncharitable thought I immediately wanted to push to one side.

Like so much else in crowded China, religion is a public practice, but still I felt that merely by my proximity I was intruding on her private communion. I shifted my weight awkwardly from foot to foot. The monk, though, was unconcerned. He stared and grinned, clearly impressed by the fluency of her praying. Turning, he leaned towards me and pushed an index finger into the middle of his forehead.

'She never forgot how to pray,' he said, his finger drilling deep to emphasize the depth of her faith. 'Those kids, they're only just starting out. They pray for silly things, like success in their school exams or getting a well-paid job, but I hope they'll keep coming here, and eventually they'll come to a proper understanding of Buddha's compassion.'

I asked him whether many young people came to Putuoshan to pray. He opened his eyes wide in emphasis.

'*Wa*, yes! Those children are from Zhoushan, so they come regularly. Their grandmothers are the ones who teach them how to pray, because their parents come from the generation who grew up in the sixties and seventies, when the monks were sent back to their villages and the monasteries fell into ruin.' My atheist taxi-driver in Suzhou must have been one of that generation, I imagined.

'The grandmothers . . .', he nodded at the old woman, who was now standing, head bowed, face in hands, '. . . grew up believing, and even prayed in secret when they could be denounced for it. It's only since the eighties that we've been free to pray to Buddha without fear, but look at how beautiful the temple has become. People come from all over the world to pray here, and some of them donate money to help themselves reach the Pure Land. *Danshi wo gaosu ni* – but I tell you – it's like we've already been reborn.'

'The Pure Land?' Chinese Buddhism had always been for me a confusing mixture of Indian roots overlaid with centuries of local traditions, with a dizzying pantheon of gods and of bodhisattvas who shunned nirvana to save human souls, plus all those disciples, celestial kings, kings of the underworld, demons . . . I could never remember the precise difference between Mahayana and Hinayana Buddhism, how many Noble Truths there were or how many *nidanas* there were in a cycle.

'On Putuoshan, we pray to Amituofo because only he can help us to be reborn in the Pure Land. Once you reach it, there are no more accumulations of karma, and you are only a short step from nirvana. Here we teach that everybody who calls on Amituofo can gain entry to the Pure Land, and that the more you call on him the greater the chance of him helping you to be reborn there.'

'And Guanyin – Avalokitesvara?'

'Ah, she's the favourite bodhisattva on Putuoshan.' He tilted his head fondly to one side and chuckled. 'She vowed that she wouldn't go to the Pure Land until she had rescued every human soul from the sorrow of existence. She's full of compassion, like your Virgin Mary.'

As I walked around that day I noticed the similarities between Guanyin and Mary. On the main road I came across an outcrop of the pinkish granite that composes the island. It overlooked the southerly Hundred Pace Beach and rose to a height of ten feet or so. A natural cleft ran through it from top to bottom, out of which sprouted stunted clumps of bamboo. In a square recess an image of Guanyin had been carved in bas-relief and the favoured intonation of the Putuoshan Buddhists, 'We pay homage to you, the bodhisattva who hears the world's sorrows', inscribed next to it. It resembled the roadside shrines to the Virgin that can still be found in Ireland and southern Europe. Though a Red Guard had managed to hack away almost the entire original Guanyin, the head and shoulders of a broken porcelain statuette had replaced her, and before it lay incense and candles offered by pilgrims.

The Ancient Well of the Immortals was cool despite the noon heat outside. I descended its dozen worn steps and entered stooping into a dank half-light. The small underground cave brought to mind pictures I had seen of the Church of the Nativity. Another porcelain statuette of Guanyin, this time intact, sat on a golden lotus in a shallow niche. Somebody had decked her in embroidered silks and gauzes and set fresh peonies and roses on the table before her. Flickering candles dripped spots of wax on to the stone floor, and their smooth domes caught the light of the naked bulb dangling from the ceiling. A rickety table in a corner supported the trappings of a working shrine – incense-wrappers, matches and spare light bulbs.

As I stood, I heard voices behind me and turned to see four old women descend into the space. I edged out awkwardly but they seemed hardly to notice me, busying themselves instead with the practical tasks of pilgrimage. They sang together dolefully as they pulled first candles, then incense from the plastic bags they each carried. These they lit and deposited on the shrine, all the while their weak, tremulous voices echoing softly in the cramped cavern. When they had finished they took it in turns to kneel and bow, the remaining three meanwhile tidying up the detritus left by other visitors. The ritual had been subsumed by the workaday normality these four friends exuded. Their actions were all so practised and undemonstrative that they could just as well have been out buying vegetables. These women had certainly never forgotten how to pray.

At the head of the well a teahouse had been built to cater to well-heeled pilgrims. Inside, yet another manifestation of Guanyin stood within her shrine, but this time the offerings were different varieties of locally grown Putuoshan tea. She looked out across the bay to her counterpart, the Guanyin of the Southern Ocean. Five waitresses were lined up like so many French maids in uniform behind a polished wooden counter. One came to take my order and introduced herself as Meiling.

When my tea arrived I learned that the people of Putuoshan take their tea very weak. So weak, in fact, that any flavour the unfermented, green leaves might have possessed was overpowered by the metallic taste of the island's water.

'It's a very subtle taste,' Meiling admitted. Its subtlety was not helped by the other waitresses' habit of politely refilling my glass each time I took a sip, with the result that it grew weaker as I drank. Meiling told me she was twenty-six and volunteered that she was too short.

'It's because seaside bunnies like us eat rice, not noodles like they do in the north, so we don't grow tall.'

'Then why don't you eat noodles too?'

'Oh, no!' She shook her head. 'I get fat when I eat noodles. I've already told you I'm twenty-six, but I've got a face like a little doll, and I'm still covered in puppy fat. I need to lose five pounds, not gain them.' Like most young women who are convinced they need to lose weight, she looked perfectly proportioned.

Meiling came from Zhoushan and lived on the island only during the tourist season, as did most of the rest of the population of Putuoshan. She shared lodgings with the other four waitresses, who joined us one by one. She had never been abroad, even though she did occasionally travel south to Zhuhai or Canton to buy video discs for the teahouse. Watching these seemed to be the girls' sole source of entertainment, and Meiling called to one of them to put a Madonna video on for their guest.

'You'll like this one – she sings in English. Do you like the Backstreet Boys?' She also liked the Spice Girls but insisted that they were a quartet of black American men. One waitress was dispatched to look for a video disc to prove this, but she returned empty-handed. I suspected she had found it but thought it best to save her friend's face. Meiling seemed innocently happy, but when she told me she would never want to visit London because she could not speak English, I sensed hidden frustration. She was in her late twenties, attractive and clearly intelligent, yet worked as a waitress in a holiday resort and had no way of bettering herself. None of the girls dared to drink or smoke because they feared their parents on Zhoushan would hear about it, and Putuoshan offered nothing in the way of nightlife. Meiling had never had a boyfriend – 'Only girls in the big cities do that kind of thing.' I had seen her and her friends slouching behind reception desks ever since I had arrived in China, on every floor of every hotel, lined up bored and sullen against the walls of every restaurant and bar, staring at the floor in every shop. It was a terrible waste.

I walked along the beach on the way to Putuoshan's one small village. Striking inland over tussocks of marram grass I picked up the road. The settlement when I reached it consisted of a straggling flag-stoned street whose every shop frontage sold an odd mixture of cigarettes, dried seafood and religious trinketry. The smell was of cured and salted fish, their boxes neatly laid out on trestles, but what caught the eye above their stiff, lifeless ivory forms was the kaleidoscopic assortment of Buddhist paraphernalia. Like the stalls outside Europe's great medieval cathedrals, with their amulets and their ampullas, their souvenirs and their bogus relics, these bore every possible device related, no matter how tenuously, to the practice of Buddhism.

There were pilgrim's satchels to receive woodstamps; jade beads, bangles, necklaces and rosaries, and more of the same in sandalwood; wooden cowry-shaped drums in all sizes; gold etchings of Buddha on credit card-sized metal tablets; countless varieties of incense, ready-wrapped or sold loose by the pound, in bundles, in stick form, in coils, and ranging from the tiny to the enormous, the biggest over four feet long and three inches in diameter; gigantic wooden necklaces, each bead the size of a conker and their whole over eight feet long; stacks of yellow paper ghost money, printed in red and gold and bound with crimson thread; yellow paper cut into the shape of gold ingots, to burn for the dead; paper coins so the dead had small change in the afterlife; coin-shaped pendants and charms; pendants in the form of Buddhas, and Buddhas in plastic, wood, plaster, porcelain or metal, ranging from the pocket-sized to the near life-sized; Guanyins in the same materials and sizes, highlighted in red, gold and blue so that they resembled Catholic Madonnas; flashy gifts each with an image of Guanyin and with flickering lights – cigarette lighters, picture frames, clocks and watches; framed portraits of Buddha and/or Guanyin; hand-held, battery-operated devices that would endlessly intone the name of Amita Buddha on your behalf, all the better for him to hear you with; compact discs of monks chanting the names of gods and saints for your salvation; pendants and mirrors bearing *I-Ching* hexagrams, just in case a Daoist should pop by; not to mention the ubiquitous tourist tat of plastic guns, comic glasses with red noses attached, seashells and handy packs of dried endangered species to save you buying each individually –

seahorses, starfish, sea snakes and others whose English names I never discovered but which literally translated as golden sea coins and white flower serpents.

In the early evening I rode the cable car to the top of Buddha's Head Mountain, from where I could see yellow water in every direction. Arthur Bestall, who for thirty years illustrated the Rupert Bear cartoons, had spent his early years in Indo-China as the son of missionaries. Rupert and his friends inhabited a world that merged the distinct backgrounds of Bestall's childhood and adult lives. Their chinoiserie land, a mixture of Tolkien and willow pattern, was of pine-covered crags rising vertically from silty yellow seas, steps twisting down precipitous cliffs to beaches and bays, and everywhere Western touches in the steamboats, lamp-posts, piers and neat topiary – just like Putuoshan.

DAISHAN

WHILE THE *Free Flying* had started life in the warm waters of Western Australia, the *Putuoshan* had in a previous incarnation plied the fog-bound islands of the Danish peninsula. Her steerage was packed three berths deep with half-naked, perspiring forms who played cards, smoked or just lay insensible in the stifling heat. The nuns and farmers who had paid 40 *renminbi* to spread out a bedroll on the deck seemed to have got the better deal.

The *Putuoshan* heaved off from the jetty in the late afternoon, treading water for an hour while a gam of submarines steamed through the Lotus Flower Strait escorted by rusty patrol boats bedecked with drying laundry. The wind got up as she finally made for Shanghai, and staying up top became uncomfortable. Instead I sat in the deserted karaoke bar and sipped a can of warm beer, all that its seasick barmaid had to offer.

At dusk we stopped at the island of Daishan. The gangplanks were rolled alongside and the *Putuoshan* exchanged one foreigner and a handful of steerage passengers for a handful of vegetable farmers bound for the big city. Then the gangplanks were trundled back and the wharves were still but for the throb of the ship's engines and the disembodied hoots of car horns from the town beyond. The ashen twilight was enlivened only by the neon characters announcing the island's name in a lurid orange from the roof of its ferry terminal.

The inhabitants of Daishan believe it to be the island the ancients called Penglai, the home of immortals. Xu Shi, a sorcerer to the first emperor of China, told his ruler of three islands in the eastern sea – Penglai, Fangzhang and Yingzhou – inhabited by immortals who guarded the elixir of eternal life. The birds and animals that lived on the islands were all pure white, he explained, while the palaces and watchtowers were of gold and silver. It was said that the islands were moored to giant turtles. They looked from a distance like clouds on the horizon but would sink into the sea as you approached, whereupon a wind would arise to blow your boat away. Nobody had ever reached them. The Emperor – obsessed by the thought that with bodily death might come an end to his power – had by then begun the construction of a great necropolis, with rank after rank of terracotta warriors and horses who would guard him in the afterlife. Better still that he should cheat death itself. He dispatched Xu Shi at the head of thousands of children in a fruitless quest for the islands and the elixir.

Under the welcome cloak of anonymity that the moonless evening afforded, I went in search of somewhere to sleep. On Penglai Road, not far from the brooding bulk of the terminal, I found a *zhaodaisuo*, a hostel that is generally permitted to accept only Chinese guests. A carpet that had long since been trampled from red into a shabby, tarry black led up a short flight of stairs to a formica desk. The owner, or *laoban*, did not look up until he had already confirmed that he had room for a traveller who wanted to stay just one night on his way to the island of Sijiaoshan.

'*Wa!* You're not Chinese, are you?'

'No, I'm English.'

He sucked his teeth and slipped a worn sheet of carbon paper into a pad of Temporary Residence forms. 'Fill this in. Do you have a *danwei*, a work unit, in China?'

'I'm just travelling.'

He thought for a brief moment. 'Did you ever study in China?' I told him I had once studied in Shanghai. 'Then put the name of the place you studied where it says "work unit". The ferry to Sijiaoshan leaves first thing, often before the police look through the new forms, so they might not realize you've stayed here until you're on board. If they get word that there's a foreigner on Daishan and come tonight, I'll say you tricked me into staying in my *zhaodaisuo*, and they'll move you to their *binguan*. It can take foreign guests, but it's not cheap. Okay?' The *zhaodaisuo* was cheap. It was worth the risk.

'Hey, friend!' The *laoban* hammered on my door as I dozed. When I opened it I found him standing in his vest and under-pants holding a bowl of rice and braised intestine which he insisted I share. 'Come and translate for us!'

In his room a television set was tuned to CNN. His daughter spoke a little English, he said. She was learning it at school, and watching television helped her. He was very proud of her progress but was eager for me to fill in the bits she could not understand in a news item of particular interest.

'It's about China, isn't it?' he said.

President Bush was leaning over a podium. An American voice explained that we were watching his reaction to the news that a Chinese airforce plane had been involved in a collision with an American Lockheed Martin EP-3E surveillance plane.

The American plane been forced to land on Hainan Island, but the Chinese plane was still missing. The President stumbled through a disjointed opinion on the fate of the aircraft, now sitting on a military airfield near the town of Lingshui, and insisted that China allow diplomatic access to the twenty-four aircrew it had detained. The Chinese must have been ecstatic at their good fortune: it was not every day that they could have their best scientists strip-search a state-of-the-art US spy plane. The *laoban* practically drooled at the thought of such a prestigious piece of hardware. It was the first of April. If everything went according to plan, I would be on Hainan in less than a fortnight. I hoped the stand-off would last at least that long.

The *laoban* hammered on my door before dawn the next morning, and I threw my clothes on and opened up.

'The police didn't come in the night, then?' We grinned conspiratorially at each other, and I left to buy a ticket for Sijiaoshan.

The independent traveller with an obsession for rusty ferries and isolated fishing villages could hop between the tiny communities of the Zhoushan archipelago almost indefinitely. The archipelago is the extension into the East China Sea of the Tiantai range of Zhejiang, its islands the peaks of submerged mountains. They grow smaller and more scarce with increasing distance from the mainland until their easternmost projection – a barren rock 150 feet high and barely worthy of its name Exalted Reef – breaks the surface. Exalted Reef is the farthest-flung point of China's curving littoral but is uninhabited and offers no place to land. My goal was the most easterly of the inhabited islands of eastern China.

Shengshan lies 122° 49′ east of Greenwich, at the very edge of a cluster of islets known collectively as the Saddle group after the outline observed by the Royal Navy surveyors who mapped the archipelago in the 1840s. Its modern name is a standardization in

Mandarin of its ancient local name of Jinshan, the Farthest Mountain. Beyond Jinshan, fishermen knew they would not find landfall until the outlying islands of Japan or Korea.

For many months after the largely land-bound PLA had liberated the rest of Zhejiang, Shengshan – like much of the Zhoushan archipelago – remained a 'black' island, the easily defended haunt of those the Communists considered pirates and criminal elements. From Daishan I planned to reach it by way of a long, clockwise arc on the ferries that serve as the locals' public transport, their delivery vans, postal service and homes from home.

I saw little of the first ferry I took, a juddering tub that toiled between Daishan and Sijiaoshan, until it had already crossed the narrow channel to Changtushan and heaved alongside its collision-scarred jetty. By then, dawn had breathed enough light into the lingering sea mist of the sheltered harbour for a person up on deck to watch the exchange of cargo.

As the ship's stern- and head-ropes were secured to the dock, goods were handed across the gap: the stiff rosettes of wedding garlands, boxes of bananas from Guangxi, tins of Hainanese pineapple chunks, cans of cola, cartons of cigarettes from the Shanghai Cigarette Factory, sacks of rice from the mainland. A steady stream of necessities was soon piled high by the roadway. Sternwards, a countercurrent of outstretched hands deposited pallets of vegetables 'for Old Li on Qushan', a reel of the green nylon the old women on the quayside were using to mend their fishing nets, and hessian sacks from whose splayed necks tumbled bruised heads of cauliflower.

Then the hawsers were thrown back on to the deck with a hollow ring, disappearing amidst a tangle of anchor chains, ropes and greased steel cables, and the ferry shuddered free of the quay, turned its nose into the light breeze and began to plough a straight, white furrow through the brown water to Qushan.

The activity at the dockside on Qushan, or Crossroad Mountain, differed only in the details of precisely who passed what to which of the waiting islanders, but even before the heaving boat had been made fast a pair of elderly fishermen leapt ashore. Their faces, deeply incised with lines and toughened into tanned, leathery masks, betrayed a lifetime's exposure to salt winds. Their legs, reluctant to adapt to the brief immovability of solid rock between voyages, swayed for a moment beneath them.

I had never before seen the Chinese as a seagoing race. The few millions who live on the islands of Zhejiang and Fujian provinces are no numerical counterweight to the vastness of China's land-bound peasantry. The Son of Heaven on the imperial throne had for centuries concerned himself with the governance of the many, had fretted over how to tame first the Yellow River and then the Yangtze that regularly flooded his land; over how to maintain the cosmological balance that would ensure the grain harvests were successful and the masses fed. These seafaring communities had watched from their fishing junks as famines came and went, as dynasties rose and fell, too few and too distant to weigh heavily on the inward-looking political centre, a source merely of curious trinkets from their trading voyages. Those concentric worlds that existed beyond China's belly were regarded as nothing more than tributary states – which, by their willingness to kowtow and to present their exotica at court, confirmed China in her world view – and beyond these lay only unreconstructed barbarians.

What this maritime people knew from centuries of exploration – that beyond China's shores lay advanced nations and cultures operating outside the Chinese sphere – was of purely taxonomical interest to the sinocentric bureaucracy of the capital. The Han sailors of these islands had more in common with the nineteenth-century British sailors who arrived on warships in their ancestral fishing grounds than with the hidebound Manchu courtiers in Beijing. Yet a century and a half ago it was they who were blown apart in their junks as their powder stores ignited, who drowned as their boats were sunk beneath them, or who were shelled into oblivion in the tangled streets of Ting-hae. Requiems had been sung for them here in scarlet temples perched on wooded summits by bonzes who understood nothing of the world of the barbarians. Tears had been shed for them behind the doors of the granite houses that clung like limpets to every slope. Their souls still resided in the grave tablets that sparkled from the hillsides of each island we heaved alongside.

At Sijiaoshan I took a minibus to the main settlement of Caiyuan – Vegetable Garden – where I re-enacted almost to the word the conversation I had had with the *zhaodaisuo* owner on Daishan. The willingness of the locals to turn a blind eye to the activities of visiting foreigners filled me with confidence that I might reach Shengshan.

At the crack of dawn the next day the *laoban* thumped on my door and pointed me in the direction of the ferry. It was a warm, still morning and, once we had left the long arm of the harbour wall, the waters of the Daji Sea were teased into the lightest of ripples. Four leagues later our port side ground a fresh layer of aggregate from the jetty wall of Lühuadao, or Green Flower Island, with a tooth-jarring screech. The women who sat mending nets looked up, grimaced, shook their heads and tutted. The familiar inventory of supplies was exchanged, the hawsers clattered back on to decks now slippery with salt spray, and with a shout of 'All clear!' we turned on ourselves to head for Huaniaoshan – Flower and Bird Island – where the same limpet houses clung to the hillsides, and the same wooded slopes glinted with graves. Another two leagues, this time across the brown of the Shengshan Sea, and we reached Bixiashan – Cliffs' Foot Mountain – scarcely a mile of pine-clad granite. Only as the propellers churned the waters of its sheltered, western bay and we swapped the lee of the island for an easterly wind from the Pacific, did I notice that the silty yellow of the Yangtze, now a hundred miles or more distant, had been replaced by the clear aquamarine and dancing white horses of the open ocean. Across this sparkling expanse I could faintly make out Shengshan as a khaki smudge on the horizon. It was not a printing error after all.

SHENGSHAN

SHENGSHAN SMELT OF the sea: not the faint, briny aroma of the fishmonger's slab but the pungent stench of rotting crab overlain with the reek of seaweed and of drying fish. I smelled it long before we landed. It pervaded every nook and cranny of the island and was at its worst as I walked along the roadway that hugged the island's southern shoreline. There, the remains of the crabs Shengshan processes for export had been shovelled on to the road and raked into a single long blanket, inches thick and yards wide, where they would dry before being crushed for fertilizer. Noon was hot, and the discarded shells with their legs still attached and their guts spilling out were food for clouds of flies that lifted as I disturbed them. I had to put a hand to my face to stop myself from retching. Every few yards the breeze would catch one of the paper-thin carapaces, sending it tumbling speckled pink across the cement where it would rest before its turn came to be crushed beneath the wheels of a motorcycle taxi. Or a gust might tug at one of the putrefying claws, which would wave ghoulishly at me as I passed.

In winter, swallows migrate towards the tropics in search of their insect food. Medieval Europeans believed they spent the winter hibernating in underwater caves. The Chinese thought of them as products of both *yin* and *yang*, with the attributes of both scaly fishes and feathered birds. Accordingly, they believed that in winter the swallows swam down to the seabed where they transformed themselves into mussels. In their smooth outlines and purple-black exteriors there is indeed a strange similarity between the two.

Gangs of women now processed mussels from the artificial beds marked by rows of floats in the bay. Hand over hand they drew lengths of muddy rope through iron rings. As the mud fell away it was sluiced to reveal clusters of shells, their silken beards torn from where they had fastened on to the coir. They were raked into piles, from which others stooped to pick them up and then crack them open. The plump, orange contents were laid out on wire mesh to dry in the hot sun. One old hunchback looked up, spotted me, broke into a toothless grin and held up a handful.

'*Lai chi!* Come, eat!' To show how good they were, she flicked one expertly into her open mouth and chewed gummily at it. The flies rose buzzing from the mound behind her.

I climbed up away from the road on a path of pounded earth. Shengshan's topsoil is just a thin layer cloaking her granite bulk and it is impossible to dig to any depth to form foundations. Her fishermen therefore construct enormous platforms of close-fitting stones on which they make their homes. As I walked I saw that each had beside it small plots of earth, demarcated by pot-sherds or loose rocks. They were green with the tender leaves of *bok choi*, lettuce, garlic and chives, and in places bristled with tall canes of aubergines and beans. Over the roofs of the houses trailed the flowers and tendrils of peas and courgettes. The steep tracks and winding stairways that connected each home to its neighbours were spread wherever my eye fell with frames of wood or bamboo where the household's catch had been laid to dry: needle-like garfish, slit along their backbones, gutted and splayed open; whole cuttlefish, their tentacles stretched out stiffly below them; flat-headed perch, butterflied into pearly white fillets; the silver bandsaw blades of elegant ribbonfish; croakers and groupers pressed flat while still whole, their eyes sunk to blank, dry caverns. I stooped to gather up a handful of granite shards from China's most easterly point to take home with me.

The bay below was thick with fishing vessels: ramshackle

sampans flitting like tick birds between wallowing rust-streaked trawlers whose decks were piled high with ropes and with lines of white floats that looked like necklaces of giant pearls. On lobster boats, baited creels were stacked one upon the other in enormous cages until they were a confused mess of steel hoops and nylon netting that would be paid out for mile after mile of ocean. Above all this grew a forest of radio antennae, navigation masts, booms, shrouds and lolling flagpoles. A canopy of red Chinese flags and dogtooth pennants fluttered in the wind. 'A souvenir on offering incense at the Puji Temple, Putuoshan. May Amituofo protect us,' read one. And then it struck me how many of the men on Shengshan wore bandages around their heads or had an arm in a sling.

A temple had been newly built on a brow overlooking the boats. On a simple cement square stood two braziers, each as tall as a man. Inside, iron scaffolds were lost beneath a thick layer of congealed wax that had trickled down from votive candles. The cramped temple hall smelt of the freshly cut pine of its timbers. Like the space outside its carved doors, the interior was plain, having none of the frippery of Putuoshan that overseas be-lievers had made possible. It was the local parish church, not one of their rich cathedrals.

Avalokitesvara and Amita Buddha were housed behind glass and had been offered thimbles of water, the steamed *mantou* the British had found so alien and unappetizing, and cigarettes that had burned themselves out in neat lines. Avalokitesvara smoked Red Pagoda Mountain, Amituofo preferred Marlboro Lights. As in Putuoshan, silk hangings attested to the universal Chinese wish that their homes be filled with gold and jade, but on the walls of this temple was something I had not seen in Putuoshan: wooden models of the trawlers and sampans the temple looked out upon. It was a seaman's chapel where Shengshan could pray for the safe return of its sailors, preferring to put its renewed faith in Guanyin rather than in the Party.

Three policemen from the Shengshan Frontier Defence Work Station of the Shengsi County Public Security Bureau came for me in the early evening, but they left once they had assured themselves that I was harmless and had confirmed that I would be leaving their jurisdiction the next morning. One of them, a middle-aged man in polyester slacks, stayed behind in the lobby of the hotel where I had been interviewed and, by virtue of simply not leaving my side, had me agree to eat with him. It was a very Chinese way of preventing lawlessness – compulsion not to do wrong by force of proximity. It would be hard for me to poke around in what was technically a border zone – I had spotted a radar station on the island's only peak – when a plain-clothes officer was entertaining me to dinner. Half joking, I suggested that first we go to an Internet café if there was one on Shengshan, which I doubted. He took my arm, skipping with me in tow up a flight of steps to a square, beyond which a row of windows burned with fluorescent light.

Besides a pool hall and an amusement arcade, where scores of teenagers sat transfixed by the bleeping of electronic games, the building housed a room lined with row after row of brand-new computer terminals, each in its own snug partition.

'A *wangba*. There's another one down the road, but this one has quicker access. It's 2 *renminbi* per hour, but you only pay for the time you use.' He looked anxious. 'Will it do?'

He pulled up a chair for me and booted up the hard drive. I had not counted on remote Shengshan being on the net and sat for a moment wondering what to do with the keyboard. I decided on a search for the name Shengshan itself, and in moments the local government's home page had appeared on my screen, a slick presentation in Chinese and English on the opportunities to be had in investing in the post-reform economy of the island. They were mainly related to fish-processing.

We ate in a private booth at a seafood restaurant his friend owned but first he escorted me as guest of honour to the glass display case where he insisted I choose what we ate. The local police would meet the bill. I ordered the crab.

When it arrived, a steaming plate of claw and shell sticking out from a bed of spring onion and ginger, he inhaled appreciatively and waved at me to tuck in.

'Crabs, now that's where to make your money these days. If you're in crabs you'll be all right. It used to be fish, but nowadays the catch is getting smaller. The trawlers have to go over to Japanese waters to land a decent catch. What else do you want to eat?'

I pointed to a string bag of mussels, kept alive in a tub of bubbling water.

'What do you call those in Chinese?' I asked.

'*Dancai?*' He shook his head. 'You mustn't eat them. We're used to them but if you're not local they'll give you terrible diarrhoea. People come from Shanghai and they're always sick.' He stopped for a moment, thought, smiled and leaned over the crab. '*Dancai* is their proper name, but we call them *dongfangchunü* – virgins of the orient.' I asked him why. He got up, bent to fish one out of the water, inserted a fruit knife into its waist and twisted it open. He held the mussel out to me and grinned triumphantly.

'Look, the hole that runs along its body is exactly the same shape as a vulva!' He was right, so I ordered the soy-braised ribbonfish.

SHANGHAI

DAWN ARRIVED OVER Shanghai's docks with a profound stillness. On both banks of the Huangpu the cranes were raised in quiet salutation, and we took a course mid-channel between its endless chilly warehouses and dry docks. To port, a weak sun slowly raised itself above Pudong's filigree of chemical works. To starboard, lines of pale green poplars glowed against the steely sky of the Shanghai riverbank. Leaning on the stern handrail, muffled against the early morning cold, I was utterly alone in a city of perhaps 15,000,000 souls.

With a phutt of compressed air and the rattle of loose glass, the doors of the bus concertinaed back and the human plug jamming its doorwell was squeezed out on to Nation at Peace Road at the heart of Jiangwan district. The spring sun of Shengshan had become a torment in Shanghai's streets that afternoon, and riding the city's buses was an ordeal.

The 'Double Ten' uprising of 10 October 1911 provided the final deathblow to the long moribund Qing, and the Republic of China was officially promulgated on the following New Year's Day. With its provisional President, Sun Yat-sen, proposing that the new Nationalist government be installed in Nanjing, only 150 miles upriver, the days of Shanghai's foreign-controlled International Settlement and French Concession were numbered.

The continued foreign presence in Shanghai was not just an irritation to the Nationalists: the success of the foreign concessions, during a period when Chinese society had crumpled, was a source of intense embarrassment. The foreigners had created their enclaves from what had been farmland less than a century before. They were self-financing, self-regulating city-states, designed to provide their merchant classes with everything they needed to turn a profit in comfort. Within a single lifespan, the paddyfields for miles around the crumbling walls of the old town had been transformed. The barbarians enjoyed metalled roads, sewerage, electricity, gas and running water, not to mention courts, postal systems, telephones, the trans-Pacific telegraph, fire brigades, police forces, prisons, hospitals, churches and public transport, while 2,000 years of supposedly superior Chinese culture had left the native city an island of filthy, dangerous alleys, shameful proof that decades of reform and self-strengthening movements in the late Qing had achieved nothing.

The Nationalists, or Kuomintang, wanted an end to extraterritoriality on Chinese soil. Indeed before his death in 1925, Sun Yat-sen went so far as to call for the destruction of the Shanghai concessions, and the second half of the 1920s saw the start of peaceful reabsorption of other foreign enclaves: Britain's concessions on the Yangtze reverted to Chinese rule in 1927 and they were soon followed by the return of Belgium's Tianjin concession and the loss of the British port of Weihaiwei and Britain's possessions in Canton. Seemingly, there was little to stop the Kuomintang from simply commandeering the Shanghai concessions. By the twenties, the Western powers, reeling from the Great War and the ensuing economic depression, were hardly in a position to halt the inevitable moves towards absorbing their territories into a single, Chinese-governed Shanghai. Yet the fact remained that the Kuomintang, supported to a great degree by the goodwill of Shanghai's capitalists, was simply not strong enough to apply the *coup de grâce*. The result was stalemate. While the Kuomintang under Sun Yat-sen's successor, Chiang Kai-shek, could neither afford to send the foreigners packing nor allow them to remain as a constant reminder of China's inferiority, the foreigners, physically hemmed in, were too weak to negotiate an improvement to their lot.

It was in this context that the Greater Shanghai Plan was conceived. The cumbersome jurisdictions of the concessions and the Chinese city would be melded into a single body, and a new centre for Shanghai would be constructed to surpass the achievements of the old concessions. The plan proposed that virgin land to the north-east be the site of Shanghai's new city centre, within easy reach of the city's lifeblood, the new docks at Wusong.

Shanghai had never been planned as an imperial capital like Beijing. The rat runs of the Chinese city and the Westerners'

boulevards had grown up organically. Those cosmological principles which underlay rectilinear Beijing in a terrestrial reflection
of the power of Heaven had been an irrelevance to Shanghai,
and so when the plan was unveiled in 1927 its proposed skeleton
of avenues running north–south and east–west symbolized its
intended status as China's economic capital.

Where imperial Chinese planners had sought to exclude the
awed Chinese subject from the seat of authority, forcing him to
approach, if at all, through a series of increasingly imposing
gates, halls and courtyards, the architects of the new Shanghai
wanted the city to be inclusive and democratic. Its spaces were
to be open and public, there were to be no walls between the
republic's rulers and its free citizens. Shanghai was to be reborn.

The centrepiece of the new Shanghai was to be the Civic
Centre, a crucifix formed by the intersection of two immense
boulevards. At its heart would be a ceremonial square with a
pagoda as its focus. Avenues were to radiate from the apexes of
each boulevard. Beyond the main square would be formal
gardens and parks. Through all of this would flow the Young
Dragon River, a man-made enlargement of a stream feeding the
Huangpu. Here would be planted willows and poplars to provide
riverside walkways for Shanghai's citizens. The organs of
government would be housed in a series of imposing buildings
culminating in the mayoral building on the north side of the
square. To its south-west, China's largest library, holding 400,000
volumes, would look out over tree-lined avenues, gardens and a
2,000-foot-long reflecting pool to the Shanghai History
Museum beyond. In addition, plans were drawn up for a municipal art gallery, auditoria for public meetings, schools, a sports
stadium and a hospital. Sadly, Greater Shanghai was overtaken by
wider political events.

In August 1937, the Japanese army, already in control of
Manchuria, engineered an invasion of the rest of China and on
13 August opened up a battlefront in Shanghai. The Chinese city

fell after bloody fighting. In the immediate aftermath of the attack on Pearl Harbor in 1941, the Japanese completed their occupation by marching into the foreign concessions. The shelling and street-to-street combat of the protracted Japanese takeover were reported to have laid waste much of the achievements of the thirties.

I doubted whether I would find more than the ghost of the Greater Shanghai Plan's street pattern but I comforted myself with the thought that I had already witnessed Sun Yat-sen's dream of a reborn Shanghai fulfilled in the skyscrapers of Pudong on the other bank of the Huangpu. There, the second of Deng Xiaoping's five-year plans had left Pudong with two of the longest suspension bridges in the world, a deepwater harbour, gas works, power plants and high-tech communications. The Shanghai underground now terminated in Pudong, and a monorail was being built to link it to its international airport. High schools, colleges and universities had been relocated to kick-start the district's own Silicon Valley, and shops, supermarkets, bars and nightclubs had been fostered to serve its growing number of residents. Pudong lay foursquare in the Shanghainese tradition of renewal and civic self-improvement. Sun Yat-sen would have approved.

I strolled up Nation at Peace Road and into Pure Spring Street. The long, straight vistas were a survival from the thirties, yet sullen housing blocks draped in a semaphore of laundry stood where governmental buildings should have been. There was nothing to indicate whether they had been destroyed by the Japanese or had simply never existed. It looked as though I had had a wasted journey.

At the junction of Pure Spring Street and Enduring Benevolence Street, two middle-aged men stood guard over a gigantic sheet of cardboard, shaped to look like a page from a spiral-bound notepad. One of them beckoned me over and pressed a black marker pen into my hand. Up close, the white surface was a jumble of cursive signatures.

'Sign our petition for us! There, up at the top where everyone can see.' The two beamed with satisfaction. I handed back the pen and asked them what the petition was for. Still grinning at having secured a foreign signature in such a prominent position, one replied.

'When there's no space left we're sending it to Beijing so that the Chinese Olympic Bid Committee can show it to the IOC. We want them to know that the Shanghai Sports Institute is fully behind the Beijing bid for the Games.' I had unwittingly helped China secure the 2008 Olympics.

'You are the first foreigner to sign our petition,' the second man began. 'I think it's very important that the IOC sees that even Westerners support the Chinese bid. Your media are opposed to Beijing, always writing stories about how the Chinese government doesn't deserve the Olympics because of the question of human rights, but what about all the good things in China? They never write about those. People are free to find jobs, earn money, to travel, to buy goods in the shops, but all your newspapers talk about is punishing us because our government arrests troublemakers and executes drug smugglers and murderers.'

How did he know so much about what was being written abroad about China, I asked.

'From the Internet, how else? My spoken English is poor, but we were made to memorize thousands of words at school, and I use my old dictionary for the ones I don't remember. There's lots of anti-Chinese propaganda on the subject of the bid.'

His friend nodded in agreement as another signature was added, this time by a tall, athletic girl in a tracksuit. 'One of the Institute's top high jumpers,' he commented as she loped off.

I had used Internet cafés in China several times during my stay, mostly to send e-mails home, but I had never thought of downloading Western newspapers, not for fear of what might happen to me if I did – as a foreigner I felt cocooned from what I imagined might be the most serious repercussions – but from an unwillingness to bring the Public Security Bureau down on the unsuspecting owners of the café. The pasted notices in each booth warning me not to access porn, or sites relating to the Falungong movement, implied strict controls. Most Internet café users – almost all of them teenagers – just sat hunched over their keyboards, logged on to chatrooms or locked in battle with somebody they had never met. So how did he manage to read the Western press? I thought the government blocked sites like that. He laughed.

'Bee-bee-sea-dart-calm.' He pronounced the BBC's web address in a lazy American drawl. 'The BBC isn't blocked, neither is *The Times* or the *Guardian*.' He paused to give the marker pen to the first of a group of students who one by one solemnly signed. 'The newspapers never say anything about the Japanese not admitting to the Nanjing Massacre, yet Osaka is applying too. Then there's Paris, but France detonated A-bombs in the Pacific, and there's Istanbul, even though Turkey is killing Kurds. I've read that in America they even execute children and mental retards. What kind of human rights are those? There are one and a half billion Chinese, but when I search the Western press all I ever read about are the few intellectual troublemakers who say we mustn't be given the Olympics. From these reports, you in the West must have a very biased view of China.' I forebore from pointing out that the converse was equally true.

'So what are you doing in this part of Shanghai? Are you a student?' I stumbled out an explanation of what I had hoped to find, showing him the architect's drawing I had photocopied from a dusty 1935 volume of the *China Journal*. He called his colleague over and put a finger on the picture of the mayoral building.

'Look! That's your office window.' His friend smiled in recognition.

'And that's where the basketball courts are.' He pointed beyond the road junction.

'I don't know about the rest, but you'll find that building behind those trees. It's the offices for the Shanghai Sports Institute.'

The central pagoda had never been built, and the spot where the observation tower had stood was now part of the Institute's dusty football pitches. The uninterrupted vistas planned for the main square were brought up short in all directions by chain fences and privet hedges. Dominating the northern side of the playing-fields, the mayoral building itself had miraculously survived bombardment and occupation but had since fallen into sad disrepair. The exquisitely detailed paintwork of its eaves was peeling off, and many of its windows gaped jagged and broken in rusting iron frames. Trees had seeded themselves between its azure tiles and nobody had climbed up to remove them. Despite its shabbiness, it had once been beautiful, and its utter lack of aesthetic sympathy with its surroundings now was striking.

It was built in a style called Chinese Renaissance. The perfect metaphor for the political changes that had convulsed China since the nineteenth century, it was outwardly Chinese but its structure was Western. Unable to rely for their legitimacy on the cyclical Mandate of Heaven that had ended with their overthrow of the Qing, China's rulers had sought to create buildings which would proclaim their power in the here and now.

Traditionally, the Chinese had relied on wooden pillars to support the roofs of their monumental buildings, and so the widest internal space possible was the single narrow span between two pillars. Constructed almost entirely of wood, such buildings were liable to destruction by fire or, less dramatically, by decay, and they rarely exceeded two or three storeys in height or survived more than a century or so before they had to be rebuilt. With the advent of Chinese Renaissance, however, architects could create buildings whose size and permanence equalled those of the foreigners in the concessions but whose external appearance was wholly Chinese. The Mayoral building retained all of the fundamental components of a Chinese monumental building, from the raised platform on which it sat to the pillars that supported the half-hipped roof with its distinctive curved lines. The detailing too was Chinese – white marble balustrades, a memorial plaque above the doorway, puppet-show figures on the roof ridges. But steel frames and reinforced concrete bore the roof and upper floors, clad in stone and cement, and modelled and painted to resemble wooden pillars and brackets. I found a side door ajar and slipped inside.

The building was unlit and at first glance unoccupied, though I could hear the hammering and drilling of workmen from somewhere within its corridors. It was being renovated. As I stood in silence, the coffered ceiling came into focus through the gloom, every inch covered in bright colours – luminescent greens, blues, reds and yellows – and highlighted in gold. Clouds swirled, dragons intertwined with flowers, and bats fluttered amongst them, homophonically bestowing good fortune on passers-by. The brass frames above the doorways, which must once have displayed the titles of the ministries they housed, now read Department of Ball Games, Department of Track and Field, Long Jump Office. Refurbishment had left the corridors crammed floor to ceiling with furniture. The sun's rays filtered through the plaster dust raised by the workmen and caught the glints of gold in the decorations, and I felt as if I had rediscovered Tutankhamun's tomb.

Tiptoeing up the stone stairs I looked out through a broken windowpane. Students were playing basketball below me. The boundaries of the ceremonial square were easily discernible. As I scanned the modern skyline beyond, two buildings stood out. Both had the same curved eaves as the mayoral building, in stark contrast to the boxy plainness of neighbouring apartment blocks. One was silhouetted against the sun's glow to the south-west, the other lit up in a streak of orange flame to its east. The library and the museum had also survived.

A brown sign humbly announced that the Shanghai Library was a Municipal Preserved Building. A larger, bright orange sign with a Nike sponsorship logo proclaimed that it was now a middle school. Here the setting sun cast long shadows. Downtown Shanghai was a knot of winding roads and tall build-ings, and at street-level dusk came quickly, but the squat blocks of Jiangwan and its straight, wide boulevards allowed the sun free rein that evening. It illuminated the solid granite of the library and its peeling plaster coat. Its scant reflection in the windows drew attention to how dirty they had become. It threw sharp shadows from the disused telegraph wires on to the walls and revealed faded communist slogans in their original, stark red.

The Shanghai History Museum's foundation stone had been hacked away until almost illegible – in 1949 the Western calen-dar had been adopted, and inscriptions that dated years from the uprising of 1911 had been destroyed – but its fabric was other-wise immaculate and it had been resurrected as the department of nuclear medicine of a local hospital. Its ornate ceilings remained, acres of primary colours supported by a forest of scarlet, but the exhibit galleries had been clinically tiled and were now lit by a sterile fluorescent light. Blue plastic chairs waited in rows outside consulting rooms as though expecting bad news, and everywhere there was the smell of disinfectant.

I came across the Young Dragon River. By now the sky was darkening, and its waters were jet black. Not the slightest move-ment was visible save a steady stream of bubbles that disturbed the smooth surface: the river was effervescent with putrefaction. A barge rusted where it had sunk or been abandoned midstream and an oily tidemark halfway up its hull that corresponded to another on the bankside willows showed where the river's flow reached at high tide. The Young Dragon River stank of stagnation, rotting vegetation and petrol. And while I stood on the ugly bridge spanning it, a loudspeaker on a telegraph pole played a distorted version of 'Annie's Song'. I was still humming it when I got back to my dormitory.

ZHEJIANG

IN THE ELEVENTH year of the reign of King Hui of the Zhou dynasty – 666 BC by the Gregorian calendar – Duke Xiao of the feudal state of Jin attacked the Black Horse barbarians. He returned with their leader's daughter, a woman he called Li Ji, the Black Horse Concubine, and she bore him a son named Xi Qi. Li Ji knew that Duke Xiao was in love with her, and she formed a plan to have Xi Qi made heir apparent in place of the Duke's eldest son Shen Sheng.

'Quwo is the site of your ancestral temple,' she said, 'while the city of Pu lies on your strategic borders. You must send Shen Sheng to govern Quwo, and your younger son Chong'er to govern Pu.' The Duke, besotted, did as he was told. Then Li Ji sent word to Shen Sheng that his late mother had visited his father the Duke in a dream, and that he should hasten to offer her spirit a sacrifice. Shen Sheng did so, sending some of the sacrificial meat for his father to eat. On the day the meat arrived, the Duke was out on a hunting expedition, and Li Ji left it in the palace for six days. When he returned, she had poison added to it before handing it to him. The Duke placed it on the floor, which bubbled up. Then he fed some to a dog, which died, and to a courtier, who also died. Li Ji began to wail.

'Your son and heir Shen Sheng sent the meat! He must be plotting to kill you!'

When Shen Sheng heard what Li Ji had done he fled, aware that if he told his father the truth about the woman he loved then the old man would be heartbroken. Unable to spread word of his innocence, Shen Sheng hanged himself. Li Ji lied to the Duke, telling of how Chong'er too had known of the plot, and he also fled.

For twelve years Chong'er lived in exile amongst the barbarians with his followers. When he finally returned to travel amongst the feudal states he often suffered great hardship. On one occasion a loyal retainer named Jie Zitui carved off a piece of his own thigh and presented it to the near-starving Chong'er to eat. Now when Chong'er was restored as the rightful Duke of Jin and set about rewarding those who had joined him in exile, Jie Zitui did not ask for reward and none was offered him. Rather than accept praise for his part in a restoration he believed was the will of Heaven, he and his mother went into hiding. Chong'er, hearing that they were living in thick forest on a particular mountain, had the forest set alight to flush them out.

For three days the fire raged, and when it finally burned itself out the two were found dead, the filial Jie Zitui still carrying his mother on his back, their charred bodies leaning against a willow, the only living tree left in the forest. Chong'er commanded that on each anniversary of Jie Zitui's death no fires were to be lit in the state of Jin, his subjects having instead to eat their food cold.

By the Tang dynasty, Cold Food Festival's message of filial piety had merged with the celebration of Qingming, when the Chinese sweep the graves of their ancestors, held on the following day. I left Shanghai on a Canton-bound train early on the morning of Qingming. Crowded Shanghai has no room for cemeteries, its dead instead being cremated, and so it was not until we left the city behind and reached the open countryside of Zhejiang that I saw signs of the day's festivities in the fields and recognized them for what they were.

Just as on the Shanghai peninsula, many of the farmers of north-eastern Zhejiang had profited from the land reforms of

the eighties and had built themselves bigger and brasher houses
that attested to their new wealth. Even so, many old farmsteads
still remained, their whitewashed walls and black pitched roofs
drowning out the notes of colour introduced by the new houses,
so that nowhere was the view dominated by the rootless self-
assertion of *arrivistes*.

The dead, like the living, were also beginning to move into
richer and more spacious accommodation. For generations here,
the ancestors had been provided with a simple conical earth
mound, a foot or two in height and topped with a wasp-waisted
pottery boss. More prosperous families had been able to afford
perhaps a small, hump-backed sarcophagus fronted by a carved
stele commemorating their ancestor's honourable name and
achievements. Countless examples of these were still to be seen,
but scattered now amongst the field boundaries and on patches
of untilled land, knee-high counterparts to the earthly houses of
the upwardly-mobile stood out, sometimes alone, sometimes
grouped like so many hamlets. Social stratification by wealth was
visible in their detail, the richer graves perfect miniaturized
versions of the full-size concrete-and-tile houses of the nearby
villages, the poorer ones using tiles of contrasting colours to
mimic a simple roof and door. The most opulent were fitted
with vestigial windows, curving rooflines, once or twice even a
lean-to garage and a tiny television aerial, and occasionally they
luxuriated behind stunted topiary hedges. In the fields, work
went on around them as usual, but signs remained that their filial
descendants had attended to them that morning.

The space around the graves had been swept with willow
twigs, and the tombs themselves had been cleaned. Now they
were adorned with bright crêpe-paper flowers and streamers in
primary colours. As the train slowed outside the city of Jiaxing
I could make out the offerings: bowls of food and rice studded
with incense-sticks and littered with the red husks of
firecrackers, and boiled eggs to symbolize the rebirth of the soul.

One farmer burned ghost money on a brazier to distract the attentions of malevolent spirits who might otherwise feed off offerings intended for his ancestors. Relatives milled around smoking, their hands in their pockets. A thin, blue smoke rose in the still air, and all the way to the horizon on the flat plain rose similar columns until the houses, trees and pylons closed in on one another.

Like all the other passengers, I had spent my time in the waiting-room at Shanghai's railway station stocking up on the necessities for train travel in China. Mine consisted of toilet paper, dried beef noodles (several kinds were on offer but the free sachet of preserved white radish tipped the balance, a choice I regretted once I tried eating it), bags of liquorice-flavoured melon seeds, tea (Oolong and Longjin), a preternaturally pink ham sausage with the texture of cotton wool, two bottles of water, and finally a plastic mug which could be filled from the carriage's boiler to provide me with a constant supply of lukewarm tea. When I inspected the mug before buying it, I saw it had a metal disc embedded in its base.

'It's a magnet,' the assistant helpfully informed me.

'Why would I want a magnetic teacup?' I asked.

'Well, it's good for your health . . . the, er . . . water in the tea gets magnetized . . .'

'And that's a good thing?'

Her explanation, that it helps the blood to circulate by making it thinner, was just getting interestingly untenable when another assistant interrupted her to agree that yes, magnetized tea was definitely better for you. Since the mug was in any case cheaper than a non-magnetized mug I kept my doubts to myself and bought it.

Aside from the familiar stampede to the narrow ticket barrier – occasioned by a Pavlovian reaction to a guard rattling her keys in the barrier's lock, and necessitated purely by the need to find space for the bags of noodles, tea, water and magnetic mugs that we all now carried – the train itself was civilized, all smoking now done furtively in the gaps between the carriages, all rubbish carefully placed in litter trays instead of being thrown on the floor or from the window, something I remembered as the norm only five years earlier. As we pulled out, the train's broadcasting room put on a doleful violin solo which made me feel immensely sad. I was alone in China, it was the small hours of the morning in England, and I prayed that my family and my girlfriend were safe.

The violin faded and the broadcasting room embarked on a stream of plasticky Hong Kong pop music which lasted until nightfall. The carriage became a beehive of contented humming during the well-known tracks and reverted to chatting and laughter during the less popular. We sat and stared from the window, read our books and newspapers, and broke open our supplies like children on a school trip.

The air of civility was broken when in the early afternoon we reached Hangzhou. Two newspaper vendors, a man and a woman, came to blows as the carriage doors were opened. The woman was in her late forties and wore an immaculate Pepsi sweatshirt, though beneath it her flowered dress was faded, her shoes scuffed and worn. She screamed like a harpy, her greasy hair flailing to reveal pierced earlobes that had become infected and had scabbed over. She had, she screamed, been there 'half a bloody day' and *she* would be selling the *News Digest* to the passengers on this carriage. The man punched her hard and unexpectedly on the chin, and the crowd descending from the train smothered and separated the pair, buying some from each by way of consolation. I bought a *Digest* from the woman, who by now was near to tears. It cost the equivalent of seven pence. Then the platform bell rang, the passengers clambered up the steps and the train jerked to a start. As we pulled away I could still hear her.

'Half a bloody day I've waited! Give me the money . . . *my*

money! Half a bloody day . . .' and she broke off in angry sobs.
I looked at the banner headline of the newspaper. It read 'US
refuses to apologize for spy plane incident', and it was accompanied by a library photograph of a Chinese jet and another of Wang
Wei, the missing pilot.

After repeating the official line that the United States must
take full responsibility for the loss of the Chinese plane and the
damage to its own, must cease spy missions near the Chinese
coast, and must apologize in full for both the damage caused and
for violating Chinese sovereignty by landing without permission, the article briefly recapped the circumstances of the acci-
dent. In the same words I had heard used each night on the
television bulletins, it detailed how the Chinese pilot 'had been
flying according to internationally accepted standards when the
American plane intentionally swerved to collide with it'. The
behaviour of the US plane had been 'contrary to international
law and to the relevant Chinese statutes', it said.

Beyond Hangzhou, the land began to rise from the sea and the
train slowly ascended into the mountains of Zhejiang. Here, the
slopes were too steep and too rocky to cultivate, and the farmers
were able to erect large graves for their ancestors without com-
promising the harvest. The graves were set into the hills, white
ornamental gateways standing vertically against the hard rake of
the stone, each surmounted by a red-tiled roof and fronted by
one or two arched openings. These were mostly bricked up, but
some still yawned in anticipation of a funerary urn.

The mountains soon gave way to a landscape of low hills
hugged by the fingerprint whorls and deltas of tea cultivation.
Now the tombs lay on the flat valley floors that curled between
these green drumlins. The ornamental gateways of the moun-
tainsides had gone. Instead, domed cement mounds two or three
feet high lurked behind large gravestones. Every few miles the
vernacular of the graves would change. Details of materials,

colour, decoration and form varied with the topography and local tradition, so that it seemed an ancestral spirit dropped at random somewhere in the Zhejiang countryside might easily navigate his way back to his home village by the style of the tombs alone.

At one point, a JCB had gouged out a hole three yards deep and twenty square. On its rim the tight rows of tea bushes with their dense foliage looked like the pile of dark green corduroy. In the middle of the hollow there remained a solitary island of bushes a few yards across. As we drifted past I could see at its centre a brick-fronted earthen mound with an inscribed tablet embedded in its front. That morning, a filial relation had somehow contrived to climb up the sheer earthen sides to press yellow bills into the cracks above the sealed entrances to the grave chambers. Their free portions fluttered in the breeze.

The soil of this region is a deep orange, almost red when freshly cut, but nature and human endeavour transform its basic rawness to a pastel palette. Cultivation, ploughing, the working in of manure and fertilizers all age the soil in the fields to a deep terracotta, while weathering on its exposed cuttings fades it to greys and browns. By contrast, on dusty trackways it is powdered and pounded to a light yellow.

By now the clear skies of Shanghai had given way to an ominous pall threatening rain. The tiled tomb frontages glinted amidst the dark velvet foliage as the last of the sun's rays illuminated the scene, and heavy drops of water began to flop into the dry dirt.

I leaned on the window and browsed through my newspaper. On one page I found an article on Qingming. It reported how thousands of Hong Kong residents were expected to cross the border to visit their ancestral tombs in Canton province, and that the customs authorities had tightened the rules on the transport of roasted meat, which was said to be the favourite food of ancestral spirits. Why? Because they feared that foot-and-mouth disease, which at the time was bringing apocalyptic scenes to farms in Britain, might be spread by some unsuspecting British visitor. Another article told of how a sixty-year-old woman in Jiangxi province had taken a poisonous snake home for the festival, believing it to be an ancestor.

> Mrs Li had to have a hand removed at a cost of 8,000 *renminbi* when the snake bit her as she fed it. This is what can so easily happen when people insistently stick to superstitious beliefs rather than thinking in a scientific manner, and when people fail to take out health insurance.

A Canton crematorium was reported to be looking at the problems posed by Qingming in a more pragmatic way. It had enforced the first 'smokeless Qingming', recognizing that even rational city dwellers go to visit their ancestors, but requiring them to do away with the candles, incense and paper money which each year cause serious air pollution in an already polluted city.

'Mum was an environmentalist,' one woman said. 'So I think she would have understood.' Another explained how her family had simply sat around their grandfather's urn and had told him what had happened that year.

'This is a very poor region,' the man standing next to me at the window mused. 'They shouldn't be squandering so much potentially productive land on those big graves.'

He was right about the poverty of the region – by now the flat paddies between sloping tea plantations seemed to have crumpled under the downpour into a mess of low gravelled hills, sparsely clothed in stunted pines and roughly stepped into terraces which bore witness to a desperate struggle to cultivate

73

every inch of land. We crawled through the deserted station of a sorry town of mudbrick and dirt roads. The man looked at the sign and at his atlas of China.

'Ah, that explains it – we're in Jiangxi now. I didn't think Zhejiang got that bad.'

Outside, the poorest of landscapes had occasioned the richest forms of ancestral worship. The graves themselves were just heaps of earth but they were littered with the sodden yellows and golds of ghost money and piled high with bright heaps of paper flowers and smouldering sticks of incense. There were charred circles on the beaten earth where greedy ghosts had been offered cash, paper clothing or replicas of household goods, and the ghosts had eaten their fill of the expensive food and drink in their living relatives' best crockery, leaving the remains for them to take back home.

'The local Party used to stop them wasting money like that, but now it's their own land and their own income and they can spend it how they want. It's all just superstition, but you can't explain that to these peasants. They just don't see that they'd be better off if they used the land to plant crops instead of building graves, and spent the money on themselves instead of their dead relatives. They think their ancestors will help them to get rich.' He drilled an index finger into his forehead just as the monk on Putuoshan had. 'But the only ones getting rich at Qingming are the businessmen who sell them all that junk.'

Pre-communist China saw the world as a succession of microcosms and macrocosms harmoniously repeating themselves on different scales. Social relationships and obligations varied little in substance but immensely in degree. At the top, the eternal workings of Heaven were reflected in the structures and rituals of the Emperor in his imperial capital, while at the bottom the lowliest of families had at its head a patriarch. The head of the household might be *yin*, or subordinate, to everybody else, but he was *yang*, or superior, to his wife and children. And just as the

Son of Heaven lavishly performed his filial duties to his imperial predecessors at the ancestral tombs, so the filial devotion of the poor farmer on a hillside was expressed with similar elements but on a much-reduced scale.

The monumental gateways to the imperial tombs outside Beijing were extravagant versions of those ornamented arches on the hills of rural Zhejiang. The lavish processions of emperors to the dynastic graves were mimicked in the snakes of threadbare farmers picking their way through the boulders and trees outside my window in impoverished Jiangxi, just as the offerings that drained the imperial coffers here became the bowls of rice and glasses of sorghum wine. Imperial ritual had ended in 1911, and its physical manifestations remained only as desiccated mummies and museum exhibits in dusty display cases, but at the start of the twenty-first century in post-reform China, the microcosm of ancestral worship was being acted out in front of me. China was reverting to being Chinese after half a century of imposing Western belief systems on itself, and today it was at its most Chinese.

Scarlet Phoenix

'In the south is the sun, its season that of summer. Its vital force is of *yang*, which begets fire, its virtues those of bestowing and of making joyous.'

Guanzi

CANTON

I HAD ALWAYS thought Canton an ugly city, and arriving as I now did at nine in the morning, in a downpour and having had practically no sleep on the noisy train, it seemed even more so. A shabby agglomeration of damp breezeblock houses and shops began to rise from the storm-lashed paddy soon after we crossed the Tropic of Cancer and almost an hour before we finally sighed to a halt. Cars and buses churned the road surfaces into a heavy spray which seemed to hang in the air defying gravity, while torrents of cyclists in wellingtons and flapping rain-capes plodded on grimly, their heads bowed.

The humid climate affected all of Canton's buildings, old or new, taking a perverse pleasure in rendering them equally mildewed and battered. Almost every single apartment and shop frontage bristled with air-conditioning units, each cradled in an iron stay and sheltered under a corrugated tin square. Their nooks and corners had been colonized by tropical greenery, ferns clinging to every niche and tendrils seeking out footholds. Rust dripped down walls in faecal smears and mould bloomed on the woodwork.

Architecturally, the city's only saving grace was Shamian Island, once just a sandbank in the Pearl River and formerly the foreign concession. Its streets comprised colonnaded colonial buildings in pastel shades, but even these mouldered in a warm, wet air of dereliction. The guidebook I had bought on the train told me that Shamian was a good place to eat and shop, but I found its restaurants expensive and intimidating, and its shops full of gimmicky name-chops and copies of Tang watercolours. Leaving the tourists to it, I walked over the putrid canal dividing the island from the rest of the city and into Canton proper.

It was lunchtime and very busy. The one small shop I found with spare seats was necessarily not the best – if it had been any good I would not have got in – but the woman who was serving wore a starched white cap, and a sign assured me that she used disposable spoons and bowls 'to avoid disease entering through the mouth'. The aluminium stockpot from which she ladled *zhou*, or rice porridge, was scorched and filthy but the contents were so hot that I could imagine them being poured from battlements to repel attackers. If anything survived long enough in there to enter through the mouth and make me ill then good luck to it. I ordered seasonal vegetables with oyster sauce while I waited for my *zhou* to cool down. The vegetables in season turned out to be oily lettuce. I had felt queasy since waking up, something I put down to the quantity of magnetized tea I had drunk the day before, and the oiliness of the food simply added to this.

And so the afternoon found me wandering the crowded streets in the rain, irritated at Canton and at having left Shanghai, a city which I loved. After a few increasingly damp and lonely hours irritation gave way to hatred. I hated Canton for its mouldy smell; for the rapacity of its shopkeepers and the sing-song drawl I imagined was directed at me; for its parades of Chinese medicine shops where vendors haggled over wheelbarrows full of beautiful species and their sorry-looking spare parts – dried seahorses, tortoise carapaces, deer antlers. The first time I had come to Canton, on a brief foray over the Hong Kong border ten years earlier, I had looked at it all with the fascination of the naïve, but now it depressed me to see identical quantities of plunder being hawked in the markets simply because the Cantonese believe that this or that will give you a bigger penis, or cleanse your blood or promote your *yang*. Whatever it was, they were wrong, and I wanted to confront them, but they outnumbered me, and in any case I couldn't speak Cantonese.

I hated upwardly mobile Canton because of the small boy who lay prostrate, shivering and almost naked on the overpass, his wild, jet-black hair curled in matted fingers on the sodden red asphalt. He held out an old tin can to catch the odd near-worthless paper note tossed to him. I especially hated the Cantonese because they had demolished the first little restaurant in which I had ever eaten in the People's Republic, and with it my first memories of the country. The Profiting the Masses Dining Hall had stood minding its own business on Shamian, serving up delicious cheap food from a single steaming wok at the back of its one room. A cassia tree grew up through the middle of it, and I could never decide which was supporting which. Now the restaurant had been torn down to make way for a nondescript flowerbed, leaving only a splash of paint and a couple of bent nails in the tree to say it had ever existed. I could not see how anyone could have benefited from its destruction, though at least I now knew which had been holding the other up.

I was not the only person nursing a grudge against Canton. That evening, after hand-washing my clothes and hanging them out to dry in the courtyard of the youth hostel, I walked out in search of a bar. A young man sidled up to me embarrassedly. He spoke in elegant, clipped British tones.

'Excuse me, but do you work for a company here in Canton?' His face was oriental, but not Han Chinese. My first assumption was that he was ultimately interested in my money. Was he, I asked, a moneychanger from China's Central Asian Xinjiang province or even Kazakhstan beyond?

'No, I'm from Inner Mongolia. I left to look for work, but I lost my *shenfenzheng*, my identity card, on the train.' And then he added sadly, 'I think it was stolen.' I had been in China often enough to understand the importance of identity cards. Without one you were practically *persona non grata*, unable to find a job, housing, medical care, sometimes even unable to buy a train ticket. An identity card could only be reissued in your home town. Why had he not turned around and gone back when he found it was missing?

'I was heading for Shanghai when I lost it. Then I heard that the employment regulations in Canton were very relaxed, and that you didn't need official papers to get a job anymore so I came here. But everywhere I've been, the first thing they want to see is my *shenfenzheng*. Do you have *guanxi* with anybody who owns a company here?' My *guanxi*, a network of mutually obliging contacts, could not conceivably have been smaller. I apologized and scratched my head, then I made to walk away and beckoned him to follow.

As we walked I asked him what had made him leave home to look for work. He had graduated from university and spoke fluent English. Could he not find work in the north?

'It's the weather. We've just had the worst winter anyone can remember in the Gobi. It was −50 °C in my village. All the animals died, so now we have no stock to raise and sell. It's terrible up there.' He stopped and looked down at the ground. He seemed to be conjuring up the Mongolian grassland, dotted with frozen carcasses. It started to spot with rain again and I held my umbrella over him.

'I should have just gone to Beijing like my family said.' He looked on the verge of tears.

I suggested that he try the British Consulate, more in the hope that he would cheer up at the thought than with any real belief that it would be of practical use.

'They might have a trade association or something, something that finds qualified Chinese employees for British firms.' This sounded like a good suggestion once I had voiced it, although I was not sure that Canton even had a British Consulate.

'Or perhaps you could try the big hotels,' I added. 'They sometimes have "wanted" boards.'

He carried on staring at the wet road as we walked, sucking his teeth, as if steeling himself to ask a big favour. I mentally totted up how much money his ticket back to Inner Mongolia might cost me if asked.

'Will you come back to Baotou with me? You can stay with my family in our village. Only I don't wish to travel there alone, and with a foreigner it might be easier. The police might not trouble me if I'm with you.' I had not expected such an offer and explained why I was in China, and that I now had less than three months to travel to Sanya, then to Ulugchat and finally on to Mohe.

'Oh, you don't really want to go to those places, do you? There's nothing to see, and Mohe is even colder than Baotou. Baotou would be much more fun!' Both our voices sounded desperate, his because he was alone in a foreign city and wanted a travelling companion, mine because I wanted to be independent and because I very much doubted that the snow-bound capital of Inner Mongolia would be any fun at all, especially as it would mean foregoing my travel plans. Chinese people invariably tell you that everywhere other than the town in which they grew up is not worth seeing. In fact I am surprised anybody ever bothers going anywhere, and it remains a mystery to me why the trains are always fully booked.

We had reached the end of the road and stood silently facing a rain-streaked pillar that supported a rumbling flyover. The Pearl River undulated in black crests and troughs below us. Then, after a painful few minutes, I said an embarrassed goodbye, wished him luck and edged away. He did not follow me, as I feared he might, but apologized for having troubled me. He did this in Chinese, '*Buhaoyisi . . .*' and I offered a comfortless apology back.

A few hundred yards on I felt terrible. Even if I could not help him find a job – I was just as much alone in Canton as he was – could I not at least have asked him to have a drink with me so that he didn't have to spend another evening on his own? I went back to see if I could find him, but he had disappeared.

On an enviable plot overlooking the Pearl River sits the United States Consulate-General. On the Sunday morning of my short stay in Canton I unpacked my shortwave radio, sat in a café from where I had a good view of the surpliced choristers filing into one of Shamian's churches, and tuned into first Voice of America and then the BBC World Service. I wanted to catch up with the Western media's reporting of the spy plane incident. A foreign correspondent in Beijing – 1,500 miles away from Hainan, the equivalent of reporting from Moscow on an incident at Heathrow – explained that the Party had been whipping up public anger. This was just what the West wanted to hear. It fitted neatly into the tidy stereotypes that explain everything that happens in China. There was talk of potent anti-American sentiments, of a state-controlled media and people blindly believing what they were told. The correspondent went on to tell listeners what the *People's Daily* was telling the man on the street to think, but he failed to mention the fact that nobody actually reads the *People's Daily* any more. Why should they, when every newsstand offers dozens of glossy women's titles franchized from the West, and any number of local scandal sheets and penny dreadfuls on sex and crime? The true state of anti-American feeling at street level was far more eloquently expressed by the long queue of visa applicants outside the consulate opposite the church. The heavily reported rhetoric coming out of Beijing did not appear to have affected the pragmatism of the average Cantonese.

I spent that evening drinking Pearl River Beer and losing at Chinese chess to the bored youth hostel staff. No matter how many times they shook their heads and explained, I would forget that generals, knights and elephants were forbidden to cross the river, forfeiting half of my turns as a result. After the fifth bottle, I forgot that cannons *could* cross the river, and this inability to deploy my heavy artillery hastened each inevitable rout.

The cleaners woke me brusquely at noon the next day when I failed to check out on time, and I had to negotiate an extra half day – my clothes were still wet, and the coach I planned to take to Haikou did not leave until the evening.

The muggy drizzle had not let up for a moment while I had

been in Canton and, when I finally did check out, my clothes were still just as damp as when I had hung them up to dry. Not only were they still damp, they had also begun to smell fusty and to grow green and white colonies of mould. There was simply not enough time to rewash and dry them, so I bundled them up in a soggy ball and shoved them into a plastic bag in the hope that Hainan would be drier.

HAI'AN

I TURNED UP at the bus station at nightfall bowed under the weight of my rucksack, and bracing myself for a scramble through a crowd of gawking peasants to plead with a bored clerk for a ticket on the overnight red-eye to Haikou, the capital of Hainan Island. So I felt a bit of a fraud when a beautiful girl in hip-hugging jeans and a silk sash advertising the Hainan bus-boat sleeper escorted me to a free position in a row of sparkling glass and chrome counters. The dot matrix display told me the price of a ticket to any destination I might care to name. I explained into the microphone that I was looking for a comfortable seat to Haikou, and within seconds my request had been tapped into a computer and a ticket printed. On the back of it, the operators of the shuttle service declared their 'Manifesto for Customer Satisfaction'. It included promises to leave punctually and to arrive on time, to provide a complementary evening meal with drinks and to maintain a clean bus with clean toilets on board. 'If you're happy, tell your friends. If not, tell us!' the manifesto concluded.

The sleeper was only half full, and another beautiful attendant in a red wasp-waisted uniform found me a double bed to myself. It was long enough to lie down in comfortably and had a sponge mattress, a pillow and a thin cotton quilt. The air-conditioning was turned on and at precisely eight o'clock we reversed out of the station and into the warm night.

We stopped at a roadside restaurant two hours later, where we were fed and watered. A handful of other coaches were there too, ranging from luxury sleepers like ours to the juddering deathtraps that carried migrant workers heading south. Groups of passengers squatted smoking under circling fans, and in the car park the registration plates bearing the provincial designation Yue – the name of an ancient southern state and now the abbreviated name for Canton – were being joined by ones displaying a Qiong, red quartzite, the mineral synonymous with Hainan.

'Whirr!'

'Pardon?'

'*Whirr!*'

I took it I was being spoken to in Cantonese. 'I'm sorry, I don't speak *Guangdonghua*. Can you say it in *Putonghua*?'

'It's English – you speak English, don't you?' For the life of me I could not work out what the man in the bunk opposite was trying to say, and my incomprehension was starting to make him lose face with the friend who peered out from behind him.

'What is "whirr" in Mandarin?' I asked.

'*Gongren!* Whirr!' It clicked. 'Worker' but with typical Chinese elision. Mandarin does not like to place certain consonants together or at the end of words, and many Chinese simply do away with the clusters rather than tackle them. I decided to lie to save him from embarrassment, even though I owed him nothing – after all, he had just shaken me awake to whirr at me.

'Sorry, your accent is very good, but I come from a part of England where we only speak a dialect of English.' That seemed to satisfy him. His English was now demonstrably better than mine, and he would waste no opportunity to prove this to his friend and to the bus at large.

'Paint!'

'Paint? *Youqi?*' An odd word to practise on me, I thought.

'No! Paint – *nongmin!*'

'Peasant! Your accent really is too good, that's why I can't understand you.' They both looked at me suspiciously. A note of sarcasm had crept into my voice. I then correctly guessed 'sore' to be 'soldier' and, buoyed up, he tried for a whole sentence, leaning over the edge of his bunk and putting his drunken red face close to mine. He smelt of *baijiu*, the vomit-tasting sorghum spirit that the Chinese mistakenly equate with malt whisky and his voice dropped as though letting me in on a secret.

'Zepeeray cayer foza whirr.' Then he broke into Mandarin. 'We're in the People's Liberation Army, and we learn English in barracks. Zepeeray cayer foza whirr. That's what we learn.' I knew that the PLA had for decades disseminated its internal propaganda very effectively under the guise of foreign language lessons. It might genuinely have 'cared for the workers', but what could possibly be the use of this soldier learning how to express his affection in English besides irritating the hell out of any invading English speakers until they agreed to peace terms?

'Zeayerfoss off zepeeray diffend ze whirr and paint fro ze agresh off fornpah.' This time I had not a clue. It had taken a good minute for the man first to remember, and then to grapple with, 'agresh' and 'fornpah', and I had half nodded off with the movement of the bus and the lateness of the hour.

'The airforce of the PLA defends the workers and peasants from the aggression of foreign powers. What do you think of the two-machines-mutually-colliding-incident?' It was the obvious choice of subject for a drunken PLA private with a captive audience and a Westerner who spoke English, if badly. I did not care. I just wanted to go to sleep. I told him that America was certainly in the wrong and that the Americans should apologize to the Chinese people. I thought this would help me to get to sleep quicker than saying what I really thought: although I felt sorry for the Chinese – they were stamping their feet because they were technologically unable to spy on the US in the same way – it seemed unlikely that a US$36,000,000 spy plane on automatic pilot had suddenly lurched towards a Chinese jet, and rather more likely that an overzealous Chinese pilot had fatally misjudged his distance. China needed to grow up a bit and accept that the US would spy on it, and America needed to be a bit more circumspect in flaunting its hardware.

'If a Chinese spy plane had crashed into an American jet in American airspace, the American people would demand an apology. We're only asking for what is right.' His friend raised himself on to one elbow, looked straight at me and nodded in agreement. Perhaps they had a point, but I had begun to drift in and out of consciousness, the ins originating from the swaying of the bus and the cans of beer I had knocked back in the roadside restaurant, the outs caused by his shaking my shoulder. The drunk launched into the stock favourite of the pub bore the world over. We might come from different countries but as long as we understand each other then we can live as one big happy family. His friend was more jingoistic.

'China's economy is the strongest in the world,' he said. 'Soon China will be the most important nation and the West will respect us. That will be good, don't you think?' I smiled weakly and agreed. As I closed my eyes and finally succumbed to the aching need for sleep, I felt his alcoholic breath waft over me.

'There are lots of black people in England, aren't there? We don't like black people . . .'

The smooth progress we had made on the motorway outside Canton had ceded to the crunching stop-start of potholed roads on the Leizhou peninsula, the Land of Thunder that curves out into the warm waters of the South China Sea to be buffeted by tropical storms. It must have been one of these jolts that brought me round again in the early hours. A full ivory moon skimmed the surface of the palm trees lining the road and bathed the flat roofs of hamlets and car repair shops in a luminous dust. The clouds had vanished and the drizzle had abated, but the temperature had risen as we drove south and a sheen of oily sweat now plastered my hair to my forehead.

In China, it is possible to tell with a fair degree of accuracy where you are from the mix of vehicle licence plates. The Hainanese Qiongs had grown more numerous, and the numbers after the Cantonese Yue had increased in size as we distanced ourselves from the provincial capital, designated Yue 01. Now we were joined by the occasional Gui – cassia tree – from the Guangxi Autonomous Region beyond the Parting of the Clouds Mountains to the west. The uneven surface of the road kept me on the brink of sleep until at 5.30 a.m. we came to an unheralded halt before the Hai'an ferry terminal.

Hai'an means Sea at Peace. It sits at the southernmost tip of mainland China. A quick, sleep-deprived walk around the town relegated it in my memory to a drab collection of slumbering hotels under stammering neon signs, serving the crowds of travellers who only ever visit with the intention of leaving. The waiting hall filled up in quiet anticipation of the six o'clock ferry. Apart from the low entreaties for alms from a woman who held out a tin can in what remained of a horribly burned hand, the Chinese were uncharacteristically tired and silent. The boat tickets handed out by the coach attendant showed a picture of a luxury liner that bore no relation to the rusty tub tied up alongside the pier. I found an empty seat, entwined my rucksack around one leg for safety, and fell asleep as the rumble of the engines rose to a muffled crescendo and the boat slipped into the Qiongzhou Strait.

The television next to my head woke me barely a quarter of an hour later and I found myself staring back at a deckful of faces. I might not have been the centre of attention at Canton bus station, but down here I could rival a Korean War film in my ability to hold the curious gaze of the passengers. I stared back. Beside the normal spectrum of Han faces – mainly the leathery tans and flat cheekbones of the southern Chinese peasant but also a few high-cheeked, ruddy complexions of the north – several faces stood out as Indo-Chinese, the delicate noses and slight features of Vietnam and Thailand unmistakeable on them. One young man, bare-chested and with freckles peppering his pale skin, sat holding hands with a girl. They spoke in a language I could not place. His neck was disfigured with red weals raised by scraping at the skin to release bad winds from the body, as is the practice in parts of Vietnam. He had probably had just a cold or a stomach upset, but now he looked as if he was suffering from some hideous medieval affliction. I had expected to see migrants from all over China who had come to look for work on Hainan, but not economic immigrants from Vietnam.

There were more people than seats, and the port gangway was choked with passengers who, unable to find a space to squat, had gathered to watch the sunrise. At barely twenty degrees north the dawn off Hainan is a hurried affair, the sun impatient to reach its distant zenith. I joined the press and squeezed into a gap next to the handrail. The horizon had already begun to blush a pale coral against the sky's polished grey, and the sea responded in the purest of aquamarines. The contrast with the Yangtze's sludgy ochre and slaty light was absolute. The water, green in its depths, was crystal clear as it dashed against our bows, and pure white as it foamed in our wake. It rose and fell in silky hummocks under a pleasant breeze.

The sun delayed her appearance until half an hour after first light. She had already risen some distance above the horizon when she broke through the light sea mist, and when she did she described a perfect blood-red disc in a crimson sward. Rising further, she outpaced her retinue of thin cloud until she was an unnatural scarlet. Soaring higher, she paled to a white-hot circle, and by the time the cranes and tower blocks of the capital appeared over the southern horizon my clothes were soaked with sweat. It was early April and not yet eight in the morning.

HAINAN

The tropical island of Hainan – its name means South of the Sea – has been part of the Chinese world since the Western Han dynasty. Lying a thousand miles south of the imperial capital Chang'an, it was feared for its savage aborigines, for the appalling difficulties involved in getting there, for its heat, its humidity, its pestilences that decimated invading armies and its dense mountain forests infested with terrifying wild animals. In Hainan, the Chinese found in their own backyard their equivalent of Europe's Darkest Africa. From the seventh century it served as China's place of banishment for disgraced officials. The Han Chinese still date their cultural genesis in Hainan from the work of these reluctant exiles in carrying the light of Confucian learning to this torrid Siberia.

In the thirteenth century, as the Southern Song dynasty crumbled, the Emperor and his court fled south, pursued by Kublai Khan's Mongol hordes and taking with them a wave of refugees. The last Song emperor, just a babe in arms, drowned in the South China Sea in 1279. Another wave of immigrants broke over Hainan when in the mid-seventeenth century the native Chinese Ming fell to the Manchu Qing. It was around this time too that the West first became interested in Hainan. The Jesuits founded a mission near Haikou to carry the light of Christian learning to the heathen Confucians but they failed to make an impact, and it was not until the opening up of the port to foreign trade after the Opium Wars that Christianity returned, first from France and later from Denmark and other European nations.

From the West's point of view, Hainan's potential for trade remained disappointingly unfulfilled. Fearing bloodthirsty pirates and murderous savages, commercial vessels would sail past the island, only stopping to carry out the most urgent repairs or to seek shelter from one of its frequent and ferocious tropical storms. In fact, Hainan's precise position was only determined with any accuracy in the 1880s, when it was discovered that previous charts had been out by twelve nautical miles. By then, Haikou consisted of a single street and some straggling settlements lining the dirty streams that fed Haidian Creek, the whole affair being partly enclosed by a ramshackle wall. Hainan's foreign trading community, barely a dozen strong, dealt principally in sugar and live pigs, while in return the Hainanese imported opium by the shipload. (In 1882, Mr Benjamin Couch Henry became one of the first British travellers to explore Hainan's interior, making his way across the island in the company of a Mr Jeremiassen, a Danish missionary who had earlier circumambulated the coast to test the supposed savagery of the natives. Henry described how Hainan's opium dens seemed to outnumber its schools, and how the male population was for the most part hopelessly addicted and forced to beg for money from termagant wives who held the purse-strings.)

From the beginning, Hainan was exploited as a *de facto* colony of China, ruled from Canton and providing raw materials for the mainland economy. Gold mined in Hainan's hills, scarlet jaspers hewed from its quarries and exquisite feathers and furs taken from its tropical wildlife were transformed into jewellery and clothes for China's nobles. Rare and precious hardwoods from its rainforests were used in building the palaces of successive imperial capitals. The Qianlong Emperor, who refused Lord Macartney the loan of Chusan, had timber from Hainan's interior transported all the way to Beijing. Mao, not to be outdone, used Hainanese wood in his Great Hall of the People on Tiananmen Square.

In the mid-twentieth century, Hainan fell victim to another imperial power. In February 1939 the Japanese conquered the island and immediately began to exploit its new colony's iron ore, coal and oil deposits. In doing so it laid the foundations of Hainan's post-war heavy industries.

On 30 April 1950, Hainan became one of the last territories to be formally occupied by the People's Liberation Army, a full seven months after Mao had declared the founding of the People's Republic from the Gate of Heavenly Peace in Beijing. The withdrawal of Chiang Kai-shek's Kuomintang armies south along the Leizhou peninsula to Hainan was so rapid that their comrades already on the island had little time to dig in defensively. Such respite as Hainan did get in early 1950 came from the fact that the PLA did not at the time possess a viable navy and was reluctant to press home its advantage across water. (The Zhoushan archipelago similarly held out until the spring of that year.) With their senior command still in disarray on Taiwan over 600 miles away, Hainan's Nationalist forces were faced not only with the build-up of communist troops barely ten miles away across the Qiongzhou Strait but also with local communist guerrillas. Disillusioned, and unable to lead a full-blooded defence of the island, the 100,000-strong Nationalist garrison collapsed within a fortnight.

Though now 'liberated', Hainan continued to be treated as a colony. Beijing, fearing that local loyalties would lie with the communist veterans who had helped secure Hainan for the People's Republic, dispatched its Southbound Work Team to the island. It consisted of cadres from the mainland, who were given preferential positions within local government, and skilled technicians and workers whose job it was to establish or develop modern industries such as mines and petrochemical works.

In 1956, under the slogan 'Let a hundred flowers bloom, let a hundred schools of thought contend', Mao loosened the constraints on criticizing the Party. The campaign seemed to be aimed primarily at garnering constructive criticism from China's alienated intellectuals, but many took the opportunity to rail at abuses within the Party leadership. On Hainan, a large number of the island's native cadres complained bitterly about the imposition of cadres from the mainland.

The nationwide clamour to denigrate Mao and his revolution threatened to undermine the Party's authority. Whether the Hundred Flowers was part of a predetermined plan to uncover the Party's enemies, or whether Mao was genuinely shocked by the bitterness it had revealed, is still debatable. Whatever the reason, the campaign was brought to an end, and those who had spoken out were purged in the subsequent Anti-Rightist campaign of 1957. On Hainan, alleged disloyalty to the Communist Party was used as the pretext for a further purge of local Hainanese from positions of power.

The Party's grip on Hainan's political and economic life was further strengthened by the arrival in the fifties of the Production and Construction Corps, a paramilitary organization that opened up Hainan to large-scale exploitation for the first time. Virgin tracts were cleared and replanted with economically strategic rubber and sugar, and Hainan's climax rainforest was felled to make way for monoculture timber plantations.

The scale of environmental destruction on Hainan was such that the island's natural forest cover, which prior to the arrival of the Corps amounted to half its land area, was by the mid-nineties down to less than one-tenth, and by the time I visited, it had almost vanished. As a result, the water table had dropped, many rivers were now dry, and everywhere there were signs of desertification and erosion.

A handbook produced in the eighties to drum up Western investment in China's newly opened coastal cities summed up the status of Hainan's ecology in the greater scheme of the reform programme. It explained how Hainan was home to 4,200 species of plant, fifteen per cent of China's total, of which 600 were not found elsewhere, and how forty per cent of its 800 species of tree were rare and protected. In conclusion it noted that 'Hainan contains China's biggest tropical rainforest, which awaits further development' and that its fauna, including flying squirrels, bears, deer, pangolins and gibbons, 'are sources of quality hides, medicines, cooking delicacies and great beauty'. The order of importance said it all.

After Chiang Kai-shek's withdrawal to Taiwan and the PLA's liberation of Hainan, the two islands had developed very differently. By the eighties, capitalist Taiwan had created an economy that far outstripped the similarly sized, communist Hainan. Just as Shanghai's foreign concessions had shamed the Kuomintang in the thirties and inspired the Greater Shanghai Plan, so Hainan's continuing backwardness compared with Taiwan was an embarrassment to the regime in Beijing whose legitimacy increasingly rested on its ability to improve the lives of its citizens.

When the economic reform programme began in 1979, the party sought a region where reforms could be tested before they were implemented on the mainland. Hainan was representative of China as a whole in terms of income, gross domestic product and social make-up but, unlike Shanghai and other major cities, failure there could be contained without threatening the centre. So in 1988 it was announced that Hainan was to become a Special Economic Zone and also, for the first time in its history, a province. The slow trickle of economic migrants who had come to Hainan after 1979 became a flood, and the island became infamous as a *laissez-faire* Wild South where the Party turned a blind eye to shady business practices and spiritual pollution, and where entrepreneurs could make a fast buck.

Sky-high growth figures of over twenty per cent each year would come mainly from the exploitation of Hainan's offshore oil and gas, from fruit-processing – every stall on every street corner in China sells coconut milk canned in Hainan, not to mention mango and pineapple juice – and from tourism. Developers saw tourism as a way of cashing in on Hainan's opening up. The building boom that followed turned into a bust when overstretched banks staunched the flow of credit. Whereas there had been only 300 tourist hotel rooms in all of Hainan before 1988, now new hotels became so numerous that they regularly closed before they had even opened. As my taxi crossed a flyover on the drive in to Haikou I could make out at a glance half a dozen high-rise shells standing empty.

HAIKOU

ONCE THE AIR-CONDITIONER had cooled the room down to a bearable temperature, I lay naked on the bed and tried to catch up on the sleep I had missed on the bus. When I awoke, the street ten storeys below baked in the noonday heat. Pedestrians were scarce, most people preferring to sit out the hottest hours of the day under shop awnings or in the shade of the coconut palms that lined the main roads. Where occasionally someone did brave the open, they cast the most perfunctory of shadows that shimmered in the heat haze at their feet. I turned on the television and emptied the ball of damp clothes from my rucksack into the sink. The mould had gone wild overnight, and only after a prolonged bout of wringing and rinsing in the bathtub did they look clean once more. I hung them on clothes hangers and then poked them through the security bars of my balcony to dry in the sun.

On Hainan TV the *China Report* dwelt on the spy plane crisis. Discussions covered not only America's Far East policy and its implications for China's relations with Taiwan, but also changes in American policy on military intervention in Europe and the Middle East. Within the space of half an hour I learned more than I had gleaned from any number of shortwave broadcasts from London or Washington, and by the time I switched the TV off, my clothes were baked dry. It was time to find some food.

The hot air hit me with a rush as I pushed aside the lobby doors. The temperature was in the high thirties but it was mercifully dry, a change from the humidity of the past week. After walking half a block in the open, however, the power of the sun beating down became unbearable and I took shelter in the nearest food shop. It specialized in *doujiang* – soybean milk – and other breakfast staples, as was clear from a sign in the window. With the melodramatic shifts of typeface one associates with patent Victorian nostrums, it detailed *doujiang's* health-giving properties.

> *Doujiang* lowers CHOLESTEROL and reduces hardening of the arteries! It expels bad *qi* and balances the ORGANS! It keeps the lungs wet and helps to unblock CATARRHAL MUCUS! It opens the intestines and facilitates BOWEL MOVEMENTS! It moistens the skin and prevents the onset of WRINKLES! We enjoin our honoured guests to drink *doujiang* regularly!

My lungs were not much drier, my organs no more unbalanced than they usually were, but the change to a diet of rice, not to mention the magnetized tea and the havoc my malarial tablets were wreaking on my digestion, made me willing to try anything to facilitate my bowel movements. I was ushered into a seat next to a fearsome air-conditioner that blew a pneumonial fog of supercooled air at me until I switched tables.

I ordered two *youtiao* – foot-long strips of puffy, deep-fried dough, the oily archetype of the Chinese breakfast – and a bowl of *luroufan*, boiled rice topped with soy-braised minced pork and served with comforting chunks of sweet-pickled mooli. They arrived with a bowl of seaweed soup fragrant with sesame. My *doujiang* came warm and sweet, the colour of clotted cream and the consistency of condensed milk. While I ate I watched life return to the street outside as the shadows lengthened.

This was not a China I recognized. I had never been so far south before and everything I saw seemed to tell me I was elsewhere –

the Philippines perhaps, or Thailand, or maybe Vietnam. On my first day in Hainan, only the Chinese characters on every surface convinced me otherwise.

For a start, there were the coconuts. Coconut palms cannot grow above certain latitudes, and in China this means that you will not see them on the mainland. But here they lined almost every street, sometimes in Indian file but often in a double row, their long, tattered leaves arching to meet in the middle and thereby providing some shade from the sun. Beneath their crowns, bunches of coconuts hung like great clusters of wooden grapes, green and smooth, their woody husks yet to be hacked away with hefty kukris by the coconutmongers.

Then there was the Hainanese Specialities Shop, the roadway in front of it heaped with produce from the interior. The largest pile was of unhusked coconuts, still attached to their thick, green stems. Beside these, a wooden stall bowed under the weight of durian, betel nut, mangoes, papaya, tamarind and pineapples. Lengths of deep purple sugarcane were stacked in bundles against a wall behind crates of pomegranates, lychees, dragon's eyes and clenched fists of tiny, fat bananas.

The Hainanese themselves seemed at first sight laid back almost to the point of loucheness. The tropical climate, the fecundity of their island home and thirteen years of economic freedom seemed to have combined to create an atmosphere of indolent hedonism. Many of the women, their hair inexpertly dyed blonde, shuffled along in flip-flops, semi-transparent baby-doll nighties and skirts that were little more than pelmets to their slim hips. Somehow they brought to mind the bored-looking young prostitutes who congregate in Thai bars, similarly dressed and exuding the same air of detached licentiousness.

Men lounged on every street corner and under every palm. Most were not local and had come looking for work in what they had heard was boomtown Haikou. Instead they lay un-employed on reed mats, their lean torsos naked and tanned, their trousers rolled up to the thigh. Some dozed, some played cards or Chinese chess. Many of them smoked and drank from bottles of *baijiu*, and all of them nudged each other and whispered *laowai* as I passed. This was often followed by a garbled halloo that was either repeated until I acknowledged it with a smile or, if I ignored it, became an irritated *wei!* – oi!

One incident later that day, as I wandered through the crowds under the palms, stayed in my mind for weeks. The migrants had been hallooing and *wei*-ing for most of my afternoon stroll, and I had ignored them for the most part, but one man squatting on his haunches with half a dozen friends on the roadway ahead of me momentarily caught my eye as he addressed me.

'*Wei! Laowai!* Do you want a fight?' He held up his fists, half in jest, like a prizefighter. In mock surrender I raised my hands, thanking him but declining the offer, and carried on. Behind me I could hear laughter. Never before in China had I encountered even a veiled hint of violence towards me simply because I was a foreigner. Had he meant it? I was unsure. Perhaps he thought I was American. It had been such a naïve, almost comic threat, yet I was disturbed that it had been voiced at all. He seemed to want to create a confrontation, only he lacked the stock vocabulary of hatred through which to articulate this. To my knowledge, no foreigner had been beaten to death in Hainan since the murder of a French missionary in 1849. I prayed that would remain the case for at least a couple of weeks longer.

The year-long saturnalia that the reform programme had created on Haikou's streets was evident when I got back to my room. While I was out, some unseen hand had pushed a flyer for a food delivery service under my door. China's hotel staff regularly supplement their meagre wages by tipping off local businesses as to which rooms contain potential customers. Foreign men are much in demand.

The restaurant supplying the service was named after

Chang'e, a famously beautiful woman who stole the elixir of immortality and fled with it to the moon. This should have given me a clue. The flyer offered dishes from all over China, which it promised to deliver promptly and free of charge to my room. Below, it listed some tempting choices, from fried wonton or *charsiu* pork steamed buns for breakfast, to set menus of seasonal vegetables, spare ribs, pig's intestines and fried beef slices, with a choice of either pig's trotter rice or 'slimy beef' rice. At the very bottom, in bold characters much larger than the rest of the menu, came the last item: 'Now we can also offer you a Thai-style health-giving massage in your own room. Just call to order your food on our hotline number and to specify whether you would like Miss Ji, Miss Xu, Miss Li, Miss Yang, Miss Wu or Miss Zhang to deliver your meal for you.' It added that a Mister Zhong was also available.

Deciding to forego food, I sat under the air-conditioner with a beer and listened to my shortwave radio for a while. A foreign reporter explained that the Chinese state-run media were preparing the people for a climb-down on the release of the American aircrew, but then the signal deteriorated and all I could find were broadcasts in what I took to be Vietnamese, Thai or perhaps Khmer from across the Gulf of Tonkin. Nothing of interest was on television, so I threw on a T-shirt and headed back out.

The streets were still sultry, the lights from the shop fronts illuminating in equal measure the families who walked hand in hand, the couples draped around each other and the mini-skirted prostitutes who stood soliciting on the pavements. A woman old enough to be my grandmother saw me, disentangled herself from a knot of friends and scuttled over on kitten heels to ask me bluntly if I wanted sex. I smiled and shook my head, and without drawing breath she tottered on past me and propositioned an elderly man coming the other way.

I came across the gateway to a covered arena. A table had been set up outside selling tickets to what a banner declared was the Hainan Kickboxing Challenge Cup. It was still early, a ticket was only 2 *renminbi*, and I was welcomed with a nod.

Inside, the oval stadium was dim and the air oppressive. Blue-painted concrete rose in tiered ranks, the topmost screened from the monsoon rains by a corrugated iron roof erected on a scaffold of trusses. The spectators sat on the concrete steps or on plastic chairs that were scattered about. The arena was slowly filling up, mainly with young men. They had the same delicate, south-east Asian features I had seen on the ferry from Hai'an, and they sat in twos or threes, semi-naked or with the sleeves of their white T-shirts rolled up over sinewy shoulders. Some guarded trophy girlfriends with tinted, spiky hair and platform shoes. Barely a head was turned to acknowledge the appearance of the lone foreigner in their midst, but still I felt a frisson of anxiety. The threat from the man on the street had unnerved me and now I was surrounded by the lowest of the migrant underclass, people so poor they had left home and come to China to look for work, people who passed the hot evenings watching violent martial arts. I mounted the seating and slid into an anonymous corner. A few heads turned, then looked away. Not a breath of air reached the ground from the roof space, and the crowd simmered in anticipation.

The only illumination came from spotlights, suspended from the roof and trained on a boxing ring in the centre of the floor, and from unshaded bulbs which lit what I took to be the judges' tables tucked in each corner and arrayed along the wall farthest from me. Behind each of these simple wooden desks sat two people who pored over sheets of paper in a pool of orange light. Spectators would sporadically approach them, exchange a few words and then go back to their seats. Otherwise, the stadium was a patchwork of threatening shadows.

The murmur of the crowd died down as a woman in her thir-ties climbed through the ropes and into the ring with as much

elegance as her tight leather miniskirt would allow but unavoid-
ably flashing a pair of red knickers as she did so. Dressed in tarty,
high-heeled ankle boots and a denim jacket, she welcomed us all
and then began to warble her way through several karaoke
numbers to the accompaniment of an overamplified speaker
beside her. As song succeeded song, the crowd grew restless.

Eventually, she stopped singing and introduced our host, a big
man with a big hairdo immobile under a layer of lacquer. He in
turn introduced the referee, who climbed into the ring and
bowed respectfully towards each side of the arena. The first bout
was introduced and the combatants removed their hooded capes
to reveal head guards, shin pads and feet bound tightly for protection. One, in his late teens and of average build, wore red
shorts. His opponent was a tall beanpole of a boy whose purple
silk shorts made him look like a Silk Cut advert. The referee
called them together and dropped his arm to start the fight. What
followed was not what I had expected.

The lanky boxer was like the kid at school who is no good at
games – all flailing legs and arms and no co-ordination – but his
reach was much longer than that of his opponent and the inele-
gant match quickly degenerated into a schoolyard fight of
pawing and shoving. The occasional lucky hit or well-aimed
kick raised roars of appreciation. A cymbal brought the first
round to a close, and the combatants retired to their corners
while the referee drew an envelope from a velvet bag offered him
by the host. He deposited the envelope in a bucket, which was
then hoisted to the ceiling on a rope.

The second round began. Eventually, the beanpole's inability
to do anything other than thrash wildly in the hope of hitting
home led to his being thrown out of the ring to hysterical laughter from the crowd. Both fighters bowed, the referee thanked
them good-naturedly and then the bucket was lowered again and
he removed the envelope.

'Southern Fist!' He held up the printed card it contained to each corner of the stadium and cries of triumph broke out. Then he replaced the card in the velvet bag, the contents were shaken for him and he withdrew another at random, depositing it again in the bucket. This I took to be the draw for the next fight, before which we were forced to sit through a melodramatic love song from our bouffant host.

The second pairing turned out to be no better or worse than the first, with the same drawing of a card between each round – this time Black Square – the same cheers, the same shuffling and replacement in the bucket. The air had stagnated as the night progressed and was now a sultry fug of sweet cigarette smoke tinged with the smell of sweat. The deadened sound of a police siren was audible in the distance.

The third fight was a mixed bout, pitching a plump girl against a much smaller boy. She laid into him from the off, bringing the crowd to its feet.

'Northern Foot!' shouted the referee. There were cheers. The number of people examining the judges' scoring had increased with each round, and now there was a constant flow of spectators moving between the seating, the lone tables and the row of hunched bodies against the wall facing me. Yet the outcome of each bout had seemed perfectly clear. There was a great discrepancy between the amateurishness of the boxing and the bureaucracy of the judging. I edged towards the nearest table to take a look.

A woman wearing a diaphanous blouse over a lacy bra took 100 *renminbi* from one of the crowd and passed it to the man on her right. She scribbled the sum and the number of the round on a pad, handed one carbon copy back, gave one to her partner and kept one for herself. Her partner, a pockmarked man with muscular forearms that glistened with sweat, tugged at the red banknote with nicotine-stained fingers to check it was genuine. Chairman Mao glared back at him. The Great Helmsman had banned gambling after 1949 along with rickshaws and for that matter prostitution. The cymbal sounded the end of another round and the woman leapt up and passed a wad of counterfoils to the row of hunched bodies, her partner's eyes following the pale thighs and suspenders now visible above the tops of her stockings.

Across the arena, the hunchbacks flicked at their abacuses and counted out the cash for the winning tickets. One man nonchalantly accepted a handful of red 100 *renminbi* notes from a teller and counted out his winnings. One hundred, two hundred, three hundred . . . over two thousand *renminbi*. Though it is hard to estimate the average annual wage in a nation with such great disparities between rich and poor, town and country, it is probably somewhat less than 5,000 *renminbi*.

As I left, the ticket-seller grinned and shouted after me.

'Did you have a flutter?' I had not brought enough money with me to have a flutter in Hainan.

'Isn't gambling illegal?' I asked.

'Of course gambling is illegal, but this is *caipiao* – a lottery. You have to be very skilful to guess which card will be drawn in each round. The odds don't change, so there's no gambling involved.'

'What are the odds?'

'Five to two.'

'But the chances of guessing right are three to one, so surely everybody must lose eventually?' He tilted his head to one side, smiled and spoke slowly, as though a foreigner was incapable of understanding the skill involved.

'Some players are supremely talented. They pray for good fortune at the temple and observe the patterns in the cards already drawn to predict the next one.'

The streets outside were still full of Hainanese making the most of the cool of the night. On the way back to my hotel I passed something I had never seen before in the People's Republic, though I had heard they existed: a discreet sign that read 'Sex

Aids'. The shop it advertised was barely a broom cupboard in size, its walls covered floor to ceiling on all three sides with glass shelves displaying a pervert's Aladdin's cave of appliances and potions. Behind the door, a melamine counter half hid the owner, a tired woman in her forties whose frumpy, flowery dress and large, thick-rimmed spectacles made her look the epitome of a respectable librarian. She glanced up from her magazine as I sidled in.

'*Wan'an*. Can I . . . just take a look round? I didn't know there were shops selling . . . these kinds of things in China.' My eyes rested on an enormous, double-ended vibrator.

'*Wan'an*. Take your time. You have these in your country, don't you? Married couples in China want to buy them too, you know.' Her schoolmarmish tone made me feel like I had been told off. I was genuinely surprised at the range she had on offer but swallowed the observation for fear of being reprimanded again. A shuffling behind me made me turn round. A man was cajoling a pretty girl to go inside. She submitted with a humph, took one look at a shelf of eye-watering dildos with protruding veins, winced, giggled nervously and ran back outside. The librarian did not blink. I presumed she had seen it all before. The man remained, however, working his way through a selection of delay sprays and aphrodisiacs.

'Is this Spanish Fly the spray-on kind?' It was, but the one he was holding was imported, and much more expensive than the Chinese-produced one, replied the owner. While they discussed Spanish Fly I looked at the rest of the stock. On the shelves labelled 'Girls' there were dildos and vibrators, butt plugs, vibrating butterfly wings, love eggs, crotchless knickers and fiendish clitoral stimulators. The 'Boys' shelves were laden with penis enlargers – one of them attached to a fearsome-looking pump – inflatable dolls with disturbingly realistic pubic hair, artificial vaginas with unrepeatable English names whose nuances I doubted could be translated into Mandarin, Arab straps, and a large assortment of condoms in all shapes, colours, flavours and textures. Everywhere were plastered the obligatory pornographer's shots of women looking lustfully at the purchaser or faking the multiple orgasms that the product promised. Most of the women were Westerners, some Japanese, a few Chinese.

One shelf was labelled 'Educational sex films'. On the sleeve of a Chinese-made DVD entitled *Sexal Intebercorse* a Chinese girl knelt demurely, naked but contriving not to show anything explicit. In the simplified Chinese characters of the communist mainland the blurb claimed that the film was intended to show couples how to enjoy sex within marriage. Grainy stills gave the would-be purchaser an idea of what he might see if he parted with 500 *renminbi*.

'Is this legal?' I asked the librarian, pointing to a freeze-frame shot of what was probably not a married couple since it consisted of three naked women. 'I thought pornography was banned in China.'

'It's to help married couples to be sexually satisfied,' she persisted. 'There's still a lot of ignorance about sex in China, even here. Lots of people get married without ever having had sex, and they're often too embarrassed to go to a doctor to admit they're having problems when they try. They can come in here, get advice and buy products that are properly tested, not that useless stuff sold by herbalists on the street.' Perhaps she was right. Whatever the case, this was preferable to the wheelbarrowfuls of dried animal parts on sale in Canton.

DONGPO

ON THE WALLS of the memorial hall to Su Dongpo, an enormous frieze narrates the story of how he civilized the Li, the aborigines of Hainan. In the same mute didactic style as the biblical murals of Europe's cathedrals, it depicts a procession of patriarchal Su

Dongpos enlightening the savages. Here we see him being banished to Hainan, and here he is, Moses-like, instructing the natives where to dig to find fresh water. In the next scene we see him imparting the gift of Chinese writing to the illiterate barbarians. Look how he taught them to make ink from pine soot and gum, and how to plough the soil and sow crops. Before he came they didn't have rice wine or the Confucian classics. The Li respected him, and he was like a father to them, as we can see from the next picture. Here, in the last scene, he is thinking deeply before writing a valedictory poem. He didn't want to come to Hainan, but look how much he regretted going back when he was finally pardoned! A ripple of knowing laughter from the Chinese tour group punctuated their guide's explanation.

Su Shi was an official during the Song dynasty. A formidable scholar and poet, a gourmand and a heavy drinker fond of experimenting with home-brewed wine, he was accused of criticizing official policy in verse and was banished to a remote region of central China, adopting the pen-name Dongpo after the place where he settled. Following a pardon, he rose again through the official ranks but in 1094 he was sentenced to exile once more, this time ending up on Hainan's remote north-west coast. His hall in the Five Officials Memorial Temple outside Haikou is a shrine to the Han Chinese assertion of cultural legitimacy on the island.

Once you have seen one memorial temple you have seen them all, and I had not planned to come to this one, but with a day spare before I left for Sanya I had decided to visit what seemed to be Haikou's sole cultural attraction. I had set out early in the morning to avoid the worst of the day's heat, but by nine o'clock I was glad to seek shelter from the sun in the arboretum that surrounds the temple. The grounds were lovingly cared for, with borders of closely trimmed, sweet-smelling jasmine and carefully labelled specimens of Hainan's exotic trees. Bright orange pods dangled from the branches of *Theobroma cacao*, bunches of green betel nuts hung beneath the wispy crowns of *Areca catechu*, and spiky red huddles drooped just outside my furtive reach from *Litchi chinensis*.

Reassured of their historical roots, the tourists strolled on through the stone-pillared colonnades and shaded courtyards of the temple with an air of tranquil superiority. In a room dedicated to the exiled officials who from the Tang onwards had sinicized Hainan, they gathered to hear their guide sermonize on their achievements.

'Before the officials arrived, the Li were very backward. When a relative died, they didn't cry like us. Does anybody know what they did?' Silence. 'They ate raw meat to show their grief!' Laughter. The guide made an attempt at mimicking a grief-stricken tribesman eating raw meat, but he just looked like a balding, forty-something Chinese making fun of the aborigines.

'They lived naked in the forests' (I was thankful he did not try to act this out) 'and hunted with poison arrows and bows made from bamboo. The Li have a story about where they came from. They say that the Thunder Spirit took an egg high into the mountains, and that the Li Mother hatched from it. She married a man who came to Hainan from over the sea to the west looking for magical herbs, and she gave birth to the Li tribe. We know that this is simply a myth. The Five Officials taught them how to farm and to write and gradually the Li became civilized.' His talk continued with the innate self-assurance of absolute hegemony.

He did not mention that there was little love lost between the Li and their Chinese rulers. Sporadic major rebellions by the Li against the Chinese presence were suppressed only through enormous financial and military effort, most notably in the sixteenth century when on three occasions the Li rose on such a scale that each uprising reportedly required the movement of 10,000 troops from the mainland to restore order, to say nothing of the almost constant minor eruptions that demanded a continuous military presence. Even as recently as 1882 the Li had risen up near Sanya in the south. An army sent to quell the insurrection succumbed to malaria in the low-lying swamps while the Li remained safe in their impenetrable jungle home. After this failure, a mandarin was dispatched to replace the military commander. He sent four common soldiers to the Li chieftain, saying that these were his own two brothers and two Chinese officials offered as hostages, and vouching for the chieftain's personal safety if he would consent to meet to discuss peace. The chieftain agreed, but when he arrived he was clapped in irons and taken to Canton where he was executed. In retaliation, the infuriated Li flayed the hostages alive.

There are now just over one million Li on Hainan, out of a total population of over seven million. They are thought to descend not from the Li Mother and a Vietnamese herbalist but from Polynesian islanders who reached the island during the Neolithic period, and until the advent of the communists they lived mainly by subsistence farming of hardy mountain rice.

After Liberation, autonomous prefectures were established and the top posts were occupied by Li cadres. Then, in the fifties, the Production and Construction Corps appropriated large tracts of the richly forested Li territory and turned them into plantations, and the Anti-Rightist campaign provided a pretext for the removal of the Li cadres and their replacement with Beijing appointees. The central government, bent on exploiting Hainan's natural wealth, had ended the brief flowering of Hainanese self-government.

Today, many Li are employed by Hainan's growing tourist industry either directly – performing the songs and dances by which the Han Chinese define them – or indirectly, producing traditional handicrafts. In Haikou, I passed Li farmers sitting in groups on street corners, dressed in grubby embroidered cottons and wearing conical hats. They sold bananas, mangoes and loose tea from wicker panniers. When I sat down to eat at one of the market stalls that appeared on the streets after dark they held out their produce and hissed unintelligibly at me until I bought something or until the stallholder chased them away. They all seemed to be old women, every mouth a jumble of betel stains and gold caps. At night, I saw them sleeping where they had sat during the day, cloths pulled across their baskets for safety.

The shadows in the temple courtyards shortened and then disappeared, and I caught the bus back to the cool of my hotel room.

That afternoon I decided to explore Haikou. A man on a bicycle vanished down a narrow alley in front of me, and on a whim I followed him. Nineteenth-century accounts written by the few Westerners who visited – naturalists, merchants or occasionally shipwrecked sailors – often referred to Haikou's rude stone buildings, solidly constructed from 'trap tuff' to survive the batterings of typhoons, but on the main streets these had been uniformly surplanted by placeless modern nonentities. In the maze of backstreets, however, I was delighted to find that those squat, single-storeyed houses, built from blocks of the black volcanic stone that composes Hainan's north, had survived. Red strips of paper flanked each doorway, their gold characters wishing the family boundless wealth and happiness. And on every street, market stalls read like taxonomies of Hainan's wildlife. The same packs of dried endangered species that I had seen a thousand miles away on Putuoshan were on sale here. So too were live turtles, entangled in string bags. The pallid, hairless carcasses of goats lay with their lips pulled back in ugly death-grins. Panniers of fish glittered like precious metals on the footpaths beside squatting fisherwomen, and elsewhere slabs of white pig fat lolled like so many blancmanges, each one speckled with flies.

One market stall specialized in lizards which hung from the uprights. Their small bodies had been dried on frames, judging from the unnatural splaying of their limbs and tails, and they were tied together in pairs, belly to belly, fingertips touching as though about to hug each other for comfort. Their necks craned forwards so that their chins met. They looked sad. The woman behind the stall broke off from her chatting when she saw me looking at them and began to shout excitedly in Hainanese, quoting what I took to be outrageous prices.

'What are they called?' I asked.

'These? They're very cheap. Buy them!' I doubted she had spoken to a foreigner before – I had not seen a single Western face since Canton – and she seemed half hopeful of a sale, half unsure of how to achieve it.

'But what are they called, in Mandarin?'

'*Feishe.*'

'What do you do with them?'

'They're medicinal. Leave them to soak in *baijiu*. Good for your health.' She looked at me steadily but uncertainly, just as the restaurant owner on Putuoshan had. I felt she was weighing me up to rip me off. I could almost hear her asking herself how much I could afford. Then she named her price.

'Fifty *kuai*.' Four pounds for a pair of lizards.

'Take them home, put one of their legs in hot water and drink it,' her friend butted in holding up a coffee jar of sickly yellow water containing what looked like a dead stick insect. Nauseated, I walked away.

'Twenty-five *kuai* . . .'

The name *feishe* – flying snakes – and their imaginary medicinal properties had rung a bell, though at the time I could not recall why. When I got back to England I found a chapter in a volume on the natural history of Hainan, published in 1870 and written by Robert Swinhoe, the British Consul in Taiwan at the time, in which he lists in detail the flora and fauna of the island.

The most remarkable . . . of the lizard group is a little flying species of the genus *Draco* . . . found in the jungles of Southern Hainan. The natives told us that it is usually met with during spring in the forests, flying from tree to tree in pairs. They catch it with small sweep nets, and when one is taken up the other falls to the ground and allows itself to be captured without difficulty. They pin them out like butterflies and dry them for the market. The use made of them is to hasten childbirth, the dried reptile being placed on the forehead of the patient. The effect on the patient would probably be produced by the instinctive horror at the touch of a reptile; but its application does not always meet with success . . . Dried specimens are called Fei-shay and sell for a shilling apiece.

Little had changed in over a century.

JINMUJIAO

THE STREETS IN some of Haikou's older neighbourhoods were still lined with the kind of colonial buildings once found in Singapore and Hong Kong. Designed for hot, wet climates, with covered colonnades at street level, decorative blind arcading on the first and second floors, and Italianate friezes above, a few also still retained their wooden-shuttered windows. They were a wonderful change from the soulless high-rises of the newer parts of town. On one particular building a vertical line of Chinese characters read 'Marxism-Leninism is Our Ideological Base!' and 'The Party is the Heart of Our Enterprise!' Above them, I could just make out a horizontal row of characters four feet high: 'Long Live Chairman Mao!' But alone amongst the three, this inscription had been chiselled away until nearly illegible. The other two were, in theory at least, still true, but here, in a street of century-old merchants' houses in free-market Haikou, they looked more out of place than anywhere else I had stumbled across them in China.

Nearby I came across a bookshop. I hunted for an anthology of poetry that included the exiled scholar-official Li Deyu's tirade on Hainan, in which he compared it to the gates of hell shortly before dying there, but the young assistants had not heard of it. Instead I bought a Chinese guidebook to Hainan and a copy of *Far from the Madding Crowd*. Their only other English novel was *Sons and Lovers*, but the sun had given me a headache and I could not face Lawrence's quivering eroticism.

That night, after Bathsheba Everdene had refused Gabriel Oak's proposal of marriage, I took a final walk around to find some food. On the side of Haikou's largest department store, enormous Smurfs cavorted in twinkling fairy lights and a flagrant breach of copyright. After the day's heat the streets were again full of life. Spotlights hidden in the undergrowth illuminated the roadside coconut palms in pale green. The glitzy stores sparkled with chrome and hummed with shiny escalators and the swish of automatic doors. Neon shimmered and winked on the advertising hoardings. I could have been in Las Vegas.

They had all come out – families holding hands; young pig-tailed women in pyjamas or, if they were more sophisticated, in Levi 501s; bare-chested muscular men showing off to the girls; Li farmers hawking fruit; and the usual whores. My apprehension had subsided after the incident on the street, and I took time to wander before I chose a plate of stick-to-the-wok fried pork dumplings in a sweet, thick soy sauce. Haikou ambled past my greasy table, now and again commenting on the fact that I was there. It was well dressed, spoke continuously into its mobile phone, adjusted its highlighted hair in the mirror it kept in its fake Gucci handbag along with its lipstick, and posed on its new scooter. For thirteen years it had been doing pretty much as it chose, and it was looking contented. If, the next day, it had woken up to news that the reforms were to be curtailed and its economic freedom reined in, I expect there would have been open revolution.

Instead, it woke up to a tropical storm. Hainan TV usefully informed me that it was raining, raining so hard in fact that even the locals had stayed off the streets, while a fearsome wind was playing an eerie minor chord on the telegraph cables. As Leizhou is famed for its thunder, so Hainan is known as the favourite playground for typhoons and violent storms. Exposed in China's warm southern waters, the island has an annual average rainfall of between 59 and 102 inches. Its highest peak, Five Finger Mountain, squelches under an annual 18 feet of rain. To put it in context, rain-soaked England gets an annual average of around 30 inches. I put the release of the American aircrew, soon after the storm hit, down not to the Reverend Jesse Jackson's threat to visit Hainan to mediate, but to the fact that the Chinese officials involved had probably been lying on the beach at Perfume Bay, down the road from Lingshui where the plane was impounded, until it rained and they were obliged to go back to work.

Since it was far too wet to venture out, I lay on my bed growing increasingly hungry as the morning wore on. I toyed with the idea of calling the Chang'e Restaurant for a Chinese takeaway, but the idea of a bedraggled but hopeful Miss Zhang, or worse a Mister Zhong, arriving at my door to deliver it dissuaded me. Soon, however, the sky lightened from dark grey to a coral-tinged white and by early afternoon the rain had eased.

The coach to Sanya was more luxurious than any I had taken so far. Our attendant handed out cans of mango juice, packets of coconut sweets and a leaf from the daily newspaper to keep us amused.

Haikou's suburbs merged seamlessly into Qiongshan City. On its outskirts we passed mile upon mile of unsightly husks of half-finished hotels and office blocks, built in the nineties during the property boom and abandoned when it became clear that there were not enough people willing to occupy them. Together they looked like a film set, an enormous *mise en scène* of bombed-out flats in Sarajevo perhaps.

We mounted the island's eastern expressway, our tyres whispering in the drizzle. Inland from Qiongshan, the coastal plain of the north rippled gently under expanses of spiky purple pineapple and storm-tattered coconut. The paddy was turning yellow, its ripening heads beginning to sag. The driver's radio crackled, and we slowed down and turned off the expressway on to the mud track it had been built to replace. The attendant was very sorry but there had been reports of a landslide and we would have to take a detour. We would be an hour or so late reaching Sanya.

The soil of the plain was a rich, red henna. In the wet it clung to the tyres of the villagers' bicycles, matted the coarse hair of their plodding buffalo like rouge, and spattered against the white plaster of their trap tuff shacks, leaving a dirty tidemark. When the inhabitants could be seen, they were Han Chinese, the same poor farmers I had seen squatting behind baskets of fruit and vegetables in Haikou's backstreet markets. In a man-made landscape of plantations and vegetable plots, the only natural features were the rivers, trudging like polished steel over auburn shoals. Swallows dipped low over their rain-teased surfaces to feed.

The roads in the larger settlements were tarmacked, and the bucolic practicality of the villagers' houses had been superseded by the efficiency of iron and cement and the security of steel grilles. The local commune would stand abandoned and mouldering on the edge of town, while now each family lived above its own shop or restaurant – here the Illustrious China Hardware and General Store, there the Shu Family's Authentic Sichuan

Food. Brickworks shuffled embarrassedly beside great red scars that had been gouged from the plain, and timber stations marshalled freshly sawn hardwoods that wept blood-red sap.

In Ding'an County the land crinkled and rose as we crossed a spur of the island's central mountains. The black tufa of the plain became lighter, almost white. In places the bedrock had been exposed in ghostly scars where logging had denuded the hillsides and rain had washed away the fragile topsoil. Elsewhere the forest was fighting back, but some mountains had been stripped bare of vegetation and nature had washed her hands of them, their pale, naked torsos left like cadavers in some vast open-air mortuary.

Lingshui Li Autonomous County looked nothing out of the ordinary. There were no signs that it was the focus of world headlines. Farmers worked their rain-drenched fields in blue plastic mackintoshes and woven bamboo hats; shiny black roofs poked up through banana groves to mark the positions of their villages. Somewhere around here, twenty-four Americans were being detained while China's top military engineers were systematically stripping their aircraft.

On a scrubby hill just south of the town were perched an outsize mottled golf ball, a small complex of buildings and a few radio antennae, the whole surrounded by a perimeter fence. The listening post faced south towards the northernmost shoal of the Paracel group, only 140 miles distant. Perhaps it was by this post that Wang Wei had been scrambled on his final mission. Out to sea, the Chinese navy was searching for wreckage from his plane, though the press was reporting that the chances of finding him alive were very small. Every evening the news bulletins showed clips of the rescue operation and pictures of his distraught wife and mother awaiting news. So profound was their grief that they had been sedated, it was reported.

I got off the bus at Dadonghai in the hope that a hotel room here would be cheaper than in nearby Sanya. The place had the derelict feel of a British seaside town in the low season, for by mid-April, when I arrived, it was already too hot for most tourists. The resort of Dadonghai – meaning Great Eastern Sea, an odd choice of name for a town that lies on a small sheltered bay on the southern side of an island – consisted of a single main street that straggled behind the holiday villas and hotels facing the sea front, and another smaller road bisecting it at an untidy right-angle to run down to the beach. Both were lined with restaurants whose owners touted for custom from the half-dozen or so individuals who wandered disconsolately around looking for something to do or see. Taxis kerb-crawled past the tables and chairs on the pavements, outnumbering the pedestrians they solicited. Everyone ignored their honking. There seemed to be nowhere to ride to anyway, so I walked to the beach.

The Chinese guidebook to Hainan that I had bought in Haikou had a short entry on the resort.

> Dadonghai is a large, natural bathing beach near Sanya, with a kilometre of firm, spotless white sand that gently slopes into the deep water. It is suitable for playing on, or for enjoying its emerald breakers. With a pleasant water temperature all year round, it has become a favourite spot for winter swimming and is famous at home and abroad.

The icon on the map showed an outline of a woman lounging under a striped parasol against a blue sky.

I was almost at the southern extreme of my journey, and it was an anticlimax. For weeks I had pictured myself stepping out of my hotel and wandering through palm groves to a white beach lapped by crystal-clear waves. Instead I picked my way across the construction rubble of yet another new resort complex. Or was it the rubble from a failed hotel that was being demolished opposite? It had stopped raining quite so heavily, but the drizzle at the tail end of a tropical storm is chilly and insistent, and it was driven into my face by the wind. As soon as I set foot on the claggy sand a Li woman jumped up from behind a palm tree and held out an arm decked with trinkets – pearl necklaces, exotic shells and strings of coral – all plundered from Hainan's natural wealth. Perhaps she had been there all day, waiting in the wet for tourists who never came. As always the trinkets on offer were *hen pianyi*, very cheap, and they looked it. I waved her away, shaking my head, and in a flash her entreaties turned to lip-curling disdain.

I kicked a plastic bottle dejectedly along the beach. Empty sun loungers, wet and gritty with wind-blown sand, were lined up under umbrellas. Some of these had overturned, and the attendants in their gaily striped marquee sat and watched as they slowly cartwheeled away. A few miles to the south-east, Jinmujiao, or Brocaded Mother's Point, was clearly visible. Several hours of daylight remained, and I calculated that a taxi would get me there and back before dark. A motorcycle rider who threw a helmet at me and gestured at his pillion seat beat the taxis to it.

'Where d'ya wanna go?'

'Jinmujiao. Do you know it?'

'I know it, but there's nothing there. I'll take you up the road to Deer Looks Back Park. Bring your camera – I'll snap you standing next to the statue of the deer. How about it?'

'Seriously, I want to go to Jinmujiao. Will you take me there and back?' He looked at me incredulously and was silent for a moment.

'Why do you want to go to Jinmujiao?' He dropped his voice and whispered conspiratorially, 'Are you an American spy?'

I laughed. 'I'm not even an American, and if I were a spy, do you think I'd be taking this?' I kicked his rear tyre. 'Anyway, you said there was nothing there, so what is there to spy on? I want to go there because it's where China ends.'

'What about Tianyahaijiao?'

'Tianyahaijiao isn't the southernmost point of China, it's just that you Chinese think it is. Look at a map. Here, I'll give you 40 *kuai*.' I strapped on the helmet and straddled the back seat.

'Fifty.'

'You foreigners, you're all mad', he said thoughtfully as we stood an hour and a half later on the edge of the damp forest at the end of Brocaded Mother's Point, tapping his temple and grinning. 'It's cost you 50 *kuai* to come here, and look! Just sea and rocks. Not even a beach.'

I chose a few shards of granite to add to those from Shengshan, and so confirmed that I was quite mad.

Since the Zengmu Shoals constitute China's most southerly territorial claim, the headland at Jinmujiao – the southernmost point of Hainan – has no current claim to any national significance geographically. In any case, the Chinese have since the Song dynasty considered the calligraphic carvings on the striking rock formations at Tianyahaijiao – 'The Limit of the Sky and the Corner of the Sea' – as putting the cultural full stop to their vast country. The fact that Tianyahaijiao lies several miles north of the featureless Jinmujiao is thought irrelevant to its status as the southernmost point of China.

DADONGHAI

'WHAT'S OUR LITTLE friend called?' The reporter stooped to bring herself down to the same level as the row of schoolchildren. The boy was called Jin Ruili, and he was nine. He had an intelligent face and a half-formed smile that tried, and failed, to hide his nervousness. He had clearly been the recommendation of the schoolmistress who hovered behind him.

'What do you think about the American aeroplane crashing

into the Chinese jet?' The reporter held the microphone out for Ruili, smiling to put him at ease. Ruili coughed and began.

'I . . . I . . . think America should . . . apologize fully to the Chinese people . . .' His words came out hesitantly, and he used the same approved formula as the Chinese newspaper reports had. The reporter moved the microphone away from Ruili and turned to the camera to wrap up the piece. Before she could speak, Ruili leaned forwards slightly and added. 'If it was my *baba* who was still missing, then I'd be very sad. Comrade Wang Wei's family must be very sad.'

The news item ended with more shots of comrade Wang Wei's wife and mother under sedation in hospital, and the previous day's footage of the continuing search for wreckage. The papers had started to admit that the likelihood of finding him alive was remote.

'*Hao chi ma?*' The *laoban* stood over me as I ate with the friendly disregard of others' personal space that is characteristic of natives of cheek-by-jowl Sichuan.

'They're delicious, thank you,' I answered politely.

'*Hen la?*' Yes, I agreed, they were very spicy.

There seemed to be an immoderate number of Sichuanese restaurants in Dadonghai. In fact, I could not recall having seen any other kind. Forcing my numbed lips into the shape of words, I asked the *laoban* why he and his fellow Sichuanese were a thousand miles from home. The front of the restaurant and the rain-drenched street were empty. He pulled up a chair, sat down, beckoned to his tiny daughter who climbed on to his lap, and lit a cigarette.

'*Chou!* Smoke!' I was only half way through my noodles. I told him I didn't smoke, but still he pressed a Zhonghua cigarette into my hand. Zhonghua is China's premium brand, expensive even when you translate the cost of a pack into sterling. Rather than embarrass him I accepted and put it behind my ear.

'The factory I worked at in Chengdu was closed down in 1998,' he began. 'If you lose your job these days you have to rely on yourself. I have a brother; he'd visited Hainan and been astonished at how much easier it was to do business here – none of the *mafan* you get in Chengdu from the local bosses who want a backhander – so I just . . . migrated.' The simplicity of 'just . . . migrating' he expressed with a flick of the hand, as if he were brushing aside a fly in mid-air. 'That was in 1999, and I don't miss Chengdu one bit. All the other *laobans* here speak Sichuanese. We're good at two things, we Sichuanese: smoking and cooking. I go back now and again. I want my mother to come to Hainan but she doesn't want to leave her home town. She's sixty-one and she's lived there all her life.' The little girl jumped down and ran after a bedraggled cat that had strayed within sight. His gaze followed her.

'If you have no money you can't support your child.'

Did he have a work unit in Hainan, I asked. He didn't.

'Then what about a place to live? What if you get sick? What about when you get too old to work?'

'I pay for it all myself.' He counted off his outgoings on one hand, tapping his cigarette against the tip of a finger as he enumerated each expense. 'Insurance . . . rent for this place . . . savings for the future . . . money to live on. I make enough in the tourist season to cover them all. And an education for my daughter – I'd like that. Zhou Enlai used to say: 'Take root in the treasure island!' That was before the reforms even, but his thinking was very rational. Hey! *Lao Ge!*' He greeted his elder brother with a shout and a wave. 'Our foreign friend has come to Dadonghai to meet you.' Then he turned to address me. 'We call him Deng Xiaoping because he speaks with the same accent. The real Deng was from Sichuan too, wasn't he, Deng?'

Deng looked sheepish. The *laoban* disappeared into the back of the shop and returned with a bottle of *baijiu* and three of Hainan Beer.

'*Naguoren?*' asked Deng. I told him I was from England.

'Have you read about the two-machines-mutually-colliding-incident?'

I said I had, and asked him what he thought of it, but he just shrugged and pushed his bottom lip out.

'*Wu suo wei . . .*' 'Whatever . . .' Then he broke into a grin. 'You know this place is called Dadonghai? Well, we call it *Dadong Hai*, because people come here to *dadong*.' He sketched the characters for *dadong* on his open palm with a free finger: 'Hit the hole', a dysphemism for sex. I was grateful I was a lone male, certain that I would not be learning half as much about the Chinese male's predilection for vulgarity otherwise.

TIANYAHAIJIAO

THE EMERALD GREEN of the mosquito coil had been consumed and now lay in a crumpled grey spiral around the pin that had been supporting it when I fell asleep. I vaguely remembered having lit it in an alcoholic daze after contriving an exit from the drinking session and returning to find several muscular-looking mosquitoes waiting up for me. My watch told me it was three fifteen in the morning, so I had slept for barely two hours. Woken by the intermittent droning of the air-conditioning as it struggled to hold down the temperature in my unventilated room, I became aware of how thirsty I was. I drained the glass by my bed and then stumbled to the table to gulp down the last of the lukewarm water in the thermos. My stomach rumbled. There was a crumpled, unsmoked cigarette adhering to the skin behind each ear but I could not remember why. I felt decidedly ill.

When I reawoke it was seven and fully light. The previous evening's rain had stopped, leaving a high ceiling of bright cloud. Though I still felt ill I decided to press on to Tianyahaijiao, but first I needed something to eat.

With the conviction of the habitual drunkard who believes that the best way to cure his affliction is to take a hair of the dog, I prescribed myself a bowl of noodles spiced with chilli and topped with finely sliced heart, intestines, liver and kidneys, and washed it all down with a bottle of Hainan Beer. At least I would have something solid to bring up if things got bad.

A bone-shaking fifteen-mile journey in a bus crammed with chain-smoking farmers is not the best way to assess an experimental hangover remedy. I sat as motionless as I could, my knees pressed against my chest, concentrating hard on the scenery. The driver became hopelessly lost not once but three times, each time taking the wrong road out of Sanya before accepting under a torrent of Hainanese curses that he might ideally be using a different route. After half an hour we were still in Sanya's construction-site suburbs, and with every cigarette and pothole my stomach was edging close to disproving the efficacy of my cure.

The road from Sanya to Tianyahaijiao, when finally we found it, was set back a stone's throw from the sea. Craning coconut palms punctuated the monotony of beach and breakers. At intervals, pillboxes still sat facing out to sea in a futile rearguard action. Placed here by Chiang Kai-shek's Kuomintang to defend – ultimately without success – the coast against the Imperial Japanese Army, they had twice changed hands by the time the PLA occupied the island in 1950. Now, half a century of subsidence and storms had left them crooked and sandblasted, a string of bleached tombstones. Their gunslits grinned at useless angles up into the tattered canopy of the palms, and pockmarks from bullets and the rust-pitted impact craters of artillery rounds were now weathered into an innocent amnesia.

Like the outskirts of Haikou and Qiongshan, the coast north of Sanya was littered with the shells of half-finished buildings. Behind a mute cordon of gun emplacements, entire estates of unwanted villas mouldered in the tropical heat, displaying the same tasteless ornamentation as the farmsteads I had seen on the way to Luchaogang wharf in Shanghai. Here a few had been inhabited by squatters who had used oddments of wood or corrugated iron to keep out the worst of the weather. The smoke from their campfires had blackened the walls, and some fires had evidently got out of control and consumed a room or a whole house. Nothing moved. The effect was of a devastated town that had borne the brunt of a full-scale coastal assault, and it reminded me unpleasantly of newsreel footage of Okinawa. This was not what holiday resorts in a tropical paradise were supposed to look like.

I missed the stop for Tianyahaijiao beach – none of the locals were getting off there and the bus sped straight past – and had to flag down a soot-belching tractor to cover the mile or so back to the entrance. In the meantime, dozens of Chinese tour groups had turned up from their Dadonghai hotels. A herd of air-conditioned coaches awaited their return in a vast car park.

'Dah, dah, dum-dum-di-dum-di-dummm . . .' I caught myself humming Tchaikovsky's *Fantasy Overture to Romeo and Juliet* as I headed down an incline towards the enormous bronze statues that had been erected on the waterfront to welcome visitors. For a while I could not figure out why until I realized that the music was coming from the litterbins. Made of plaster, they were unconvincingly disguised as tree stumps. On closer inspection each had a built-in loudspeaker that proved to be the source of the muzak. *Romeo and Juliet* faded away and a nearby lamppost struck up a tinny 'There's no place like home'. The sentiment was echoed from a tree a little further on, while a toddler provided a surreal finishing touch by hurtling up and down the pathway, each tottering step accompanied by a loud squeak from his comedy flip-flops.

'Be it ever so humble . . . squeak, squeak . . . there's no place like home . . . squeak, squeak . . .'

The choice of statuary in the pleasure park was telling. Here, on the very edge of the Chinese world, framing a cluster of rocks lying a short way out to sea, two Han dynasty generals were mounted on horseback, brandishing their swords. Inscriptions on their pedestals attested to their role in making Hainan Chinese.

Li Bode was a general under the Western Han dynasty who in 110 BC conquered the island and divided it into two administrative commanderies. One of the seats of government that he created is now the site of Sanya City, and the Han citizens of Sanya look on Li Bode in the same way many white Americans look on the Pilgrim Fathers. During the subsequent Eastern Han dynasty a second general, Ma Yuan, put down the aboriginal revolts that racked what was known as the Island of Scarlet Cliffs. That the Communist Party had chosen to anchor its territorial claims to the Spratlys in this seminal period of Chinese history seemed no coincidence.

'Yesterday . . . squeak, squeak . . . all my troubles . . . squeak, squeak . . . seemed so far away . . .'

A pleasance of winding paths and lawns led through outcrops of pink-grey granite to the beach itself. The Chinese passion for controlling the natural environment, for emasculating and dominating their surroundings, had achieved its fullest expression here. Doggerel poems had been carved on wooden boards in the undergrowth lining the footpaths, evoking images of birds singing in the branches, of bubbling crystal streams, mist-veiled mountains and fragrant flowers. None of these existed amidst the dull artificiality of Tianyahaijiao, but for the tourists who stopped to recite them they conjured up the classical landscape of a mythical China, the written character sufficient to embody its meaning.

Here and there women posed for the camera, gently holding the tip of a dangling palm frond or leaning lightly against the frail bamboo. They posed with the shackled elephant in the same way. A tap on the tusk from its mahout, and it wrapped its calloused trunk around the giggling tourist's waist and raised her to deposit her feet on one tusk. A second prod and it reared up on its hind legs – *Snap!* – and back down for the next photograph. The elephant had intelligent black eyes that might have seen through the pretence that here were intrepid Han dynasty colonists, latter-day Li Bodes come to subdue the threatening animals and savage natives. That, after all, was why they had paid their entrance fee.

In the verdant monochrome of the 2 *yuan* banknote, the Southern Pillar of Heaven, lashed by waves and spray, looks proud and untamed. When I stood before it, the rock that supported the ancient Chinese sky in its southern quadrant was little more than a prop in the tourist fantasy. Secular pilgrims busied themselves around the megalith, taking turns to hold each other's bags and cameras and chattering through the various permutations of rock, pose and family member. Barefoot, they paddled into the weary surf, the women hitching their skirts up around their thighs, the men leaving their trousers to flap about in the foam with affected nonchalance.

The crowds grew thicker as I crossed the sand and neared Tianya Rock, the Limit of the Sky. This was the point where the world ended and the sea began. China knew of the nations beyond this place, but here her hegemony ended and she contented herself with waiting for tributary states to come to pay homage. The tour groups took turns to line up, the shortest at the front, the tallest at the back. Behind them, two large characters declared the rock's name in scarlet paint. Barely visible beside them, a ghostly hand wished Chairman Mao 10,000 years of life.

Twenty yards south across an empty stretch of strand, the smaller Haijiao Rock, the Corner of the Sea, was unvisited. None of the tour groups was interested in defining themselves in terms of where the rest of the world started. Just one lone foreigner, visiting from beyond the Corner of the Sea, scuffed aside the sand at its margin to look for some pieces of granite to add to his collection.

*

I wandered back toward the Li Cultural Village, intent on watching the performances. I had paid for an all-inclusive ticket and wanted to get my money's worth. On the way, a shelf of books in the souvenir shop caught my attention. Amongst the familiar trinkets my eye settled on a book entitled *The Ethnic Minorities of the PRC*, the characters of the title embossed in gold down its spine. It was divided into four sections, dealing in turn with the minorities to be found in China's north, south, east and west.

From the earliest written histories the Chinese saw themselves as surrounded by the barbarians of the four directions: in antiquity those to the north they named the *di*, those to the east, the *yi*; in the south all the culturally non-Chinese tribes were termed *man*, and in the west *rong*. Very old habits clearly died hard. Yet, as experience of non-Chinese peoples grew over three millennia through war, trade and peaceful assimilation, so the terminology used to describe the ethnic groups with whom the Chinese came into contact did nonetheless become more subtle. After Liberation, the Party set about systematizing the way in which China's minorities were defined. As a result, all of China's citizens are now deemed to belong to one of fifty-five ethnic nationalities. The largest is the Han, comprising 94 per cent of the population. The rest range from the Hui – native Chinese Muslims, or Tungans – found all over China and numbering in the tens of millions, to the Lhoba, who live only in southern Tibet and who number barely 2,000. Every Chinese citizen's *shenfenzheng*, or identity card, states his ethnicity.

Intentionally or otherwise, the author of this volume had resurrected the ancient four-fold division as the framework for his broad categorization of modern China's non-Han peoples.

Under the Party, each ethnic group was defined in terms of how far along a scale of economic development it had progressed. The scale began with primitive society and slave society, and then developed through feudalism and capitalism before reaching the ultimate goals of socialism and communism. In order to raise each of China's minorities to the higher stages, so the theory went, it was first necessary to define the position of each on the scale. Only by knowing where a minority nationality lay on the path to communism could policies be tailored to suit its development and so allow it to catch up with the Han who were already well advanced. In the years after 1949, ethnographers travelled all over China to study and categorize the country's ethnic make-up. Through countless measurements and photographs they built up a picture of each group. Their results had been summarized in cold detail in the book I now held.

Set against a scenic backdrop of their typical locality, stiffly posed shots of individuals in traditional costume headed each entry. With few exceptions they were women and girls. Below were listed each minority's physical characteristics, in language similar to the pseudoscience the Nazis employed to justify the extermination of Jews, gypsies and the mentally retarded. In the happy faces of the Zhuang, the Salar and the Bulang, I recognized the tense sepia of non-Aryan subjects measured, photographed and condemned as inferior by eugenicists. The categories included morphological face indices, PTC taste-blindness frequency and ABO blood-type distribution: populations reduced to statistics. Some teetered on the brink of pathological ghoulishness: average age of menarche and menopause, wet-type earwax distribution, the number of creases on subjects' hands. In places the author had inadvertently added a touch of humour. The Lhoba were known for their methods of divining the future by chicken livers; the De'ang of Yunnan 'know no beggars. Those in hardship do not complain.'

My final destination lay at the extremity of Heilongjiang, and so I turned to the section on northern China. The names sounded exotic: Oroqen, Ewenki, Daur and Xibo. They had been transliterated from the complex phonetics of Siberia and the Altai into the more cumbersome mono- and disyllables of Mandarin. Tired of the heat of the tropics, I felt a cold thrill at the prospect of seeing their birch-forested homelands.

A man had sidled up to me as I read.

'You understand Chinese! Are you interested in our minorities?' He wore a white shirt that had started to yellow at the collar, black polyester trousers that made me sweat just looking at them, and a pair of scuffed slip-ons. Beneath one arm was tucked the insignia of Chinese middle management, a zip-bound, black leather wallet the size of a sheet of A4. Into these are typically fitted a *shenfenzheng*, papers from the office, pens and, when travelling, a toothbrush, a comb, a flannel and a change of clothes. He was the first person that day who had accosted me without wanting to sell something and he seemed delighted at his discovery.

'Actually I'm more interested in how you Han see them.' He looked at me blankly.

'Let's watch the Li perform in their village,' he said. 'I'll show you where it is.' He put the book down for me and led me by the arm. 'I hope you don't mind me talking to you like this, but I don't often get the opportunity to speak to *waiguoren*. What did you mean by "how you Han see them"?'

'I meant that you Han always portray the minorities as women or children. That book had one photo for every *minzu*, but they were almost all females. It's as though you're afraid of admitting that the minorities can be strong and masculine. You need to pretend they're all submissive females and you Han are the dominant males.' Again, he looked at me blankly. I was unsure whether it was my ideas he had not understood or the way I had expressed them in Mandarin, so I continued. 'We British did the same. We came to Africa, Asia and Australia, and represented the natives as children who needed to be fostered by the British Empire. We told them they were inferior culturally but that if they would just learn from us they could aspire to be British too.

Do you understand what I'm trying to say?' As we neared the Amorous Garden he stopped walking and turned to me.

'*Ni jiao shenme mingzi?* What's your name?'

'My Chinese name is Lin Jie.'

'I'm Hong Weiguo. Lin Jie, I understand your words, but I'm not sure I understand their meaning.' His tact was admirable.

The performance had begun, and consisted of pairs of Li who sat on rocks placed hard against, and on opposite sides of, the bases of a dozen or so palm trees. They peered coquettishly around the thick trunks in a display of the Lis' traditional courtship. An announcer explained to the crowd of tourists that the symbolism behind the ancient ritual had now been lost. Nobody seemed to have noticed the extraordinarily phallic significance of placing two rounded boulders at the base of a palm tree. I was surprised they had got away with such filth for so long.

'Weiguo, you see those Li performing a traditional courtship? More than half are women. Don't you find that a bit strange?'

'That's because the women wear the most colourful costumes, I imagine. Look, that one's a man!'

'But he doesn't not even look like a Li. He's a Han dressed in Li costume.'

Weiguo shrugged. 'That's not important, you're meant to enjoy the performance. This is what they do in their villages. We're lucky to see it.'

'We missed the last performance of the traditional dancing. What a shame.' The Singing and Dancing Hall was deserted, much to Weiguo's disappointment. I had been rifling through my dictionary as we walked and was now armed with the vocabulary I needed to get my meaning across.

'Another thing, Weiguo. The Han always define the minorities by their dancing or their singing or their costumes, all those shallow cultural differences that don't threaten the fact that the Han are the most powerful, and that what they say, goes.' He expressed his disagreement in the characteristically polite way the Chinese have. Eyes directed down, he smiled and shook his head, one hand raised in front to wave my opinion gently aside in a manner that was half dismissive, half the good-natured parental indulgence of a naïve child. It was accompanied by a softly chuckled '*Bu, bu, bu . . .*'

'No, no, no . . . You have to understand that the minorities are genuinely very . . . backward economically. They're still feudal. They need the help of the government to develop.'

'The government wants to develop their island but doesn't want them to threaten its authority, you mean?'

'Lin Jie, you're purposely trying to misunderstand their situation. It's a very difficult question.' He used the approved form of words for ending an awkward conversation. 'Look, here's the textile weaving and dyeing workshop. And there – the pottery workshop. You see, they still make clay pots – I told you, they're backward.'

'I've never been to a real Li village, and I suspect you haven't either, Weiguo, but I bet they only make those to sell to the tourists.'

Come nightfall, we were seated in the dimly lit lobby of my hotel.

'My family home is in Anhui province, but I'm working for the Customs Bureau in Haikou. I'm here to deliver some documents to the Bureau in Sanya.' He tapped his document case, which sat on the table between us as proof for all to see of his management status. 'Here's my address and telephone number. Call me when you get to Haikou again and I'll take you to meet my friends at the university.' He slurped the last of his coconut milk, refused my attempt to pay for the drinks, shook my hand and left. 'My meeting you today was *mingyun*.' Fate.

JIANFENG

FOR DAYS THE Li hunter had pursued his quarry, a shy Hainan deer, across the grasslands of the island's west coast. The hunter knew the deer was so proud of its beautiful antlers that it would stay in the open rather than risk harming them on the branches of the interior's dense forests. He stalked it south, along the ever-narrowing coastal plain. It fled before him along the sandy spit of land where Sanya now lies. Reaching a dead end at an inlet of Sanya Bay, it stopped and sniffed the air.

The hunter was now bearing down on the deer, and it turned and swam the narrow channel to the peninsula beyond. The hunter too swam after his prey, which soon came to the tip of the peninsula. Before it stretched the vastness of the southern ocean. The deer knew that it could run no more, and turned its head to look the hunter in the eye. As it did so, it transformed into the most beautiful woman the man had ever seen. Straightaway the two fell deeply in love, and the hunter threw down his bow and arrow, vowing never to hunt again.

The high cloud, which had dissipated the heat during the day, broke as I rode back to Dadonghai, and blades of orange now pierced the canopy of trees fringing Deer Looks Back peninsula as the sun set beyond it. To the east, Brocaded Mother's Point was illuminated in a final ethereal glow, before a shadow swept across its cassia face and only the pinpricks of stars told where the blanket of the earth became the veil of the night sky. I sat on the beach looking out at the sea. It struggled to raise itself from its bed, rolled languidly over the coral sand, and flopped back with a sigh. Fairy lights, invisible during the day, began to twinkle in the beachside palms. Just as the sun in the southerly latitudes seems to hurry to reach its zenith after a brief dawn, so dusk there is just a short interlude before the light vanishes. As the western glow of the horizon visibly faded, I began to make out patches of yellow against the ink of the sea. They rounded the headland, slowly circling across the horizon in the distance then sweeping towards me, back across the curve of Elm Forest Bay in a silent, unearthly ballet. As they neared, the patches of yellow took on the texture of the water's rippling waves. Behind each patch appeared first a silvery bow wake and then the dark form of a trawler's hull. Then came the soft, rhythmic beat of their engines.

Under the humming striplight back in my room I pored over the list of sights recommended by my guidebook. Jianfeng Mountain National Forest Park it claimed, was 'the largest, best preserved example of primeval tropical forest in China'. Never having visited a tropical forest, and having by now a few days in hand, I got up early the next day to see about getting there. At Sanya bus station I asked if there was a luxury coach to the township of Jianfeng at the foot of the mountain. The woman behind the counter tip-tapped my destination into her computer.

'I'm sorry, the luxury service uses the high-speed expressway to go directly to Number Eight Township nowadays, but for Jianfeng you'd need to get off where the old road divides just beyond Eternal Peace Village. Take the standard service and tell them to let you off.'

'Standard service?'

'It means you have to sit on a urine-stained bench while the driver plays deafening pop music to drown out the noise of the caged cats fighting to the death on the back seat.' Or at least that is what she should have said.

The old coast road hugged the base of the mountains as it snaked its way westward. A hot sun glanced off bald slopes whose thick mane of trees had been shaved and whose thin scalp of earth had washed away. The bus clattered on past Nose Point to emerge on a coastal plain. We stopped at Number Nine Township, and the Li women squatting by the single-roomed bus station climbed up to sell us bunches of bananas, eggs hard-boiled in soy sauce and tea, and spring rolls filled with sour vegetables. When I returned from the toilet – a wall in the midst of a rubbish tip for the use of which an old woman had demanded 2 *mao* – a farmer had taken my window seat. I sat down next to him and he offered me his copy of the *Hainan Daily* by way of compensation.

'That article's about Jiusuo, where we are now.'

The headline read 'Thousands join in search for pilot'.

'Searching high and low for the missing Wang Wei is our duty.' These are the heartfelt words I have heard spoken today by the local cadres and fishermen in Number Nine Township, in Dragon's Perch Bay and in Lookout Tower Port while investigating how these coastal regions of Ledong Li Autonomous County are helping in the rescue effort. For days now, several hundred trawlers and over 3,000 cadres, militia and fishermen have enthusiastically joined in the search operation along the county's 62-kilometre shoreline.

In the small fishing hamlet of Dragon's Perch Bay, with its population of only 1,127, people are concerned for the safety of Wang Wei, listening out for news on their televisions and radios. When they realized that they lived within the search area decided upon by the county government, they began to congregate soon after dawn every day to comb the beaches.

Number Nine Township searches in the afternoon, which it considers is the best time. Four squads, composed mainly of local militia, scour the sea and the beach for any unusual objects. In Lookout Tower Port two fish and prawn merchants, Ke Qiuyun and Chen Yanong, are both willing to do a little less trade for the time being, instead taking their motorboats out to search in deep water.

Li Zhangchong and over fifty other fishermen set out each night with searchlights to look for the pilot. They all agree that, even though they are tired and losing money, they feel it is worth doing.

In Oriole's Song Township, He Hanguo and Wu Boge began to search in their fishing boats ten days ago, and their example has led to over 300 similar sorties from other fishermen.

The trawlers in Elm Forest Bay had been trawling not for fish but for wreckage.

The townships we passed through on the plain – Burst Bank, Yellow Current, Buddha's Net – all seemed to depend for their existence on buying and selling fruit, mainly the green, milk-laden coconuts piled high in their warehouses and on the backs of grumbling lorries. Beyond the limits of their bustling markets the countryside gasped for moisture. The plain's natural cover had been stripped off long before to make way for plantations, and the desiccated scrub that had in turn replaced these was unable to hold the friable soil together. The dust was whipped by an onshore wind into swirling white clouds that descended like gauze. The bus dropped me off, alone, at the point where the path to Jianfeng branched off the tarmacked road and struck inland through this arid brush.

I saw the dust storm that shrouded my transport long before I could make out what it was – a Lanzhou bus, named after the city in Gansu province where they are believed to originate. They are a common sight in rural China, each consisting of a three-wheeled chassis with a small, noisy engine mounted centrally in front. Behind the driver's cab, the flat back is covered by a steel frame on to which is riveted a metal skin. Slits let in air and choking dust in equal measure. The rear wheel arches are boxed in with plywood, and planks nailed on form a rudimentary bench. The conductress, who will hammer on the roof when a passenger wants to get off, perches on the rear bumper and grips the walls to avoid being flung clear.

Jianfeng – Pointed Peak – was a one-street hamlet of wandering chickens that scratched in the dirt, pot-bellied pigs and barefoot children who ran laughing after the man with pale, hairy legs. I asked if anyone could drive me to the top of the peak.

The temperature dropped sharply as the motorcycle and sidecar that I had hired wheezed in first gear, at barely more than walking pace, higher and higher into the cloud. For the first time since arriving in China I delved into my rucksack and pulled out a heavy overcoat. It was creased and misshapen from weeks of incarceration. My driver stopped watching the road and turned to watch me. The slope was so steep, the going so slow, that it would have mattered little if he had driven with his eyes closed.

'What do you want to wear that for? I thought you said you were English. I saw a programme once about England. Don't you have to send teams out to search for cars buried in the snow?' Demonstrating the action involved in prodding long sticks through snowdrifts, he pretended to discover imaginary cars, whereupon he would emit a clank and look unjustifiably surprised.

It was not the temperature itself so much as the unexpected change in temperature that had made me feel cold: at sea level it had been hot and humid, the low cloud acting like a blanket to retain the day's heat. Above the cloud base a thin shirt and shorts were far from adequate and I had erupted in goose pimples.

The thick cloud swirled around in tangible drifts as the wind eddied through the forest. It swallowed the sounds of the engine and of the occasional birdcall, carrying them from their source and sublimating them into an eerie, disembodied whispering. I broke the unnerving silence by asking him what he thought of the US spy plane.

'The two-machines-mutually-colliding-incident? I haven't

really discussed it with anyone. Are you interested?' I hunched my shoulders into my coat for warmth and shrugged. I had hoped for some more vociferously partisan views, but Hainan did not seem to be the place to find them. After a few minutes he spoke again.

'It used to take me about two or three hours to get to the top of the mountain before they built this road last year. Every time it rained the whole surface would turn to mud. When it was dry, it was as hard as iron. But after a shower? Forget it!'

'Why did it take until last year to get around to building it?'

'Tourism. We're getting more and more tourists coming here, so now there's money involved. There are a few hotels up around the lake. Some of the local Party members have got business interests there and the right *guanxi* to get roads like this built.

'Listen! That was a monkey. You sometimes hear them up here, but you have to be lucky to see one.'

We reached the cusp of a small valley, beyond which the mountain rose even higher through the mist. As we cleared the watershed and began to gain speed, he switched off the engine and coasted to save petrol.

'The money to build roads like this comes from public taxes, but the people who really benefit are the people who run the hotels. If the money they make means the government doesn't need to give the conservation zone as much financial support, then the work unit that runs it gets praised as a good example of self-sufficiency.'

'That doesn't sound a very good way of protecting the environment,' I commented. He switched the engine back on as our momentum was lost. 'I mean, isn't the government just encouraging people to find ways of making money from the park, rather than giving them enough money to conserve it as it is?'

He nodded. 'To get rich is glorious. The environment isn't as important as making money.'

*

137

Evidence of the gangs that had hacked the roadway out of the mountainside was still visible. Every few hundred yards overgrown shacks, little more than corrugated iron and strained tarpaulin, leaned where they had been abandoned against rock faces that still bore the red scars of mechanical excavators. Makeshift stoves of fire-blackened cement were dotted near each camp. Piles of hardwood, cut from the trees felled to widen the track, lay in ricks or hung precariously over the void where they had been bulldozed. Telegraph poles had been erected to carry telephone lines to the hotels, their progression a gaping wound in the forest cover. Where the trees had been logged to make way for cars and communication, the earth was eroded in deep, orange runnels. For an area of environmental protection, there was a lot of needless destruction.

We reached the top of a long rise that opened on to a vision of sparkling blue water and emerald slopes. We were above the clouds. My driver pointed out the hotel I planned to stay in, and I told him I would walk the mile or so around the lake to reach it. The sun was shining, but the air was pleasantly cool at altitude. The only noise came from deep within the forest. It sounded as though somebody had switched it on and turned it up but had forgotten to tune it in. To a background shortwave static of cicadas had been added the avian whistles and pops of a valve radio, a time signal's chronometric beep, the crackling of a Geiger counter. Despite the volume, the only wildlife I saw was a warbler that hopped from reed to reed on the lakeshore, a few sand spiders scuttling away as I approached, and the briefly glimpsed long, red tail of a bird as it escaped into the tree line.

At first sight, the Lake of Heaven cradled beneath the many summits of Jianfeng Mountain National Forest Park was invigoratingly unspoilt wilderness, but as I walked my mood began to sink. At the water's edge, the lower slopes were artificially terraced and planted with close, green bands of tea. The road twisted, revealing construction sites that had been hidden from higher up. Villas and holiday homes were being built. The earth had been churned by the tyres of heavy machinery while wet and, now dry, had set in ugly peaks and troughs. The path crossed a dam. Even the lake was man-made.

The hotel was built on an artificial promontory. Its teenage staff were friendly but clearly bored beyond belief. I appeared to be the only guest that day and easily bargained them down from a ludicrous 300 *renminbi* to a steep 100 *renminbi*. That they refused to go lower was due only to the impossibility of my leaving before the departure of the hotel's motorcar for Jianfeng at six o'clock the following morning. They got their own back by overcharging for a plate of greasy noodles in their depressingly empty restaurant. I went back to my room, hung my mosquito net from the lamp on the bedstead and, when I found that there was no electricity to power the television until after dark, went outside to read. Surely somebody could arrange for a power line to be hacked through the forest, I asked, only half-joking.

A long, sandy spit of land, dotted with some large boulders where guests could sit and look at the scenery, jutted into the water. From it the hotel was invisible and out of earshot, and I was surrounded on three sides by glassy water. The opposite shore was just a few hundred yards away, but while I had been eating, a thick cloud had descended on the lake's surface from beyond its encircling peaks. It blotted out the sun and the blue sky and drew an impenetrable veil across the forest. I tossed a pebble into the haze and it plopped softly out of sight. *Far from the Madding Crowd* was comically apt, and I read a few pages before falling asleep where I sat.

When I awoke, the cloud had thinned to reveal a village of wooden huts ahead of me. Retracing my steps I found a point where the path branched off to it, but instead of a Li settlement I found an abandoned entertainment resort, reached by a chain-and-board bridge. Its holiday huts had fallen into disrepair and their tidy borders had gone to seed. Straggling cacti and vines now grew through their ramshackle plank walls and thatch of reedstalks, and the intense fragrance of wild jasmine and dog rose hung in pockets in the moist, still air.

The road led back to a collection of down-at-heel dwellings that did not merit the title of village. The local shop was a shack built from oddments of timber and bamboo through whose cracks trailed the tendrils of creepers that had seeded themselves in the surrounding bare soil. Bamboo staves supported an awning that cast a square of shade on a patch of beaten earth where crude trestle benches and a melamine table had been arranged. Here the local men sat drinking a ruby red tea from tiny glasses and smoking. One man looked up, saw me and beckoned me over.

'Where are you from?'

'England.'

'Good – if you'd said you were American I'd have had to demand a fight.' He glared at me as though he meant it, but I thought I detected the faintest hint of a smile in the corners of his eyes.

'Really?'

The hint of a smile spread to the corners of his mouth, and his neighbour answered on his behalf.

'Don't worry about him, he's just annoyed because the airforce didn't phone to ask for his help in the search.' The group burst out laughing. The first man nodded his head pensively in agreement.

'It's true. You'd think they'd have at least called,' he pouted.

'*Qing zuo, he cha.*' Another invited me to sit down and take some tea. 'Do you like it? Guanghua's brother grows it on the other side of that hill over there.' I liked it very much. It had been dried and fermented, and was powerfully smoky, far better than the insipid brew Avalokitesvara drank on Putuoshan. He nodded towards Guanghua, who turned out to be the man who had first called to me. Guanghua smiled back and stood up.

'*Lai!* Come! I'll give you a tour.'

Back on the road up which I had come that morning, Guanghua turned his motorbike into a gateway that I had not noticed on the way up. Two posts supported a metal signboard that read Educational Base Area in thin, unwelcoming characters. He switched the engine off and left the keys in the ignition.

'Nobody's going to steal it up here,' he commented with an air of resignation. He was Han, he said, a poor farmer descended from mainlanders who had arrived in the centuries before Liberation, but he did not know exactly when, or where they had come from. Native Han farmers like him were at the bottom of the pile, he said. At least the Li had preferential birth-control policies, and those Han whose families had arrived in the fifties, or after the reforms, got the good jobs and the opportunities. He had had only the most cursory education and he struggled over the characters in my guidebook. I pretended not to understand them either.

Guangha's face was unwashed and lined from the sun, his hair was cropped short and stood madly to attention, and he walked with a slight stoop, hands in pockets. He wore the standard uniform of the poor Chinese farmer, a Western-style two-piece suit of navy polyester, the arms rolled up to the elbows and the trousers rolled halfway up dirty calves. It was engrained with grease, and I doubted it had ever been washed. Under it was what should have been a white vest. He picked his way expertly along the rough stone path that had been laid through the dense trees, and for the first time I noticed that he went barefoot. He spoke to me without turning round.

'How old are you?'

'Thirty. You?'

'Eleventh of December 1970.' He was exactly one week older than me.

'During the Cultural Revolution?'

'That's why my father called me Guanghua – Glorious China.

By the time I knew what was going on around me, all that was over and Mao was dead. You have to be at least in your forties or fifties to have had anything to do with the Cultural Revolution. What does it matter anymore? It's history.' He stopped to offer me a cigarette. 'Watch out for *mahuang*! You get a lot of them in the forest.'

'*Mahuang?*'

'I'll show you if we see one. Keep an eye on your shoes.'

A machinegun clatter of birds rattled through the canopy. Hardly any light reached the forest floor – a thick, dank leaf-mould – and dead vegetation lay rotting in the dark convolutions of the tree roots. Guanghua stopped and bent down to examine something. He held out a feather.

'Look! A wild quail.' Farther on, he stopped again and this time produced a small fruit kernel. 'Something's been eating that, but I can't say what it is. Look at the teeth marks. It must be quite big, not an insect . . . There! That's a *mahuang*. Here, let me.' Squatting, he lifted the hem of my trouser leg to reveal a thin brown leech that was heading for bare skin. I recalled reading Benjamin Henry's account of how his coolies' feet and legs would stream with blood after being bitten by these hill leeches.

'You're a guest. We don't want you getting bitten and falling ill.' He drew on his cigarette and held it close to the leech, which convulsed and fell to the ground. 'If there are wild quail around I'll have to come back with my shotgun this afternoon.' Straightening up, he took aim into the canopy with an imaginary gun. He pulled the trigger and it kicked against his shoulder. 'If you're lucky, you can kill one or two.'

'You shoot birds? I thought this was a protected reserve.' He carried on walking ahead of me but said nothing. Now I knew what I was looking for, I too spotted feathers and fruit stones, along with the crimped red plastic of shotgun cartridges.

*

Guanghua's brother had felled half an acre or so of forest slope to plant row upon row of tightly packed tea bushes. He lived in the hut he had built from the proceeds of selling the tea in Jianfeng and in Number Eight Township. I knocked on the door but he was out.

'When there's demand, he can get 80 *kuai* a pound for the best stuff,' Guanghua boasted. 'He grows it without using chemicals.'

'Are those the regulations for the forest park, then – no artificial chemicals?'

'No, it's just that we don't need to waste money on them. The climate and the soil here are perfect.' He was so matter-of-fact that I felt stupid. 'Try one of those fruit, they're my brother's too. They're a speciality around here. We sell them in Jianfeng.' They were small and purple, a little like plums but very sour. I pretended to like them.

On the pounded earth outside Guanghua's home, he pointed out the orchids he grew in terracotta pots.

'If I sell any, fine. If not, then I just carry on repotting them. That one's a chilli plant. They grow well up here, so I don't need to spend money on chillies. That's garlic . . . those are onions.'

The sun was shining brightly now, though it was nearing the rim of the mountains. It burst in oblique rays through the cracks in the flimsy walls of his hut, catching the dust that hung in the air and illuminating the interior. He led me from one room into the next, as if he needed to show me how little he had, although he never said a word until we had finished the inspection and sat down at his table.

'My home is very poor, very backward. I'm embarrassed to show it to you.'

I did not know what to say. I had never seen such poverty, but admitting this would benefit neither of us.

'In England, we say that it doesn't matter what your home is like, it's still your home.'

'But it's still a hovel, isn't it?' Far from ignorant, he sensed I was avoiding the issue and pressed me to agree, but I couldn't. To break the awkward interlude we drank water poured from his greasy thermos flask and I asked whether he had ever travelled anywhere else in China. As soon as the words left my lips I bit my tongue. It had been a thoughtless question.

For a moment he said nothing, as if weighing up his answer. Then he replied.

'I've been to Haikou and Sanya. They're okay.'

The floor inside his hut was also pounded earth. A column of bricks supported the reed thatch roof and acted as the firebreak for a stove that was nothing more than a clay pot resting on three bricks above a pile of embers. In the corner, his bed was a bare board raised on more bricks, with a washed-out mosquito net draped over it. Blackened pots and pans hung from nails in the roof timbers. A plastic washing-up bowl contained two small carp in a few inches of water. He nudged the bowl with his foot, and the fish began to swim.

'My dinner for tonight. I caught them in the lake this morning.'

'Do you often manage to catch fish here?' I asked.

He shrugged. 'Some days. It's really a matter of luck.' There seemed to be a lot of luck involved in living on the mountain. Shooting quail, getting a good price for your tea, catching fish for supper. Luck is a word people tend not to use if they feel in control.

'You never see the people who are meant to be managing the reserve,' he went on. 'They don't really care what happens up here. I don't think their hearts are in the job.' He pointed to a rusty gin trap lying on the bare earth. 'I set that up in the woods. I've caught wild boar a few times. The monkeys aren't heavy enough to spring it, but once I caught a tiger.'

'You killed a tiger? But they're very rare! I didn't even know Hainan had any left.' He looked me in the eye and grinned.

'Lin Jie, you should see your face.'

We drank together outside the local shop. It had no refrigerator and the beer was warm, but the evening was too cool for cold beer. On the walk back to the hotel I read a slogan painted on the wall of the hamlet's only brick building: 'Protect the nature reserve – do not fish in the Lake of Heaven.'

Back in the hotel, the electricity did not come on at six as promised. Instead, one of the maids tapped on my door and left two candles and a box of matches. I sat in semi-darkness listening to the radio until at 7.30 the room burst into light and the television crackled awake. Outside, above the white noise of cicadas, I could hear the hum of the generator. Every now and again it would struggle and splutter, and my bedside lamp would dim from bright white to yellow, and finally to a glowing orange tungsten coil.

On television there was a documentary on Monkey Kingdom, a kind of simian Jurassic Park on a peninsula near Lingshui. The monkeys 'performed' for the tourists: the reporter used the same verb – *biaoyan* – as had the announcer at the Li village in Tianyahaijiao. One animal timidly approached a six-foot pole set in the floor of a small arena. Holding a slow match in one paw, it shinned to the top and lit the touch paper on a string of firecrackers. They blew apart in a long, loud staccato and the terrified monkey jumped down and ran off to cower behind the trouser leg of its trainer. The crowd applauded. A second monkey ran a Chinese flag up a flagpole, and another donned glasses and rode a tiny motorized scooter up and down in front of the audience.

'Some are easy to train and love to perform,' explained the trainer. 'We reward those ones. Others don't learn at all well and they get chastized.'

SANYA

BACK IN DADONGHAI, as I sat down to an evening meal of *kungpo* chicken and rice, I looked at the copy of the *Hainan Daily* on the table beside me. 'Our island attracts tourists from home and abroad', ran one headline. Eventually I gave in and read the text of the article. It said that Hainan was famous worldwide for its spectacular scenery, its mild climate and the warm welcome its natives offered their guests. It was said to be attracting more and more overseas visitors.

I could see why Chinese tourists would travel here. There was no need to go through the long application procedure to obtain a passport, nor any question of a cash deposit to ensure a return from an overseas trip. The food was familiar, the climate reliably good, and most of the natives spoke Mandarin. But why on earth would Hainan's closest developed neighbours, the Japanese, Singaporeans or Australians, holiday here when they could just as easily and cheaply fly to Queensland, Bali or Hawaii? And as for the thought of hordes of picky American tourists putting up with the constant staring, the strangulated halloos, the over-charging and the offers of a fight . . .

When I had finished eating, I went down to the beach with some cold beers.

'This is fo' you.' A hand appeared beside my shoulder clutching a carton of orange juice. It was followed by a thin, tanned arm and ultimately by a girl I placed in her mid-teens. She sat down next to me and carried on talking in faltering English. 'Whe' a' you fro'?' I put her out of her misery.

'*Yingguo.*'

'Oh, I'm so glad you speak Chinese. I've been sitting over there with my little brother trying to pluck up the courage to come and talk to you. You're the first Westerner I've ever spoken to. Yes, really. I have an English exam next week, listening comprehension, but we never get the chance to listen to real English people.

'Oh! Say some more! It sounds so nice, far better than my teacher. Are you studying Mandarin here? Oh, I see. Mohe? But there's nothing to see in Heilongjiang. I have to take my brother home now, but I can show you Sanya tomorrow if you like. Well, let's say ten. Here, call me on my mobile.' She scribbled the name Gistlaine and her telephone number on a sheet of paper and handed it to me.

I woke at eleven, heavily entangled in my mosquito net and dreadfully hungover. A thirsty-looking mosquito stomped up and down on the telephone by my bed. I remembered what had happened the previous evening and fumbled for the piece of paper and the receiver. To my mild surprise I got through, and Gistlaine answered. She sounded worse than I felt.

'Uh? Oh, it's you . . . I fell asleep waiting for your call.'

'Sorry, I overslept. I think I've got a cold. Do you still want to show me Sanya?'

We arranged to meet on the corner of Harbour Construction Road and Liberation Road. When I got there she ran up to me but at first I didn't recognize her. The night before, she had been dressed girlishly in a flowery skirt, a red blouse and plimsolls. Now she wore a white halterneck top, Levi 501s and a pair of slingbacks. Over one shoulder was a black handbag, and sunglasses were perched on top of her black hair.

'You look very nice,' I said, trying hard not to sound as though I was chatting her up.

'Thank you, it's the first time I've been allowed out on a date alone.' She dropped the English word into the sentence.

Date? I had not realized I was to be responsible for any nascent expressions of sexuality, and I didn't want to hurt her feelings.

'Really? How old are you?'

'Seventeen.'

'Gistlaine, when you were born I was already studying at secondary school. I think I'm a little old to be dating you.'

She tilted her head and looked at me quizzically. My next

sentence I finished in a whisper that only she could hear, for by now several people had stopped to stare at us, the only mixed-race couple in Sanya.

'I'm too old to, you know, be your boyfriend.' She threw her head back and let out an embarrassed laugh.

'Is that what *date* means? I'm sorry, I looked it up in my dictionary. How should I translate *yuehui*?'

'In this instance, I'd recommend meeting or rendezvous. That's your first English lesson for the day.'

We walked along Liberation Road, she muttering 'meeting' over and over before starting on 'rornvoo', I firing questions at her as I noticed fruits and trees whose names I wanted to know in Chinese. It was a very odd rornvoo. Later she pointed out Sanya's sights for me – the tall apartment block nobody would live in because it had been built on unstable ground and had developed a worryingly visible list, the wholesale market where all the dried animals and sea creatures I had seen at Putuoshan and since had originated, Sanya's central chicken and dogmeat dealership, and the teahouses that had opened in the city's many half-built villas and office blocks.

'Why Gistlaine? Isn't it a strange name for a seventeen-year-old Chinese girl?' I asked as we sat at our table in the garden of a hotel, a large stick of mosquito repellent burning between us, and Gistlaine flicking through a magazine full of pretty, coiffured women.

'My teacher chose the name Betty for me, or Mary or something. Her English isn't that good – to tell you the truth, I don't think even she understands the tapes she plays to us – and she always chooses such boring names. I made Gistlaine up. Do you like it?'

'I do. It sounds very historical. I think there's a lady in English mythology with a similar name.' She seemed delighted at the thought that her English name had a ring of both authenticity and mystery about it. She sat up in her plastic chair and preened herself.

'I'd like to go to England to study, or perhaps Canada or Australia, but my father wants me to learn German so I can study in Germany.'

'Why Germany?'

'We can apply for a full scholarship there, but in England we have to pay our own tuition fees. My father says he'd rather I went to a college in Germany than elsewhere, since it's he who'll have to pay.'

'He's very sensible. Do you know any German?'

'*Mein Vater hat mir ein Buch gekauft, damit ich Deutsch lernen kann.*' It was strange to hear a Chinese person speak a foreign language other than English. The assumption throughout China is that all white foreigners speak English, to the visible chagrin of French tourists. 'But I work so hard at school that I barely have time for even my normal studies. We start at 6.40 a.m. every weekday, and we don't finish studying until after 5 p.m.

'There's competition for the best university places, and our parents want us to get well-paid jobs so we can support them when they retire. The state doesn't always provide them with an iron rice bowl anymore. My father came here in the seventies as a soldier with the Production and Construction Corps, but instead of going back to Guangxi he stayed on and went into business when the reforms started.' Her handbag rang and she opened it to take out her mobile phone. 'Yes, I'm fine. With the Englishman I met at the beach. Not too late, no. *Zaijian.*' She turned back to me.

'My mum likes to check up on me. She wants me to go to a good university, but I'm not so sure. I don't know what I want to do with my life yet.'

'If it's any consolation, Gistlaine, I still don't know either.'

'It's different for you, though, Lin Jie. You're a man and you come from a rich country. If you want to come to China to travel to – where was it? Yes, all those places – then you can. My parents will want me to marry before too long, and it's even harder when you've been to a good university.' I raised my eyebrows. 'Well, the women who go to the best universities and get the best jobs are the A women, then come the B women at the not-so-good universities, and then the Cs and the Ds. Chinese men want a woman who's their inferior – they're very traditional, even though officially men and women are equal.

'So the A men want to marry a B woman, the B men want a C woman, and so on. See what I mean? So the A women and the D men are left unmarried.' She intertwined her fingers in front of her, women to the right and men to the left, and wiggled the digits that corresponded to each happy couple. Sure enough, the woman at the top and the man at the bottom hung partnerless in space to prove her point.

'This is Lin Jie, from England. Don't mention the Li, you'll never stop him talking.' Hong Weiguo, the customs official whom I had met at Tianyahaijiao, introduced me to his two friends at our pre-arranged meeting-place, a Haikou restaurant specializing in the food of their native Anhui.

'This lovely lady is Chunyu, and this reprobate who hasn't bothered to put on any decent clothes for the occasion is Liangde.' He cuffed Liangde playfully around the head. 'I'm older by two years, so as elder brother I'm allowed to reprimand him for being impolite.'

We took our seats outside, and Weiguo explained how he and Chunyu had come to meet.

'I was in the same class as her at Haikou University. We both studied law, and now she's a postgraduate. I'm doing my exams to become a fully qualified lawyer with the Customs Bureau here. Liangde overheard us speaking Anhui dialect and now he won't leave us alone. He's from Bengbu, the railway junction in northern Anhui. We're both from the capital, Hefei.'

It is the custom of Chinese from the same province to band together when in internal exile, though this can make for some strange bedfellows. The size of the country, its many mutually unintelligible dialects and its varied cuisines and cultures tend to make people feel more attached to their roots when in a foreign province, and they seek out and form what are often their strongest friendships with fellow provincials. Provincial associations exist in many Chinese cities to help newcomers find their feet.

Liangde was a peculiar creature. His face wore a constant look of surprise, while his hair led a life of its own, sticking up and out in unkempt clumps. He had an adolescent's bumfluff moustache and he fiddled hyperactively with whatever was nearest to hand as we ate. Mostly this was his mobile phone, which rang once or twice, making him jump. He was twenty-two and had just started a postgraduate course in computer science, but he bought and sold shares on the stock exchange to support himself.

'The rise or fall of any single company's value is limited to ten per cent on any one day, and you can't sell shares on the same day you bought them,' he explained in answer to my remark that it must be a risky business. 'So many people were losing all the money they had – hundreds of people even committed suicide – because they genuinely thought the stock exchange was nothing more than a way of getting rich quick. To stop the market being quite so volatile, the government introduced rules that capped the losses you could face or the money you could make on any one day. People still don't really understand that the exchange is just part of how a capitalist economy works. Most people think it's just a gift from the Party to reward people who follow their line on self-enterprise.' Here Chunyu interrupted.

'Liangde, you always assume that other people aren't as clever as you – the Party didn't have to introduce the stock exchange, but it's benefited many people who want to be economically independent and not have to rely on the state.'

'That's where you're wrong, as always. The Party did have to open stock exchanges in China. They can't pick and choose when it comes to reforming the economy – either they want a market economy or they don't. World economics doesn't listen to their silly slogans. And there's nothing economically independent about throwing yourself off the top of an office block in Haikou. My friend's father did that when he lost all his investments. Apparently when he hit the ground . . .' Weiguo held up a hand.

'Liangde! Our guest doesn't want to hear . . .'

Our first dishes arrived and we began to eat.

Landlocked Anhui is one of the poorest provinces of China, and it expresses its poverty eloquently through its food. It is a cuisine, if cuisine is the word for it, of the preserved, the salted and the fermented, its ingredients reflecting the necessity of laying down reserves in good years for the bad years its farmers know will come. First to arrive was Weiguo's favourite, a casserole of rotten beancurd and salt pork. The beancurd came in firm, pressed slices and was speckled black with a preservative layer of mould. The lactose-intolerant Chinese neither drink milk nor eat cheese, and fermented beancurd is their nearest equivalent to the latter. Slowly braised in a clay casserole dish with strips of pork, whole garlic cloves and a cloying, brown sauce, it tasted better than I had feared it might, and at least rotten beancurd was in no danger of being hunted to extinction.

Chunyu's choice had been salty beans – broad beans preserved in brine. They had been stir-fried together with the pallid honeycomb discs of lotus root. Liangde liked smelly beef. When it arrived he tucked in, but not until he had scooped up some of the larger slices and placed them in my bowl.

'It's been smoked to preserve it, then hung up and left to go rotten,' he explained. The meat had been sliced paper thin and melted in my mouth. It was indescribably fatty and smoky, and it was also strangely addictive.

Hong Weiguo, as a responsible member of the Customs

Bureau, was less hotheaded than his two student friends, less willing to question the status quo in public. As the conversation turned towards politics he stayed judiciously silent, showing he was still paying attention only by a noisy inhalation of breath through gritted teeth when the subject became too controversial and opinions too loudly expressed.

'Lin Jie, you're a foreigner. Objectively, what do you think China's biggest problem is at the moment?' Chunyu asked. I hesitated before answering. China, like Britain, has many problems. I did not want to give offence.

'It's a very difficult question. Corruption, probably. China wants foreign investment, and foreign investment needs the rule of law. And of course it goes without saying that people in China suffer if their local cadres are corrupt.'

'That's what made Hong Kong so successful,' said Chunyu, interrupting. 'We need the rule of law for all of us, not just for investors.' I seemed accidentally to have hit on her pet subject. As a lawyer, she was likely to follow the Party's line more closely than most, but she too recognized the problems. 'Liangde, you often say the Party is holding back China by not allowing an independent judiciary. The reality is that all judges are appointed by the Party, so all judges owe their position of power to the Party. No matter how much we might want them to be independent, how can they be? It's all window-dressing. The primary means to achieve the impartial rule of law would be to have all our judges and lawyers appointed independently of the Party. I can't see how that can happen so long as we have the Party leading the nation.'

'You've made my point for me,' replied Liangde. 'The Party is coming between China and the impartial legal system the constitution says we're entitled to.'

'But the Party's in a difficult position.' She turned to me. 'What do you think was the cause of the Tiananmen Square incident in 1989?'

'The media in the West always reported that the students wanted democracy, but I've read that people were angry about official corruption, and the fact that the workers were getting involved is what finally forced the Party to . . . you know.' I noticed that Weiguo was gazing down at his rice.

'I know Liangde disagrees with me,' continued Chunyu, 'but the Party isn't stupid. They must have believed that what they did was the lesser of two evils. Think how your economic reforms would have been damaged if in 1989 we'd had the army breaking ranks, or if the Party had been overthrown. You wouldn't be sitting here now with your mobile phone and your stock deals, because China would have fallen apart.'

'Rubbish! They're scared of competition, that's all. If they're so good for China, let them hold elections. What have they to fear?'

Weiguo brought his hands up to his face and let out a groan. 'This always happens when I bring these two out together.'

Liangde and Chunyu veered into Anhui dialect and I lost the gist of the argument. If anything it seemed to become more par-tisan, the left-leaning postgraduate lawyer and the maverick, wheeling-and-dealing computer expert firing broadsides of opinions across the lukewarm remnants of our meal. Drinks were ordered, and two pots of Anhui tea arrived, Yellow Mountain Hair Peak and Taiping Monkey Chief.

'Lin Jie, I'm twenty-two. I was nine years old in 1989.' Chunyu had reverted to Mandarin to address me. 'Just because I'm a student now doesn't mean I understand what was going on in the minds of students when I was a little girl. I don't expect to understand what they hoped to achieve, what made them believe they could succeed, or how much their movement was hijacked by troublemakers. What's true now is that the Communist Party has staked its future on the reforms that Liangde is benefiting from, and all of China has staked its future on the Party's reforms working. Sometimes he forgets that.'

White Tiger

'Wood, residing in the east, governs the *qi* of spring. Metal, in the west, governs that of autumn. For this reason, wood governs the processes of life-giving, and metal governs those of death-dealing.'

Dong Zhongshu, second century BC

BEIHAI

DAOISM, THAT MOST calculatedly asocial of China's philosophies, had recolonized a patch of land on the crest of a long, low hill in Beihai, a city of a quarter of a million people in the mainland's Guangxi Autonomous Region. I had scarcely slept on the ferry from Haikou the previous night, and my tired eyes were watering from the dust. The road running past the temple was bleached white by the sun, and barely another soul braved the heat. At first I mistook the redbrick, windowless walls for a factory or a warehouse, then, as I neared it and could distinguish a red lacquered door, for a teahouse. Fingers of pale pink paper, pasted at their upper extremities to the door, beckoned to me in the wind. On each of them was the name of a benefactor and a sum of money painstakingly executed in longhand.

China's only native, vernacular religion, Daoism arose in the Warring States period partly as a reaction to the doctrines of the Confucian school, obsessed as it was with social class and the artifice of morality, as the Daoists saw it. Daoism instead took a non-ethical view of man, placing him on an equal level with all else in Nature. In Confucian eyes Daoism dehumanized mankind, removing the tenets by which man was placed above the rest of Creation, and by which the Confucian gentleman was placed above the rest of mankind. In Daoism, man became squarely a part of Nature, emancipated from the feudal strictures of daily life. At first Daoism did not promise worldly goods or riches or sons. Neither did it offer the comfort of rites and rituals, gods to see and believe in, or the immutability of holy days and festivals to prove its eternal truth. All of these it was to develop, first as Confucianism retreated to become the cult of the state, leaving ancestor worship as its social footprint, and later under the influence of Buddhism's success in fulfilling people's longing for comfort in this world and a promise of happiness in the next.

The temple guardian was watering his plants in the small courtyard between the first double door and the innermost hall. His tiny eyes were set like currants in a brown, gingerbread face, and his dishevelled moustache protruded insistently beyond the tip of his flat nose. His arms were so thin they looked as though they would break under the strain of his watering-can, while a pair of equally thin legs dangled from within baggy shorts. He saw me contemplating the innermost door.

'Have you come to pray?'

'No, I'm afraid I don't believe in . . . this isn't a Buddhist temple, is it?'

'*Bu, bu. Daojiao.* Come, come inside.' He held the handle and shifted his lean frame until the door's weight gave and a gap opened up. He encouraged me in, following close behind as I squeezed through. The hall was in near pitch darkness and was thick with incense. I shivered. It felt almost icy after the heat of the sun.

The room was small, barely five or six yards square, but the roof vault seemed much higher than one would have guessed from outside. A few thin, etiolated beams of sunlight filtered down through the chill, smoky void from cracks in the tiles. In this place, the unknowable Way of Nature was approached through darkness and rarefaction. Amongst southern China's *yang* resided here a grain of *yin*; the feminine, yielding, negative balancing the gaudy pandemonium of Buddhism. In Daoist thought, the more one tries to define the Way, the farther one gets from understanding it, and so in the cold and the darkness, followers are thought better able to glimpse it. The contemplative atmosphere of the temple felt like that of a church or a mosque, God invoked by silence.

'I'll light a lamp, if you haven't come to pray, so you can see better.' He hobbled over to a corner of the hall, and presently one end was lit by a pale glow that grew until its dim fingers probed the middle distance. The farthest shadows, where we had

entered, remained untouched. The halo revealed the man to be
standing beside his bed, a simple wooden frame on which was
spread a mattress, the two of them covered by a mosquito net
that had been yanked back to allow the bed to serve as a daytime
chair. He sat down and nodded his head encouragingly at the
altar that his oil lamp had unveiled.

'Take your time.'

A long hassock, like a badly stuffed draught-excluder, lay on
the ground before a table of gifts – incense, silk flowers, hump-
back ingots in gold-painted plastic. None of them had the edible
practicality of Buddha's offerings. A heavy velvet curtain hung
behind, its folds deep and threatening. In front of it stood five
immense incense-sticks, each the girth and height of a small tree.
Five red spots of light hovered in the darkness above.

'What's behind the curtain?'

'Three gods. The Three Pure Ones. Their names are . . . let
me think.' He thought for a while before listing them. When
they emerged, they were long and barely pronounceable, his
elderly tongue tripping over their syllables like a novice stum-
bling over the Latin names of the saints.

'The first rules over the past, the next over the present, and
the last over what is to come.' A holy trinity of tangible manifestations of the intangible Way, a practical response to the
layman's need to visualize the unrepresentable.

'Are they actually there, behind that curtain?' He gave a self-
deprecating chuckle.

'We Chinese are not like you Westerners. We still believe in
spirits, demons, ghosts . . . we are not scientific like you.' What
did he mean?

'They,' he indicated to the ceiling, and beyond to a higher
authority, 'they say there aren't any spirits or gods, that we're
"blindly following superstition". But – do you know? – the
cadres on the street, the ones who say it's superstition, they come
here too, and at home they've all got altars where they pray to

Buddha, pray for their ancestors. None of them will admit it to their *laoban*, but even their *laobans* pray.'

'We're not really scientific in the West, either,' I replied. 'You can't replace religion with science. You must have been told for decades that you couldn't come to the temple, but it didn't stop you believing, did it?'

He looked into the middle distance and went quiet. He must have been in his seventies at the very least. I suddenly realized how little I understood of what his life might have been like. In his late twenties, at Liberation, had he been an enthusiastic PLA soldier or one of Chiang Kai-shek's retreating army? A Daoist monk or just one of the *laobaixing* – 'old hundred surnames'? I did not even know when his belief had begun or how deep it was. I had sub-consciously ascribed to him the stereotypical role of the devout believer, compelled to practise his faith in secret to escape perse-cution. The young monk on Putuoshan had pointed out the old women who had never forgotten, and novels on modern China revel in the pathos of the oppressed believer. A picture of collect-ive madness has been painted, where we are invited to draw the conclusion that the abrupt change after 1949 from the universal and public practice of traditional beliefs to the sweeping away of superstitious religious thought was just one of mutual deception; that everybody still believed but nobody dared to stand up and be counted; that even the persecutors prayed in the dark. At best such a view leaves everybody equally complicit in a history that need never have happened. At worst it seeks to deny that totalitarian-ism had its willing accomplices, laying the blame instead at the door of the men at the very top, the Maos and the Stalins. I was reluctant to embarrass or insult the custodian by asking him where he had stood. I was after all here for my personal gratification, not to conduct a sociological survey or to interrogate old men over lives I could barely hope to understand.

'The temple was demolished after Liberation in Mao's "sweeping away the old". We rebuilt it a few years ago.'

I took to his mention of Mao in an effort to move away from the subject of his own past, and asked another question.

'Almost every taxi I've ridden in China has had a talisman with Mao's picture on it hanging from the rear-view mirror. Don't people remember what he did?'

'Mao Zedong . . .' He held the name gently in his mouth, as though afraid that he might harm it, half in reverence, half in the daydreamy sadness by which the elderly sometimes conjure up wounds that had once hurt but that time and experience had healed. I did not ask which.

'Mao Zedong. We say he was seventy per cent right, thirty per cent wrong. You should know that already.' I nodded. It is a well-known saying. 'He swept away so many bad things: the foreigners who had carved up China like a watermelon, the Japanese bandits, the opium, the landlords. He tried to sweep away religion too, but now it's come back. Perhaps he was wrong to try. What's the point in losing sight of the good he did? Now we can have both the good things and the memory of Mao. Isn't that much better than losing him? Even though the Party still says we are ignorant to pray to Guanyin, to the Three Pure Ones and our ancestors, we all have shrines at home. Mao was a Chinese, but he wasn't China. China is bigger than Mao. It was here before him and now he's part of it, in its heart.'

I walked Beihai's backstreets that evening after the light had faded and the heat had dispersed. Lit from within, each of its single-storey homes threw an electric yellow pool over a patch of the road outside. Windows and doors were uniformly lashed open to let the air into their sultry recesses, and through each without exception I could see the shrines the temple custodian had spoken of.

Scarlet rectangles served as the foci for ancestor worship. In every home one was pasted to the wall, directly facing the front entrance so that the souls might come and go as they pleased.

On them, underlined by a small shelf bristling with unlit incense-sticks in stubby vases, framed black-and-white photographs of past family members stared rigidly out into the street – the long dead in traditional costume, the more recently deceased stiffly posed in their best Western suit, each one wearing an expressionless mask as if they were passport photos for the journey into the afterlife.

Which afterlife they had reached was unclear. The shrines professed a syncretism of not just ancestor worship but also Buddhism, Daoism, even communism. Statuettes of Guanyin and of Caishen, the deity of wealth, rubbed shoulders beside plasticky *yinyang* swirls and octagonal mirrors surrounded by the eight trigrams. All possible bases were covered. Wherever their loved ones had ended up, by attending to the rituals of each school their descendants might guarantee their well-being. Little wonder that China rarely experienced religious persecution until the arrival of Christianity, Islam and Marxism. Syncretism has the advantage that nobody is ever wrong, even Mao.

The Great Helmsman shared wall space with the monochrome faces, here a fresh-faced young revolutionary in olive green tunic and cap; there the familiar elder statesman in blue cotton, his black hair plastered back over waxy temples. He smiled demurely out over the joss and the offerings of fruit and into the busy street, as though satisfied with his new status of demigod.

The street I walked was choked with spectres. Against the malevolent roar of gas burners gaping cauldrons belched steam into the black air. People stood tending them, stirring their depths with long, dark paddles. In the blunt light of unshielded bulbs, hunchbacks sieved and riddled the boiling contents and, in a wretched *danse macabre*, reeled back and forth under their weight to disgorge basketfuls of steaming shells on to low tables. A red plastic lightshade splashed streaks of infernal fire across the scene.

Silhouetted by the light from each window, squatting figures toiled to transmute the burdens into piles of glistening meat and discarded shells. All around them, shadows scurried to and fro, and by degrees the piles of shells were collected into heaps, the heaps into mounds and in this way slowly into putrid mountains. As far as I could see through the tree-lined gloom, pannierfuls of tiny, yawning cockleshells had been tossed on to the crests of dunes. In the heat of the day they had mouldered, and the flies that fed on them now rose, now settled in suffocating clouds about the heads of the bowed workers as the emptying of each new load disturbed them. The workers gritted their teeth and returned with their empty baskets to the cauldrons. Dehumanized by the never-ending task, they were the tortured souls that Buddhism teaches are bound to *samsara*, the eternal wheel of death and rebirth, or Daoism's living ghosts born of man's inferior soul.

YINTAN

THE TAXI-DRIVER I had hailed at Beihai's ferry terminal that morning had known the whereabouts of the hotel my cabin mate had stayed in several weeks before and had recommended. But by the time we reached it, it had already been demolished, its raw constituents now no more than a pile of rubble that was being picked over and sorted into heaps of bricks, splintered wood, metal and shards of glass. No matter – the taxi-driver knew a *zhaodaisuo* that would take me without getting the necessary permission from the Public Security Bureau. The *laoban*, overweight and sweaty, had slouched back on his worn-out rattan chair in a string vest and underpants, more intent on watching a Peking opera that flickered in a grainy falsetto than concerned at the arrival of an illegal guest. The room was on the top storey, its roof exposed to the full force of the sun. Now when I returned after dark it was oppressively hot, even though I had left the window wide open all day. The TV made a noise like a boiling kettle, focused its beam to a single spot of white, and threatened to explode if left to its own devices in the dingy room, so I unplugged it. The tap in the bricked-off corner that served as a bathroom sneezed when I turned it on, then held its breath for a moment before coughing rusty water at me. I decided I had to leave Beihai.

It is strange how sometimes the smallest of pleasures can change the way you view a city. The next morning I caught the smell of the tiny bar of jasmine-scented soap that had been left for me beside a threadbare but clean towel. The sun was fully risen and tugged hopefully at the rends and tears in my curtains until I swept them back to let it in. I breakfasted on a mango and a papaya that I had bought the night before and drank green tea made with a sachet left by the thermos. When I went downstairs, the street was perfumed with the blossoms of the most beautiful, red-flowered trees. Immaculate white hens and proud, crimson-tailed cockerels scratched and strutted in the dust.

I headed for the station, hoping to buy a railway ticket north to Chengdu, but there was no scale to my map, and after twenty minutes' walking in the escalating humidity I discovered I had made scarcely any headway. Instead I found myself in what had once been the Roman Catholic enclave. A white church with blue glass windows sat back from the road, facing what was once the palace of the Roman Catholic Bishop of Beihai. A sandwich board declared in handwritten characters '*Haliluya, Yesu Jidu fuhuo le!*' Hallelujah, Jesus Christ is risen! Opposite, a monument to the city's history recorded how Beihai had been a base for the quasi-Christian Taiping rebels and their leader Hong Xiuquan, the self-professed younger brother of Jesus, during their mid-nineteenth century uprising. Presumably Rome had insisted on founding a cathedral here, once the port was opened to foreign trade, to exorcise Hong's heresy and to preach its own Christian truth.

The houses fronting the street opposite were graced with high, Flemish façades, stepped gables alternating with pitched, and beneath the shade of cassia trees Beihai's citizens drank tea. I sat down at an open-air family restaurant with a copy of the *Guangxi Daily* and ordered the patriarch's recommendation: pig's tongue, braised aubergine and a bowl of boiled rice. The front page was dominated by the continuing story of the missing pilot, by now presumed dead. On page two a smaller article announced that he had been awarded the title Defender of Maritime Airspace.

I abandoned my intention of walking to the railway station and caught a bus. The attempt to develop the land between Beihai – on the north coast of a peninsula that sticks out like a crooked finger into the Gulf of Tonkin – and Yintan Silver Beach, to its south had met with a predictable, unsightly fate. The depressing vista of roads laid out with surveying poles and lined with parched poplars and crumbling cement shells had dogged me since Suzhou, only the transient details of the scene giving any indication as to where I was. Here, a herd of goats grazed on what should have been the manicured lawns of the office of an exporter of cultured pearls, one of Beihai's major commodities, and prudish vegetation was slowly covering the defunct company's name. And as the bus, the only vehicle on the road, clanked south in a trail of yellow dust, we passed row upon row of mock Tudor houses, Sleeping Beauty castles and Amityville mansions, each empty and staring.

The ticket-seller had only one kind of ticket for sale, a hard seat to the city of Liuzhou in the north of the province on a train leaving the next morning, and in desperation I bought it rather than face the long trek out to the station every day in a vain attempt to buy one direct to Chengdu. Outside the station another bus was waiting to ferry people to Silver Beach.

I had high hopes of China's Number One Tourist Beach. The girl who stood behind the counter at the *zhaodaisuo* had told me

I would enjoy it, for this was where Beihai's gilded youth spent its weekends; but its open spaces were filled with the by-now familiar piles of building rubble and its beachfront hotels were the same shoddy pastiches – Black Forest hunting lodges executed in lavatory tiles – that I had seen elsewhere. Beyond a row of trinket shops the beach swept out of sight to the south-east. Coastguards' lookout towers were lined up as far as the eye could see like so many animals come down to a watering-hole to drink. Black dots marked the bobbing heads of the few off-season swimmers who splashed and laughed and waved to the speedboats that powered up and down. Further out, a flotilla of fishing junks, their decks a mess of tarred boards and hawsers, tarpaulined shanty cabins and fluttering red flags, held its position noisily against the ebb tide. On the oily sand at the mouth of a small creek, the skeletal ribcages of sunken sampans shared their gravespace with beached, high-bustled junks.

But Silver Beach's uniquely odd aspect was a collection of miniature windmills. They were scattered amongst the palms and the yellowing lawns, like enormous souvenirs from a gentleman's Grand Tour of Europe. Beside each stood a signboard explaining how its style reflected the national characteristics of its builders.

The Welsh windmill 'displayed a natural use of wood, and was conservative'. This was because the Welsh 'were sentimental and liked to bring the countryside into their industrial cities'. The French windmill was predictably 'romantic', though in fact it resembled the Welsh one in nearly every detail other than that its vanes stood broken and immobile. The English windmill too was 'conservative', and the 'industry and efficiency' of an identical German windmill were held up as a model for China's market reforms.

I pumped three rounds from an air rifle into a tin can on the shooting-range, handed my prize teddy bear to the child who stood watching me and caught the bus back to Beihai.

*

'*Jintian bu nuli gongzuo, mingtian nuli zhao gongzuo.*' If you do not work hard today, then you must work even harder to find work tomorrow. Now that the iron rice bowl had been snatched away, it seemed that the local work units of the People's Railway had been charged with spreading the word that state employees who slackened off would lose their jobs. The sign painters had been out in force up and down the line from Beihai to Liuzhou, and the warning echoed from the brick walls of whistlestops and halts along the way. If you lose your income it is no longer the Party's fault. You have only yourself to blame, even if you are blameless. A nation of over one billion people was being gradually and painfully weaned off its reliance on the state.

Guangxi's coastal plain was a sunbeaten, dusty green that matched the utilitarian paint of the train. Tabletop prospects of ripe, pendulous paddy were scattered with parched villages and the shellburst sprays of feathery bamboo groves, accentuating the vertical at the expense of a scaleless horizontal that receded into a khaki heat haze. The bleached horizon was a wall of gently waving fronds, of gnarled, top-heavy pines and larches, that resolved when we reached it into the same middle distance we had just passed through, while behind us the recent detail of village, track and stubble field faded to a closed wall of pallid vegetation. The carriages played a sinuous game of follow-my-leader into the bare foothills of the Hundred Thousand Mountains, dragging their heels as though insensible from the midday sun. The ragged, olive curtains down one side of the carriage were drawn to shield us from the worst of the heat and the dust. They complained fretfully at their confinement, whipping back in billowing skirts as they escaped from under sleepers' folded arms or from the heavy bags of fruit and dried fish – presents for country cousins – that had served as stays. With each billow, dust blew in and settled on our sweating bodies. We mopped our brows with moistened facecloths and sipped tea from recycled coffee jars and decapitated Coke cans.

The drumlin slopes merged and raised themselves into dry whorls of tea, and behind their barriers the hot wind dispersed and subsided. The paddy terraces grew wetter as we inched higher, and by early afternoon they carpeted the flat valley floors, arching gracefully and architecturally along barely perceptible natural contours, piled on top of each other in retreating tiers of silvery looking-glasses pricked by a myriad of filaments. Ahead, the tender emerald shoots coalesced into endless lawns of greensward, as smooth as the baize on a billiards table, over which our humming diesel engine rolled, on and on.

As we pulled through the railway town of Black Pond, shadows spilled over the crests of the hills and cascaded into the valleys. A steely glow hung in the west for a short time and then faded. With the fall of night, life within the carriage turned in on itself, cards were produced, evening meals were cobbled together from the contents of plastic bags, and morsels forced on fellow passengers. Bottles of *baijiu* were snapped up from the dining-car and rounds of frenetic toasting began to make their mark in red faces and tired, bloodshot eyes. I woke up as we reached Liuzhou and staggered stiffly on to the platform where a guard asked me where I wanted to go. Within a few minutes she had produced a much sought-after ticket, had invented a supplementary booking fee and had sat me down in the soft-class waiting-room to await the 11.30 p.m. train to Chengdu. I was thankful to be spared the ordeal of Liuzhou. I had passed through it once years before and had no desire to revisit the impoverished, damp streets I recalled.

GUIZHOU

IN THE EARLY hours of the morning the Chengdu train crossed into Guizhou, south-west China's so-called Precious Region, larger than England and Wales combined and comparable in size to Washington State. In 1999 Guizhou had a population of nearly 36,000,000, and in recent years this had been increasing by fourteen and a half per cent annually. This I learned from the *Atlas of Guizhou Province* that was pushed toward me by my neighbour as I ate breakfast the next day. I propped my bowl of rice porridge between my knees and noted down some of the more interesting facts.

The abbreviated name for Guizhou – *Qian*, an obscure character meaning black – is taken from the name of a territory within the southerly Warring States nation of Chu. It is a poor province, lying on the mountainous Yunnan–Guizhou plateau, and only one-tenth of its area is suitable for ploughing. The locals say it has not three consecutive feet of level ground. Its thick forests are one of the richest sources of traditional Chinese medicines. During the Anti-Japanese War large numbers of people retreated before the advance of the Japanese Imperial Army to the remote wastes of Guizhou where they sat things out in the best of traditional Chinese health. They might have spent their time drinking the famous Ximaojian tea from Duyun, each of whose leaves is said to resemble a sparrow's tongue. Guizhou also produces over half of China's mercury and phosphorous. Its deposits of silica, iodine and bauxite are China's most important, and western Guizhou is known as China's south-west sea of coal. Over one-third of its population are ethnic minorities, including the Miao, Buyi, Dong, Tujia, Yi, Gelao, Shui, Hui, Bai, Zhuang and Yao peoples. A full quarter of the population is illiterate.

'It's pitiful. How poor must you be, when to spend your days picking old scraps of cloth from a rubbish tip is worthwhile?' My neighbour sat on the fold-down stool that was the twin to mine and leaned on our shared window-ledge table. We were travelling at barely the speed of a suburban car, and trackside images hung before us long enough for us to take in their details. A couple of dozen men and women turned to look at the train as it passed, their ruddy, peasant faces appearing like the rash of some infectious disease against the pale skin of the spoil heap.

The train slowed down to a jog to negotiate the endless twists and turns of this part of the Yunnan–Guizhou plateau. It was as though our giant engine were traversing a Lilliput of miniature valleys and scale-model hills. Tunnels were briefly heralded by a press of scruffy grass walls before the scene was lost in blackness for five or ten seconds. Then an exclamation of sky, a sigh as the crescendo in the carriage dropped in pitch, and we were met with the same scene as before, only now in an indistinguishable, neighbouring valley. For hours a succession of steep-sided dwarf hills abutted each other, separated by narrow ravines and scored by rivulets. The locals were right – there were not three consecutive feet of level ground. The slopes overlooked each other so closely that the valley floors, even when every available square foot had been cultivated, were clearly insufficient to support a population of any size. In desperation, the farmers had struck upwards, clearing the hills of vegetation to their very crowns. Their fields, a buff patchwork of lichens, clung to even the steepest of angles, each delineated not by gracefully sculpted walls but by untidy lines of turf sod. The luxuriant growth of the previous day's Guangxi plain had given way to a feeble stubble interspersed with rocky scars where the near-constant rains had scythed away the thin soil.

'You can't separate the question of poverty from the question of *renkou* – population,' said my neighbour. 'Everything in this province is so poor – the soil, the transport, education – that the people rely on male offspring for their future. You see the steep rake on those fields, the piles of rocks they've hacked out so they can till the ground? That's not girls' work.' He conjured up a massive boulder on the table between us, which he heaved with both hands from the table on to the floor where it blocked the narrow gangway. 'So they need more than one son, and so they have more mouths to feed, and so they get poorer. It's a very backward area.' *Renkou* – literally person mouths – and backwardness: to the Chinese these are the two inseparable absolutes of their great south-western provinces. If neighbouring Sichuan was anything like Guizhou, I could see why the noodle-maker in Dadonghai had left.

My neighbour was a teacher, and his pet subject was illiteracy. He stared out through the rain-spotted glass. The rain was so fine, and the speed of the train so slow, that the droplets never seemed under any obligation to coalesce or to fall.

'If you have ten people doing a job that one can manage, then either you have to lay nine of them off or you have to pay everybody ten times less,' he said. 'In the region where I work – in Guangxi – the adult illiteracy rate is said to be five per cent. We have slogans around the village just like those.' He nodded at a daub on a passing wall that challenged the scavengers to 'Stamp out illiteracy'. 'It must be worse for them here. We try to spot the gifted pupils early on, during primary school, and then we scrimp on expenses, turn a blind eye to the odd falsification on the class register, find extra time for after-school lessons, and try to fund them through middle high school. We call them Produce of Hope students.

'In the villages that supply my school there are some good people, people who've got rich under the reforms and who are socially aware, who feel a responsibility to others. The local Party says we should all contribute to local schools through the local scholarship funds,' here he slipped into English, 'but we all know that most of the money ends up in the cadres' pockets.'

'How much does it cost?' I asked.

'After a pupil leaves primary school, at least 1,200 *renminbi* a year.' He looked out of the window and sucked his teeth, as though hopeful of soliciting a contribution.

The monotone shouts of *Ganzhe!* and the hollow clang of the trolley as it negotiated the gangway could be heard long before the white-overalled attendant appeared in our carriage selling sugar-cane. For a few *renminbi* we each chose carefully from the smooth purple lengths on offer and waited patiently while the skin was removed with a filthy knife. The teacher offered me his copy of the *Guilin News Weekly* to read and I stood, sugarcane in one hand, newspaper in the other, happily munching away while Guizhou crept past outside the window and the sugary juice crystallized in sticky clods on my lips and on a week's growth of stubble.

On the front page, alongside an article on Zhejiang's first transsexual (reportedly so unhappy with her new self after eight years as a woman that she was now suing the hospital that had performed the operation) and another on a controversial pro-gramme of euthanasia for sick camels in Liaoning province, there was a grainy photograph from the sixties. A crowd brandished automatic weapons, rifles and rice sickles in celebration of the capture of an American airman. His mugshot was tucked away in the corner, a frightened, sweating contrast to the jubilation of his captors. It was clearly intended as an editorial comment on the incident in Hainan – China and the United States had been through this before, and in the previous instance of American incursion the Chinese had won.

Further down the page, in language that resonated with the official line being put out over the US spy plane's breach of Chinese territorial integrity, the *Records of Fangcheng County* for 1968 were quoted.

> In 1964 the US launched a war of aggression against Vietnam, and time and again sent warplanes to intrude on our airspace with the aim of provoking retaliation. In order to severely punish the flying bandits and to protect our national sovereignty, mili-tary commands in twelve counties bordering Vietnam established anti-aircraft positions, manned day and night to spot enemy aircraft.

Lu Guanlin, a twenty-five-year-old temporary worker on a commune in a village called Banba in Guangxi's extreme south, was in the rice fields early in the afternoon of 21 August 1967 when, from the direction of the Vietnamese border to the west, he heard the roar of jet engines. Almost instantly the planes appeared overhead, two silver and one black. The silver aircraft were firing constantly into the fuselage of the third, which sent out a ball of flames and sparks as one wing was torn off. Fragments showered the ground where Guanlin stood watching, and some of the women in the field began to cry. The aircraft let out a strange scream and a plume of thick, black smoke, and then slammed into the side of Turtledove Mountain behind his home, sending the onlookers' conical straw hats flying with the force of its wake.

Through the smoke, Guanlin could make out two white dots, one small and one larger. The small one hit the ground first and at speed, the second veered to land more slowly nearby. There was no time to fetch his gun, and so he shouldered his bamboo carrying-pole as a weapon and raced to the spot where the parachutes had come down.

The body of the pilot was laid out stiff and straight below the tree where his unopened parachute had snagged. Commander Jimmy L. Buckley's right hand had been severed, his right leg had been holed by bullets, and his face was awash with blood. Guanlin felt for a sign of life, but he was already dead. Then a People's Militiaman arrived on the scene, and together they went to look for the second airman.

In a thicket nearby, Guanlin came across signs that the foliage had been disturbed. A rustle of leaves and a pair of flying boots betrayed Lieutenant-Commander Robert J. Flynn, who was found with both hands shielding his face, his breathing laboured. Guanlin recalled how Flynn's automatic reaction, when he shouted at him to put his hands up, had been to reach for the pistol on his belt, and that he had lashed out at his hand with the bamboo pole to stop him. More Chinese arrived, and Flynn was bound and led from the thicket, trembling from cold and fear and limping from a leg wound.

For the benefit of the *News Weekly* reporter, Guanlin recalled how surprised he had been to see such a giant of a man, with blue eyes, blond hair and *such* a big nose, his pale skin visible beneath his tunic and shorts. By now several hundred people had surrounded Flynn, and more were still streaming up the hill as the news spread. Eventually there were over 2,000 people on the hill, and they began to chant 'Down with American imperialism!' as they paraded their trophy back down the hill to a waiting army truck.

That evening, Guanlin and others were detailed to guard the crash site and Commander Buckley's body, and the next day reporters arrived to shoot footage and to take photographs of the scene as propaganda. Late that second day, once his usefulness as a dead flying bandit had been exhausted, Commander Buckley was buried where he had fallen. His gun was found a year later in a stream by a child tickling for fish.

Only later did Lu Guanlin hear that a second aircraft had been shot down in Guangxi on the same day. This second aircraft had been part of the same flight, which had been launched from the USS *Constellation* on a mission to attack a railway marshalling yard north of Hanoi, and which appeared to have strayed into Chinese airspace to avoid a large weather front. No survivors were found by the Chinese, nor any remains of either Lieutenant-Commander Trembley or Dain V. Scott, even though Americans came to comb the area in the seventies. They are still listed as Missing in Action. According to Chinese records, Commander Buckley's body was disinterred years later when an American delegation arrived to repatriate his remains. Guanlin was surprised at how beautifully preserved the body of the airman was when the grave was opened. Some villagers commented that Americans were better nourished than the Chinese, others put it down to the rich soil of Banba village and said that the pilot had benefited from his time there.

Lu Guanlin and the MiG pilots who shot down the American aircraft were fêted as heroes in China. Honoured by the Central Military Committee in a triumphal parade, Guanlin was presented with a certificate of merit, *The Selected Writings of Mao Zedong*, *The Sayings of Chairman Mao*, *The Poems of Chairman Mao* and a Chairman Mao badge. Flynn spent almost six years imprisoned in China before being repatriated. The article concluded by reporting that one of the wheels from the downed aircraft was said still to be in daily use as a school bell near the crash site.

By the time I finished the article the scenery had shifted. The now-you-see-me-now-you-don't press of tunnels and ravines had widened and fallen away into a richer, flatter world where the background spine of hills had through lack of necessity been spared the depredations of the farmers' axes. They were clothed in pines and maples, a band of dark natural green sandwiched between the gold of ripe paddy and a nicotine sky. At dusk the teacher got off at a station in northern Guizhou, wishing me *yiluping'an* – good luck for my trip – over one shoulder.

The few isolated farmsteads that we now passed were endowed with an unearthly beauty by a pale moon that tried to break through thinning clouds, their white plasterwork assuming a near spectral luminescence between lines of black timber. Eaveloads of drying maize were softly lit by the orange glow of oil lamps or starkly silhouetted against the brilliance of naked bulbs. Pearlescent threshing floors were streaked with moon-shadows cast by the rakes, hoes and winnowing baskets that dotted their surfaces or leaned against invisible walls. Lying on my bunk, my chin resting on a crooked arm, I peered out at the blackening hills as we heaved north towards Sichuan and fell asleep.

CHENGDU

COME DAWN, A heavy mist had reduced the Sichuan Basin – the size of Britain and home to the majority of Sichuan's population of 120,000,000 – to no more than a quarter of a mile of damp, tree-flecked fields stretching away on either side of the railway. Beyond this the white sky descended to merge with the white vapour exhaled by the soil as it awoke and began to stir.

The Sichuan Basin's fecund soil is watered by a tapestry of rivers and ancient irrigation works, and its fertility is legendary. From before the time of the first emperor, Qin Shihuang, rulers coveted the basin as a source of staples to keep the bellies of old hundred surnames full. Wheat, barley, rice, sesame and beans thrived here, and later crops from the New World: the sweet potato, maize, tobacco and the peanut, which the Chinese named *huasheng*, born of the flower, from the way the fertilized flower stalk burrows down into the earth where it transforms itself into the familiar pod. Pomeloes from Fuling were presented as tribute at court, so sweet did they grow in a subtropical climate that rarely drops below freezing. Aficionados of *zhacai*, the mouth-puckeringly pungent, salt-pickled mustard greens the Chinese find an indispensable accompaniment to any meal, will argue for entire train journeys over which part of Sichuan produces the freshest, most fragrant version. The most sought-after beancurd milk in China is said to come from Sichuan, as are the tenderest bamboo shoots and the best strange-flavour beans your *renminbi* can buy.

My hotel in Chengdu was just a place to rest for the night, for I had secured a soft-sleeper ticket to Urumchi leaving the following day. On the way back from the railway station the bus stopped while two policemen dragged the body of a middle-aged man by the ankles to the side of the road. I had long ago become hardened to the sight of dead bodies on China's roads, but I still wasn't used to the lack of human dignity accorded to them. The dead man's arms splayed outward and back at that painful angle that only the unfeeling dead can perform, and his suit jacket rucked up behind his head as it grazed the tarmac. His eyes were open and he looked mildly surprised, as though he remembered stepping out but couldn't recall reaching the opposite pavement. Passers-by stopped to stare. Some pointed or laughed, most just gawped, a few covered their mouths with one hand or shook their heads. He was manhandled to the gutter where he would not cause an obstruction, his feet were let drop, and the bus inched past him and then accelerated. All that was left on the road was a neat trail of blood, as though a thick, red highlighter pen had been swiped across it.

The soft-class waiting-room at Chengdu railway station was an exemplar of the funereal comfortlessness that passed for luxury under Mao and which, with a little digging, one can still find in Chinese backwaters. A pair of heavy doors, in smoked glass and varnished wood, insulated the frowsty atmosphere inside from the airy celebration of life on the hard-class benches outside, swinging back quickly and noiselessly on tight springs. I trod my way silently to where a uniformed attendant sat half-hidden behind her service counter. In a put-upon whisper she demanded to see my soft-class ticket. Only once my status was confirmed was I entitled to enjoy the dubious luxuries that came with it.

I ran an eye over the dusty relics on the glass shelves. They were the same as were hawked up and down the corridors of every Chinese train: cans of cola, orangeade, eight-treasure congee, bottles of *baijiu*, boxes of dried noodles. What I wanted was some water for my magnetic tea. I began to ask, but my voice seemed to reverberate around the nave-like space in a profane shout and I reduced it to a self-conscious whisper.

'Do you have any hot . . . sorry, do you have any hot water

for my tea?' I stood like a communicant before the altar rail and presently received hot water from a thermos. I sought out a pew, a brown leather sofa that looked as though it had been plushly upholstered in the fifties or sixties but which had become hard and parchment-like from lack of use. In the melancholy stillness a vision of the mangled body in the road the previous day flashed unbidden in front of me.

Above the counter a clock ticked away the hour or so before the Urumchi train was due to leave. The sun shone through a chink in the window's floor-to-ceiling net curtains. On the ceiling had been fitted a mirrored globe and a ring of spotlights, angled so their beams fell on nothing in particular. Three were lit, one green, one yellow and one red, and they threw pale splashes of colour on the wall as though the sun were shining through a stained-glass window. The sacristan, asleep behind the counter, stirred, coughed and mumbled under her breath. Above her, a clock ticked away the seconds.

Presently the doors were pushed apart and once again swung apologetically back. A young man surveyed the interior, spotted me as the only other passenger there, smiled, and approached me. Any company was better than an hour's wait in gloomy isolation, I thought. He spoke in English.

'Hi, my name's John. Mind if I join you?' His hair was cropped to within a whisker of his scalp, and a pair of round, wire-rimmed spectacles were pushed high up his nose so that they left an impression in his thick eyebrows. He had a small, perfectly circular face and a furrowed brow that made him look like he was permanently deep in thought. As he spoke, he looked me up and down, as though weighing me up before deciding that I was worth talking to.

I introduced myself and complimented him on his English. A Chinese person's reaction to praise of his ability in English is often the best indicator of how accustomed he is to Western company. The dabbler, who likes to talk to foreigners merely to show off to his friends or to gain status in the company of strangers, will invariably become coy, one hand brusquely waving aside the praise which in all likelihood he believes is well-placed, regardless of how poor his English is. The more experienced, on the other hand, will generally explain briefly how he came to speak the language, so accepting the praise by default. John fell into the latter category.

'I've been in business on my own for several years. I have a lot of American friends here in Chengdu.'

'What line are you in?' The idiom did not confuse him.

'This and that, as you say. Working for myself is better than having a *laoban* who you're obliged to suck up to or be fired.'

'What makes you say that? Did your *laoban* fire you?' He had seated himself in the pew facing me and grinned as he looked me over once more.

'Well guessed. Is it that obvious?'

'You don't strike me as the kind of person who'd be satisfied earning 200 *renminbi* a month sitting behind a desk.'

'A rebel without a cause.' He smiled, and I smiled with him.

'You work with Americans. Have you ever been to the US?' I asked. His answer was instantaneous, expressed in a quick tensing of his eyebrows and a tightening of the jaw. His words when they came failed to achieve the same depth of resentment.

'The US? No. I'm planning to travel there, but I need to apply through the local police station for an exit permit. They can make things very difficult if they want. Have you ever been?' I felt ashamed that I could travel so freely if I wished but had never managed to fly across the Atlantic.

John pulled a dog-eared book from his bag and flicked to where a business card was serving as a bookmark. He began to read. The cover featured a Chinese businessman in a lounge suit holding forth from a podium. Behind him a graph climbed in an exponential curve, visible proof that the businessman was doing well. I fumbled around in my rucksack for Thomas Hardy and turned to my place a few pages from the end. I sipped at my tea and saw Gabriel and Bathsheba happily married before I put the book down and addressed John.

'Do you play on the markets?'

He looked up.

'I've been known to. What I want to know is this: if the author of this book has cracked the secret of the stock market, why is he writing such rubbish when he could be earning thousands of dollars sitting on his fanny tapping away at a computer screen? Cigarette?' I shook my head.

'What do you think of China?' he asked bluntly. It is the one question that I always dread. Some ask only because they want to hear praise for the way in which China is developing, and they generally do so in front of friends, and in Chinese, so that they can all bask in the answer. Others want to hear the exact opposite. Whether this is from a misplaced Chinese sense of self-effacement or from a genuine bitterness at how backward they imagine China to be in comparison to an idealized West I am never sure. Here, however, we were almost alone, the only other person within earshot was fast asleep, and we were speaking in English.

'Do you really want to know?'

He drew himself to the edge of his pew and nodded.

'Well, it strikes me China could have a great future,' I began, 'but I also think it might slide into a very dark period.' I was unused to having to give details beyond the obligatory comment that the reforms have made China a great power but, just as in the restaurant in Haikou, I was glad to find myself on new conversational territory.

'Take unemployment. I've read statistics that claim there are 150,000,000 people in China who are either unemployed or just marking time in a temporary job. It doesn't matter how many young graduates go abroad to study, or work in a joint-venture firm, or earn a small fortune and talk into a mobile phone all day:

150,000,000 people is enough to overturn a government if they get organized. In Britain our Prime Minister makes a statement to Parliament if a factory closes and 1,500 people lose their jobs. Do you know the saying "The devil finds work for idle hands"?'

'I can work it out.'

'But they probably won't ever get organized, will they? Mao understood that revolutions are led by the middle classes, and so long as the middle classes are making a tidy profit from the reforms, with their children going to the US and their parents settled in a nice, cosy home like in all the soap operas, then all the Party need do is act as the broker between foreign capital and your 150,000,000 unemployed peasants who'll work for a pittance.'

'It's a simplistic explanation, but at least you're trying.'

He slumped back on the sofa and then sat up straight again.

'*This* is the problem.' He pushed his wire frames even further up his nose and let out an animated sigh, as though frustrated that only he knew the answer to China's problems and that nobody else could see it, least of all the people concerned. Then he leaned forward.

'The new middle class, as you say, is getting richer, though most people are actually a lot worse off than they appear, but that's a different issue. In terms of money, lots of people are doing well – some very well. Outwardly, they're getting more advanced, more developed.' He leaned further forward until he was as close as the low table between us would allow. 'The problem is that what's in *here*', he tapped vigorously at one temple, 'isn't developing at all. In our heads we're still communists, not in the sense that we believe in Marxism any more, but because we let the Communist Party do all our wider thinking for us. The Party comes out with slogans and we repeat them. The only reason why China held together when Eastern Europe and the Soviet Union fell apart is that after Mao died, Deng Xiaoping realized that the slogans had to change if the Party was ever going to survive in power, but they didn't disappear. Instead we were told that "It doesn't matter if the cat is black or white so long as it catches mice" and that "To get rich is glorious" . . . '

'And "Work hard today, or work even harder finding work tomorrow"?' I suggested sarcastically, but there was no stopping him.

'The Party admitted that people work better if you allow them to act selfishly. The basis of our reforms is that people are best motivated by self-interest. The Party remains at the helm, of course, steering the economy in the greater national interest, and they call it Socialism with Chinese Characteristics. The assets that used to be owned by the Party on behalf of the people have been given to local government officials instead, so the officials owe a debt to the Party for having given them power and wealth. If the Party's legitimacy were removed, the local officials wouldn't be able to justify the windfall they inherited, and so they have to support the Party if they want to go on enjoying the benefits of the reforms. What about people like me, though? I don't need a legitimate Party in control to justify why I have money, because I earned it instead of being given it. Even if the Party loses its legitimacy, my money is still my money. Eventually the local officials will get to a stage where what they've done with the assets they inherited outweighs the fact that it was the Party that handed them out in the first place. That's when the Party might find itself out of a job.

'Then there's all that rubbish about making China a strong nation so it can take its place on the world stage. We've got one billion people and nuclear weapons! If we aren't already a major player in world politics then what the hell is wrong with us? The average Chinese person equates having a pager or mobile phone with being developed and Western. That's our yardstick of success – that, and going abroad . . .' He was standing up now, carried away with his thoughts. He had acted out the words pager and mobile phone by conjuring up enormous belt pouches, and now he leaned backwards to underline the size of an immense imaginary wallet that weighed him down. 'And having lots of cash in our back pocket. They confuse being cash rich with being developed.' He sat down and lowered his voice as though tired of the whole business. 'But in their heads they're not developing beyond the stage of seeing within the boundaries set out by the Party. We're all like little kids who believe what our parents say. Do you think we'd carry on like this if tomorrow the slogan suddenly became "To get rich is bad"? Of course not. We'd all blindly follow the new slogan instead.

'All kids start by believing that their parents are the most powerful people in the world, but then most grow up and realize that they're only human. They come to accept that their parents won't be making decisions for them any more, and at some point the parents accept that the kids have grown up and don't need to rely on them. We Chinese haven't reached that point, we haven't grown up yet.

'We can travel abroad much more freely than before, but we can still only go if our parents allow us. We're like children who can only go out of the garden to play if mom lets us, and if we don't come back when she calls us, we're punished. People in China forget this, because they're so pleased at just being allowed outside to play. We're like little children. We don't even have the freedom to decide to do nothing with our lives if we want to.' He paused to light another cigarette.

'The big cheeses all strut and puff and think they're so important because they've got money, but when getting rich means being either corrupt or a hooker for foreign businessmen, then getting rich confines them to a child's mindset. It's not development at all, just arrested development. Of course, the West can't get its pants down quick enough when it comes to taking advantage of our cheap labour.' He acted out the West leeringly unbuttoning its flies. 'And China is so childlike, it can't repel their amorous advances. It's tantamount to paedophilia!' I snorted loudly and the attendant looked up over her arm through a pair of bleary eyes.

'This spy plane – do you know about it?' asked John.

'I've just passed through Hainan, but they wouldn't let me call in on the aircrew to say hi.' He ignored my attempt at a joke.

'How is China reacting to it? The Party puffs out its feathers like a rooster, and us hens – the Chinese people – watch it standing on top of the henhouse making a great noise, and we're all very impressed. The reality is that we can't do anything about the US spying on us apart from making a noise and holding hostage an aircrew that was delivered straight into our hands – how difficult can that be? There's no way we can admit publicly that the US can spy on us at will and that our pilots can't even fly a plane safely. When a country has to resort to such simplistic nationalism to get the people on its side . . .' The Tannoy drowned out the end of his sentence.

'*Qianwang Wulumuqi de lüke, qing zhunbei jianpiao!*'

'Your train.' I nodded, pushed Hardy towards him, and stood up. I threw my luggage over one shoulder and held out a hand.

'Take care, Liam – the Uighurs are nothing but a bunch of thieves.'

Soft-class ticket holders are allowed on to the platform first so that they don't have to face the anarchy of hard class. Once I had found my berth, turnstiles somewhere within the station were flung open, the hard-class ticket inspection commenced, and soon a flood of passengers burst from the wide mouth of the platform underpass and lapped the length of the carriages. Their possessions were slung about them in old fertilizer bags or bulging tricoloured nylon bags, and they clutched their tickets and stared slack-jawed at the train as if they had never seen one before. Then like sheep being driven from pen to pen, they began to search for their carriages, each wearing the same look of incomprehension and urgency. Some tried to climb on board my carriage, unaware of the differences in class. The attendant on guard waved them away in irritation, and obediently and blindly they surged off down the train looking for the hard-seat carriages.

The Chengdu-to-Urumchi train brought to mind the nineteenth-century steamers that crossed from Europe to the New World. Here were the steerage-class passengers headed for Xinjiang, China's New Frontier province, to look for work and living space away from the overcrowding and poverty of the south-west. Just like the complement of the westbound Atlantic steamboats, whose lower decks never caught sight of an American face nor sound of an American accent, not one among them bore the Turkic features of the indigenous minorities of China's Great North-west – the Uighurs, the Kirghiz, the Kazakhs or the Tajiks. Instead I was witnessing a mass migration of Han, a colonization by force of numbers. They would spend three nights and four days cramped in the rigid, upright seats of hard class or, if they could only afford the very cheapest 'no designated seat' tickets, sprawled on the spittle-smeared floor between the carriages, occasionally stealing a few minutes' questionable comfort when a seat was vacated by its owner as he went to the toilet or to stretch his legs at a station stop.

A well-dressed couple disentangled itself from the herd and strolled toward my carriage. Entering the four-berth compartment, they acknowledged my presence, loaded their luggage into the rack above the sliding door, produced a polythene bag of food and began to lay out delicacies on the window-ledge table – chickens' feet and wingtips, cold roast duck, sliced beef, *zhacai*, and red roast belly pork.

Out beyond the suburbs of Chengdu, the western edge of the Sichuan Basin was sticky with the moist heat of early summer. The rape had already flowered in its brief shout of bright yellow, ripened and dried. Now it was laid out on the loamy, mist-dampened fields in fan-shaped fistfuls of lifeless brown. The bamboo-and-wire scaffolds which during Qingming had preceded the families like regimental colours as they processed to their ancestral graves now poked at odd angles from the humpbacked mounds. Their colourful bunting infill and paper streamers had rotted away in the wet air and what remained hung in sad tatters. I stood for a while in the corridor as the train left the floor of the basin and climbed into the forested mountain valleys of northern Sichuan. Then the fourth passenger in my compartment, a man in a white shirt, beckoned me inside.

URUMCHI

'HEY, WAKE UP . . . *wake up!* What's your name?' I raised myself on to one elbow and tried to focus on the uniformed shape in the doorway.

'Lin Jie.'

'Okay, Lin Jie, check your belongings . . . Have you had anything stolen?' It seemed a stupid question. I had just put my head down for a few minutes' sleep after a lunchtime drink with the other passengers. It was still light. To keep the man happy, I felt under my T-shirt for my money pouch. It was still there. I couldn't understand what was going on.

'Open it.'

It was empty but for my passport. Then I noticed sickly yellow bruises on both my forearms.

'Lin Jie, what do you remember about yesterday?'

Yesterday?

The policeman assigned to the train had a podgy, kindly face, with dark eyes set back under a mane of hair that he pushed aside every few minutes. He sat opposite me, on the bunk where I dimly remembered chatting with my fellow passengers and sharing the couple's food and drink the day before. Was it really the day before? I had absolutely no recollection of anything beyond finishing the final round of toasting – the two men with *baijiu*, myself drinking the beer the woman had brought – and climbing on to my bunk for a rest.

'What had you been toasting?' It was the woman's birthday, that's why she'd brought a cake for us. Despite having been out for seventeen hours I was still half asleep, and each time I closed my eyes I was faced with a swirling pointillism of primary colours that formed themselves into taunting Chinese faces and images of myself lying motionless and staring on the bed. I stopped the trolley in the gangway as it passed and bought a bottle of water with some small change that hadn't been taken. I felt dehydrated, and I gulped it down without stopping for breath. Then, a few seconds later, I lurched like a drunk to the toilet where I threw it back up.

'The third man, where did he go?'

'We took him off the train at the last stop. He had things stolen too. The other two must have got off somewhere in the night. They left this.' He patted a plum-coloured suitcase beside him. 'It's empty apart from a couple of toothbrushes and a flannel. What did they look like?'

I tried my best to describe the couple, but my explanation in Mandarin sounded just like the stock description of any Han face: black hair of average length, a yellowish complexion, brown eyes. I remembered the man brushing aside my offers to pay for some of the food and drink, telling me it was *mingyun* – fate – that had put us in the same compartment.

Despite my struggling to keep them open my eyelids kept closing. The man's watery, bulging eyes and excited face came back to me. He twitched and stammered, babbling away in the same peasant drawl I had struggled to fathom the day before. He was laughing at me. Terrified that if I fell asleep I would not wake up, I forced them open again, though they felt as leaden as my limbs. The policeman slipped out of the half-open door and returned with a bottle of sweet green tea.

'You've been drugged. This will make you feel better. Sip it slowly.' He looked at me with a mixture of pity and annoyance. He could not help but feel sorry for a young Westerner who had been duped and robbed, but still his questions betrayed his incredulousness at just how much money they had stolen – US$3,000 was a substantial fortune to a transport policeman – and only half hid an irritation that I had chosen his train. He asked whether British policemen were ever tempted to accept bribes because they were poorly paid. I said on the whole not. He sighed. All this would mean the head of the regional transport police would want to interview me in person, he explained wearily. Lots of paperwork. If it had just been that Chinese man who had been – here he brought himself up quickly – who had been robbed, it might have been more easily dealt with. But when foreign guests were involved? A real headache. He shook his head jokingly to cheer me up. Despite feeling sick and scared I felt sorry for him. I was his responsibility, and he had not asked for it.

'Try to get some sleep, Lin Jie. The chief radioed to say he would be on the train by tomorrow morning. He'll want to ask a few questions, take a statement.' He pushed aside the quilt on the bunk where the third man had been and drew the curtains for me. 'I'll get the attendant to lock the door from the outside so you feel safer.'

I was safe from another theft, though I had little left to steal, but when I lay back on the bed and gave up trying to stay awake, I could not escape the cascades of sparks and flashes of light that coalesced into leering, dancing demons. I snapped my eyes open, but this waking nightmare lay in wait each time I succumbed to the desperate need to sleep. I spent the rest of the day in this unforgiving semi-consciousness, now staring at the formica base of the bunk above me, now trying to will myself into a deep and demonless sleep. When night eventually fell, I gave up the struggle and dreamt of dead bodies laid out on mortuary slabs and of hideous mocking faces.

A chalkdust smudge against the graphite of the Dragon's Head Mountains to the north-east heralded dawn. I drew the curtains back. It hurt to move. It had been over forty hours since I had sat watching the steerage passengers on the platform at Chengdu station. While the rest of the passengers had slept for the second night, and while I had tossed and sweated alone in the stifling compartment, the train had traced the invisible line of the tracks into the Gansu Corridor.

The Gansu Corridor defines itself best by what it is not. It is not the crumpled, parallel ranges of the Qilian Mountains that skirt its southern edge, the farthest echoes of the ancient clash of continents that created the Himalayas and the Tibetan Plateau. Nor is it the waterless wastes of the Tengger or the towering megadunes of Inner Mongolia's Baidan Jaran Desert that press down from the Gobi to the north, threatening to suffocate it. At the corridor's narrowest point, barely seventy miles separate the freezing Tibetan Plateau from the unforgiving desert sands. That morning the weak light of the rising sun cast olive shadows that raced down from the Dragon's Head Mountains to envelop the railway, and its tentative first rays grazed the foothills of the distant Qilian Mountains beyond. The icy whispers of light in the sky were answered in the landscape by the pale glow of hoarfrost that streaked the stony floor of the corridor. Then the hoarfrost melted to reveal a speckled landscape of greens and dull browns, an introvert palette of buff sand, dust and dappled pebbles extending away on both sides and rising through green velvet slopes to the mountains' saw-edged profiles.

Our caravan of wagons rumbled along the old Silk Road and the day wore on. Subtle differences in shade that had been striking close after dawn were burned away under the glare of the sun at noon, were caressed into revealing themselves again by dusk's long fingers, and then finally vanished beneath the russet shadows from the west. The semi-desert was never more textured than when sunset spotlit every pebble and blade of scrub grass and cast for each its own tapering shadow.

The section chief boarded the train to see me in the heat of midday. He looked like somebody's grandfather. On behalf of the People's Railways he apologized to me. It was a terrible occurrence. He had never come across anything like it on any of the trains under his jurisdiction. He would get to the bottom of the case, but he needed me to give as much detail as possible so that they could arrest the culprits. I knew the couple might have got off the train anywhere within a 500-mile stretch of the remote mountains on the borders of Sichuan, Shaanxi and Gansu, but I thanked him for his kind words anyway.

Sitting at the foot of one of the bunks he took off his nylon jacket, let out a long sigh as though painfully aware of how much work my lack of caution was going to demand of him, squared up the pad of paper before him, uncapped a fountain pen, and turned his tired-looking, care-lined eyes on me.

'You speak Chinese. Can you understand what I'm saying to you?' I did. He turned to the constable. 'That'll save us waiting until Urumchi for an interpreter.' He turned back. 'Tell me what happened, in your own words.'

For three hours the conversation went back and forth, I stating what I could recall of the events of two days before, the chief holding a hand up to interrupt me while he wrote or to interpose questions to clarify my meaning, and occasionally bringing the constable into the conversation to check my account against what he knew of timings, station stops and so on. It became clear that the last recollection I had of that day could not be given any precise time. I could not even recall with any certainty whether or not it had been daytime when I put my head down for a short rest. The chief complained under his breath that this was all a waste of time. He pressed me for the most insignificant of details – what brand of beer had she bought, how had she opened the bottles, what subjects had we talked about? – requiring me to recount time and again what I remembered. His thoroughness surprised me, but I knew that little of what I told him was of any practical use. Finally, I was invited to read through my statement, four sheets of closely written characters, to ensure I agreed with his interpretation of what I had said. I was too tired to correct the few minor mis-understandings, so I told him it was correct and was asked to write, in strokes that looked painfully childish and unlearned beside his elegant, cursive hand, the words 'I have read the above and agree it is an accurate account of my statement'. Satisfied, he produced a wad of cotton soaked in blue ink, the kind that comes with children's printing-sets, and indicated where I was to dab my forefinger.

'Here, on the date and place of the interview . . . here, on your name . . . here, where I have changed a word . . . here, where I have written the sum stolen . . . here, on the number of the page . . . again, here, on the number of the following page . . . here, where the final number of pages is confirmed . . . here, on your affirmation. I think that's all. Be more careful in future, won't you.'

The white sheets, as thin and crisp as cigarette papers, were now stippled with blue whorls and deltas. He folded them into his shirt pocket, put his jacket back on, shook my hand and left. The constable left with him but soon returned, sat down and closed the door. One of the chief's questions, which at the time had seemed nothing more than a passing thought, had unsettled me.

'What did the chief mean when he asked whether from where I was lying I could have seen them kill the other man, the one in the white shirt?'

'What he said was, "*if* they had tried to kill him while he was on the berth below you, would it have been possible for you to see what had happened?"'

The attendant assigned to the carriage, a kindly woman genuinely upset by how listless I had become, looked in on me that afternoon with a cardboard tray of rice and another of fatty belly pork, braised soybeans and fried cabbage. I managed a mouthful. She sat down opposite me and pushed the door to.

'I shouldn't really say this, but we all know it's true. Society has become very chaotic lately, there are more and more people like that around. Things get stolen, thieves take other people's bags off during the night, but I've never come across this before. *Kepa!* Frightful! Once the doors to the compartments are locked at night we don't know *what's* happening inside.' I shivered. Soft sleeper on the People's Railways had always seemed a sort of cocoon, a safe bolthole where, if you were willing to spend the money, you were made immune from the prying, the endless questions, the irritating curiosity of the lower end of Chinese society. Now my compartment, with its white lace trim and velvet edging, felt like a walk-in coffin, and I longed for the communal watchfulness of the packed hard-sleeper carriages.

The gangway that ran along one side of the soft-sleeper carriage, and on to which the doors to each compartment opened, had been empty ever since the robbery had come to light. I could not decide whether the constable had asked the other travellers to allow me some peace, or whether they had voluntarily shunned somebody they thought to be associated with a death. The officially atheistic Chinese remain surprisingly superstitious on that score. I had no evidence that the fourth man had indeed been found dead, just a feeling of unease, but I was too scared to press the constable for the truth. Instead my fevered imagination read into others' actions and words an assumption that he had been carried dead from the train before I was woken, and that I alone amongst the passengers was not meant to know this. I had overheard one woman say: 'There was blood every-where.' It was only days later in Urumchi, as I looked up at the white crest of Mount Bogda, that it struck me I had misheard the word *xǔe*, snow, for *xùe*, blood.

And so I spent a further night lying on my back, wide awake despite the throbbing pain behind my eyes. We were pressing deeper into the western desert, and a crack in the window seal that had worked itself loose with the motion of the train let in an acrid mix of ash from the engine and sandy grit churned up from the trackside.

I had neither washed nor slept, nor eaten more than a mouth-ful, since boarding the train three days previously, surviving on boiled water and the occasional sip of cold tea which I had bought with the few *kuai* that had by chance been in my pocket. So when the constable tapped on my door to be let in and asked what my plans were when we reached Urumchi in the late morning, I begged him to arrange for a police car to drive me to the biggest Western hotel in town, the Holiday Inn. I knew I simply could not heave my rucksack that far without help.

Urumchi is as far from the ocean as it is possible to get. To reach the nearest coast, you must travel due south for 1,550 miles before you arrive on the Bay of Bengal, and in doing so, you must cross the Tian Shan range, the eastern edge of the deadly Taklamakan Desert, the entirety of the Tibetan Plateau and finally the Himalayas at one of their highest points. After this it is an easy 400 miles, downhill all the way. Alternatively, you can choose to head north-by-north-west, crossing the Gurbantunggut Desert and then the Altai Mountains before trekking 800 miles across the uninhabited steppe, tundra and permafrost of the Western Siberian Plain, finally reaching the Gulf of Ob on the Arctic Circle, but this would needlessly add 110 miles to your journey, and the beach is reportedly no better. Even the Chinese regard Urumchi as remote. It is as close to Moscow as it is to the tip of Taiwan.

The city is the capital of the Xinjiang Uighur Autonomous Region. Its name means fine pasture but it sits on the stony slopes of the great Tian Shan, the Celestial Mountains which cut Xinjiang in two, commanding a low pass in the range that links Xinjiang's northerly Dzungarian Basin to its southerly Tarim Basin. Beneath the snow-capped peak of Mount Bogda, the city's suburbs sprawl in an ugly crust of slum dwellings and filthy apartment blocks. Even so, after the horrors of the journey, I was overjoyed to be there. I wanted to hug the manageress of the Holiday Inn just because her bellboys were dressed so smartly, and I choked back hot tears while my credit card, hidden in my luggage in case of emergencies, was swiped and transformed into a shiny, magnetic key to a room where I could watch Hollywood blockbusters, order room service, and shower.

As I explored the streets of Urumchi over the next few days, I began to feel increasingly irritated by the Han Chinese. In eastern China I had been prepared to grin and bear their calls and stares, born I knew of genuine though impolite curiosity. There they were on home ground. Here in Chinese Turkestan they all seemed outsiders, more alien to the landscape than I was. Their inane hallos and gawkish staring infuriated me, and more than once I wanted to lash out. Perhaps my experience on the train had soured me, but now I felt they were all sizing me up to rob me, if not by stealth then with their petulant overcharging. The economic opportunism that had brought them all here, and their idiotic belief in the patriotic slogans on the opening up of the Great North-west, I found almost unbearable.

By contrast, I was enchanted with the Middle Eastern features of the Uighurs, with the sounds of their Turkic language and the way in which they greeted each other with a boisterous *assah-lahmu alaykum*. Relieved to lay aside the tonal singsong of Mandarin, I *salaam*ed old Uighur men in restaurants and on the street, and used the Turkic greeting of *yakshimusis* when I bought yoghurt from stalls in the old town or a slice of *matang*, the local fruit-encrusted nougat loaf, carved from a slab by the roadside.

Day by day I managed ever-larger portions of *laghman* – noodles accompanied by a bowl of spiced lamb and green bean stew – or *suoman*, the Uighurs' pasta squares that come with a garlicky mutton and tomato sauce that reminded me of Italy. I drank endless glasses of black tea at open-air markets, where it was freely offered with none of the mercenary penny-pinching of eastern China, and devoured skewer after skewer of mutton kebabs whose meat alternated with bubbling hunks of pearly fat. For the first time in weeks I ate bread that had been baked in an oven rather than steamed: the *nan* came in hot, flat rounds, pricked in swirling patterns to help them bake, and strewn with onion seeds, sesame or caraway. I found a shop where the bearded proprietor would respond to my attempts at greeting him with an amused *wa'alaykum assahlahmu* and then sell me meat and potato *samsas* that looked like palm-sized Cornish pasties. My mind raced less, the adrenalin of the train subsided, I could walk for more than a few minutes at a time without needing to sit down, and I began to sleep for a few hours each night.

The constable arrived at the Holiday Inn one afternoon with two colleagues from the Public Security Bureau. They apologized for my mistreatment at the hands of two of their country-men and then interviewed me again for several hours, but I could tell them nothing more and I did not recognize the pencil sketches of a wanted couple that the constable produced. They left with another wad of paper covered in my fingerprints, and asked me to call them if I wanted an update on the search, or if I changed my address. They would need me to make an identification if they arrested the pair.

As they left my room, turning to apologize once more and to wish me a pleasant stay in Urumchi, I held the constable back by the arm. He closed the door. There was one more thing.

'What is it?'

'The third man. You said he was taken off the train before I was woken.'

'We took him in for questioning at the local police station once he reported there'd been a robbery. Why? What else do you know?' I was still too afraid to ask outright whether he had really been taken off the train alive.

'I . . . nothing, honestly . . . I just wondered.' Sometimes ignorance is bliss.

Out of curiosity I called the number I had been given, but there was no reply. It was May Day week and they were in all likelihood on holiday. It was time to put the episode behind me. If they arrested them red-handed with my travellers' cheques then all well and good, let them face their punishment. But I did not want the responsibility of identifying them in a police cell, knowing that I would be signing their death warrants. One morning, I slipped away from the hotel and took a hard-sleeper berth on the overnight train to Kashgar.

XINJIANG

FOR THE FIRST hundred miles, the train headed east, retracing the route I had travelled a few days earlier under the brow of the Bogda range, but at the rail junction of Daheyan, Great Riverbank, on the brim of the searing Turpan Basin, we switched tracks on to the Kashgar line. To the south-east, across thirty-five miles of gently sloping moonscape, lay the oasis of Turpan, the lowest point of China and, after the Dead Sea, the lowest on earth. At the salt-encrusted shore of Lake Aydingkol the basin dips to over 500 feet below sea level. There, during the long, rainless summer, the temperature climbs to nearly 50 °C in the shade, only there is no shade.

The view from the carriage was awe-inspiring. On one side,

the khaki buttresses of the final folds of the Celestial Mountains stretched away in both directions and receded overhead to powdery peaks; on the other, the ground gradually fell away to a distant, invisible horizon. The view was so enormous, so featureless, so silent that I felt I could almost hear the earth's low rumbling as it revolved.

I felt more at ease surrounded by Turkic faces. More than half the passengers were Uighurs and there was a sprinkling of Kirghiz men too, bound perhaps for my final destination, the Kirghiz town of Ulugchat, and instantly recognizable in their high-crowned, white felt hats with upturned black brims. I asked the man beside me to teach me the Uighur words for one to ten, and pronounced them until he stopped looking pained.

'*Bir, iker, uch, töt, pash* (I could never remember six or seven), *sakkuz, tokkiz, on.*' In four, *töt*, I imagined I could hear a vague echo of Russia's *chetirye*. Five, *pash*, fascinated me. It reminded me of the Russian *pyat'* and the Sanskrit *pañca*. We were in a region that bordered both Russia and India, I reasoned to myself. The other connection that sprang to mind, between *pash* and the Welsh *pump*, seemed fanciful. Then again, I had read about perfectly preserved mummies, 2,000 years old, excavated in the Taklamakan Desert, whose hair was ginger and who had been buried in woollen clothes with tartan designs. They had Indo-European features. People had argued that here were the speakers of Tocharian, a now-extinct language that had been discovered on manuscripts in the abandoned cities of the Turpan Basin and which bore similarities to both the Latin and the Celtic tongues. A Tocharian counting from one to ten might have been half understood by a modern inhabitant of rural Cork.

The Chinese authorities had reportedly reacted to the discoveries by storing them away in museum basements for fear that evidence of early non-Han settlement of what was now Xinjiang might give ammunition to Uighur separatists demanding the establishment of an independent East Turkestan. Their fear stemmed from the widespread Uighur assumption that they were the aboriginal inhabitants of Xinjiang, and that therefore any archaeological remains must be those of their ancestors. It was also intimately linked to the view amongst certain Uighurs, not to mention the Chinese, that Uighur identity is inseparable from Islam. Although it makes no difference to how the average Uighur sees his link to the land or his religion, or to how the Party will continue to bury or misinterpret evidence that undermines China's claim to the region, the truth on both counts is more complicated.

The Uighurs first entered Chinese history as the most powerful in an eighth-century confederation of nomadic tribes in what is now northern Mongolia. In the middle of that century they toppled the Turkish khanate that held sway there and created a new power base, its focus in central Mongolia but extending as far as Lake Baikal, the Altai Mountains and the oases of northern Xinjiang. Here their territory straddled the Silk Road, the great overland route to and from the world's most advanced nation during the height of that most outward-looking dynasty, the Tang. The Uighurs took advantage of their position astride the trade route, and barely a decade after the establishment of the Uighur nation in Mongolia they were heavily embroiled in Chinese affairs, coming to the aid of the beleaguered Tang during the prolonged rebellion of General An Lushan that came perilously close to toppling the dynasty in the mid-eighth century. Only with the help of the mercenary Uighur cavalry – always willing to defect to whoever would reward them most richly – did the Tang regain their lost capitals, Chang'an and Luoyang, and control over China.

Exposure to the sedentary agricultural and commercial life of China affected the Uighurs deeply. Especially around the Turpan oasis they formed settled, sinicized trading communities. Knowledge of the new religions that had travelled eastward along the caravanserais of the Silk Road transformed the shamanistic Uighurs. In AD 762, under the influence of Sogdian missionaries at the Tang court, they adopted the eclectic dualism of Manichaeism as their state religion.

An invasion in the mid-ninth century by the fearsome, nomadic Kirghiz from the north broke the power of the Uighurs' Mongolian capital. They fled along the Silk Road, some ending up in the oases of Kashgaria and Central Asia but most settling in the towns of the Turpan oasis where they re-established their capital at a place named Khocho. The Uighur city-state of Khocho flourished under the Tang and successive dynasties, and by the time the Mongols' Yuan dynasty took over the reins of power there in the late thirteenth century, Uighur culture had become a rich mixture of Persian Manichaeism, Nestorian Christianity and Buddhism.

Knowledge was highly esteemed, the result of the Arabic learning which followed Islam into Kashgaria. Uighur society's ruling class was highly educated in the fine arts, in astrology and in the Arabic sciences. The Uighurs' Turpan oasis city-state like-wise gradually turned toward the Islamic beliefs of the powerful Moguls, who in subsequent centuries were to conquer India, and in the mid-fifteenth century it too finally converted to Islam, putting behind it a long history of religious pluralism. The term Uighur remained to describe that portion of society that did not convert to Islam, and it was with the end of the practice of other religions some two centuries later, and the universal adoption of Islam amongst the oasis dwellers of Xinjiang, that the term dis-appeared.

When the Communist Party began its program of defining and categorizing China's ethnic groups in the fifties, 'Uighur' was resurrected to refer for the first time to the Turkic Muslims of Xinjiang. Although not historically accurate, the definition was accepted by both the Uighurs themselves and their Han rulers.

*

Metal, residing in the west, governs the processes of death dealing, and the volatile trinity of ethnicity, land and religion has indeed proved in recent decades to be a source of violent conflict in Xinjiang. The *Selected Works of Chairman Mao* – his little red book – contains a shrewd observation: 'We say China is a nation whose territory is vast, whose resources are rich and whose population is large. In fact, it is the Han nationality whose population is large and the minority nationalities whose territory is vast and rich in resources.'

The People's Republic desperately needs the territory and resources of Xinjiang. Its coal deposits have been mined for decades. It is a source of gold, nickel, lead, copper and manganese, and rare metals for industry: beryllium, gallium, lithium, niobium and tantalum. Beneath the shifting, baking sands of the Tarim Basin huge reserves of fossil fuels have been found, and a highway has been driven across the centre of the Taklamakan not for the convenience of the Uighurs in the southern oases of Hotan, Keriya and Niya, but for the exploitation of the desert's oil and gas. Besides, Xinjiang is China's Bikini Atoll, its highly prized backyard Mururoa. Since the sixties, China's nuclear tests have been conducted in the remote saline desert of Lop Nur in eastern Xinjiang, where the only people who might be affected are impoverished, powerless minorities.

Strategically, Xinjiang borders some of the world's most politically sensitive regions: Kashmir, Afghanistan, Pakistan, Russia; the former Soviet republics of Kirghizstan, Tajikistan and Kazakhstan; and the Autonomous Region of Tibet. India still disputes China's occupation of 12,000 square miles of the barren Aksai Chin Plateau in the Himalayas. Secessionists, who see China as a foreign presence in what they regard not as China's New Frontier but as their own East Turkestan, are agitating for change against this impossible background of national necessity and geopolitics.

The recent history of separatism in Xinjiang is closely linked to events in other parts of Central Asia. The creation by the Soviet Union of autonomous republics in the Central Asian steppe forged unifying, nationalist identities for the local nomadic communities which had previously been bound only by tribal loyalties. Under first Brezhnev and then Gorbachev, local leaders gained political power, and when the Soviet Union split apart in 1991 the Central Asian republics declared independence under native, rather than Russian-led, governments.

The subsequent rise of fundamentalist Muslim groups in the former Soviet sphere beyond the Tian Shan put an end to the experiments in religious liberalism that had been going on in Xinjiang since the end of the Cultural Revolution and the start of the reforms. (The Cultural Revolution had been particularly destructive in Xinjiang. At its height in the late sixties, pitched battles had been fought between factions of Red Guards and Uighurs.) While the eighties saw a revival of Islamic practice, with the founding of religious schools, the renovation of old mosques and the building of new, and the opening of borders for *hajj*, by the late nineties policies had changed. Chinese fears that the Muslim republics on its borders were seedbeds for anti-Chinese rioting led to an agreement in 1996 with Kazakhstan, Kirghizstan, Tajikistan and Russia on the suppression of funda-mentalist groups within their own borders to their mutual benefit.

Nevertheless, anti-government protests and violence con-tinued and increased. In 1997, bombs exploded on buses in Beijing and Urumchi. The government retaliated with a number of executions of suspected terrorists, but the unrest continued. Self-styled Uighur *mujahideen* were known to have been trained by, and to have fought alongside, the Taleban in Afghanistan. Posters on walls all over Urumchi detailed the latest prohibitions on the possession of guns, grenades, explosives and even mortars, in a chilling indication of what must have been happening but which was never reported in the press. Just as Churchill's wartime

Ministry of Information attributed Hitler's V2 rocket attacks to exploding gas mains to avoid sowing panic, so there had been an unexpectedly large number of badly stored propane cylinders igniting in Xinjiang.

The threat of secession by such a strategically important region has added new force to the government's policy of sinification. When Xinjiang was liberated by the PLA in 1949, its Han population was barely 200,000 strong. Now it numbers around 7,000,000. Hardly any of the new settlers ever bother, or indeed need, to learn a single word of Uighur, nor do they mix with the indigenous inhabitants. Already the Uighurs may be in a minority in their own land.

The carriage baked that night. On the topmost of the three tiers of bunks – the only option if I was to leave on the day I bought my ticket – there was not the faintest hint of a breeze. The windows were locked shut to stop the sands of the desert from creeping in, but even so a fine grit settled evenly over sleeping bodies, over crumpled, sweat-moistened sheets, over window ledges and floors. It matted my hair and adhered to my face, and when I awoke I found it in my nostrils and between my gritted teeth. I climbed down from my bunk in the darkness to get some water and pulled back the corner of the curtain. Thin streaks of yellow flame were visible far away in the Taklamakan: tiny razor-blade slashes in a borderless black cloth, gas flares on oil derricks.

Miniature dunes the same colour as the desert outside formed and mutated in the wind-lapped spaces between the carriages. Come daylight I stood there and looked out over the featureless heat haze of the Taklamakan. Flares were still visible, some so distant they were no more than an occasional white shimmer in the hot air, others close enough for me to make out the dark lat-ticework of the needle stacks supporting them.

An elderly Uighur in a heavy woollen cardigan joined me amongst the dunes.

'*Wa'alaykum assahlahmu*. Good morning. Do you speak English?' He had mischievous eyes and bushy eyebrows, and wore an expression of amused curiosity.

I replied that I did and asked how he came to speak it.

'I teach it at a university in Urumchi. Would you care to take breakfast with me?' I was determined that my experience of Chinese hospitality on a train was not going to spoil my acceptance of Uighur hospitality and accepted, albeit with a certain nervousness. Breakfast was mutton and *nan*. The mutton he took from a plastic bag, still attached to the hefty knuckle on which it had been boiled, and sliced off several fat, stringy chunks. We were seated at the window-ledge table, while opposite on the two bottom bunks sat what looked like an extended family: one old man wearing a *doppa* embroidered with grape leaves; one matriarch stifled in layer upon layer of leggings, stockings, underskirts, overskirts, aprons, blouses and waistcoats and topped by a flowered headscarf; a younger man in an unwashed two-piece suit, his hair closely cropped; and a small girl wearing what had once been a bright white, sequined dress and white stockings but which were now worn and tinged with grey. Her fair hair stuck out adorably on either side from glittery, plastic hairgrips. The old man was speaking. The others listened intently, interrupting him from time to time to make him repeat what he had just said.

'This gentleman is telling a story. It's about a man called Afanti. We are very fond of these stories, they allow us to imagine we are Afanti, who always gets the better of his rulers. Would you like me to translate?'

We started some way behind the old man, but with good-natured heckling from his family we soon caught up and my interpreter worked alongside the storyteller.

'One day during one of Xinjiang's bitter winters, the heralds announced: "Hear ye! The king has made a pronouncement! He will give the hand of his daughter and half of his kingdom to anybody who will stay out naked on the city walls of Khocho all night!" You should visit the ruins of Khocho,' my interpreter added as an aside.

'Afanti heard this and thought there would be no harm in getting the better of the king, who was forever cheating his subjects, and so he went to the palace and announced that he was willing to accept the challenge. The king was astonished, but he ordered his attendants to strip Afanti and take him on to the walls. Before he was led away, Afanti asked the king to have a huge boulder placed on the wall beside him. "You fool," said the king. "You're bound to freeze to death! What would you want with a boulder?"

'"If there is no boulder then the deal is off!" said Afanti. The king had the boulder hauled on to the wall and the ladder taken away. He was sure Afanti would die of cold.

'It was very cold that night, but instead of lying still, Afanti heaved the boulder to and fro on the ramparts, and so he passed the night keeping warm from his exertions. At dawn, the king and his advisers were awoken by a voice. "Phew! It's so hot up here! Get me down!" The ladder was raised, and Afanti climbed down panting.

'"Most honoured majesty," he said, "I have spent the night naked on the wall of Khocho as you asked. I now require your daughter's hand and half your kingdom!" The king had no intention of fulfilling his promise. How was he to know some fool would try his luck and survive? He thought and thought, and then he asked whether Afanti had seen the full moon the night before.

'"Of course!" Afanti replied.

'"Aha! So that's how you did it! Keeping warm by the rays of the moon! I'll teach you to cheat me!" Afanti was thrown out of the palace and went to live in the desert, near the mouth of a *karez*, an underground irrigation channel.

'One very hot summer, the king was out hunting with his

ministers. They rode back and forth looking for water until Afanti's hovel was spotted. "Hey! Head of the household! Bring the king water!" they shouted. "He's dying of thirst!"

'Afanti came out. "The king's wish is my command!" he answered, and he went over to the *karez*, whereupon he cut the rope and buried the bucket in the sand. Soon the king became impatient and sent a servant to fetch him. The servant returned and said to him: "Sire, he says that if the king wants water then let the fool fetch it himself!"

'The king was furious. "The wretch!" he shouted, and he took his men into the hovel. "Where is my water?" he cried. Afanti casually pointed to the *karez*.

'"Wise majesty, look into the *karez*!" The king did so and roared. "Imbecile! How can I quench my thirst by just looking at the water?" Afanti smiled. "Majesty, the rays of the moon were enough to keep me warm for a whole night on the city walls. Surely the glistening of the water is enough to quench the royal thirst?"'

When he had finished his tale, the old man sat back and smiled. The punch line must have been apparent for some time – this could scarcely have been the first occasion on which the old man had been asked to tell the fable – but the family seemed to delight in the familiar. The mother exhaled a satisfied breath and tidied her skirts, and the young man slapped his hands purposefully on his knees. The little girl stood staring like a besotted puppy into her grandfather's wrinkled, smiling face.

'Is that story about the Uighurs and the Chinese?' I asked.

'We identify with him as the underdog. He does our rebelling for us.' I thought of the migrant Sichuanese on the platform in Chengdu. 'What do you think is the future for the Uighurs?'

His answer was swift and emphatic. 'There is no hope for us Uighurs. Unfortunately we are a small population of poor farmers who are unlucky enough to inhabit a strategic region with some powerful neighbours. If it had not been the Chinese it would have been the Russians or perhaps British India. No, most likely the Russians. They were here during the Anti-Japanese War.

'The Party needs to control Xinjiang. Already there are as many Han as Uighur here, and from this year there will be no more Uighur-language schools. All children must either learn to speak Mandarin or remain uneducated.

'If a Uighur wants a good job he must speak Mandarin, but for us it is a very foreign language from a completely different language group. English is much easier for our tongues to pronounce. Yet if we master Mandarin then we have accepted that the Han future for Xinjiang is the right one. The Bingtuan gives all the best land to the Han migrants. They have constant irrigation. They take all the best jobs. No, there is no hope. Here, take some more *nan*.'

Few people outside China have heard of the Bingtuan, or Production and Construction Corps. Its role in controlling Xinjiang is not as newsworthy as the PLA's role in Tibet, and the Muslim Uighurs are not as popular a cause as smiling Tibetan Buddhist monks.

The Bingtuan is not a new concept in Xinjiang: the Chinese have used military labour to colonize and farm the region since the Han dynasty over 2,000 years ago. Even under the Qing, paramilitary agricultural colonies provided cheap muscle in the form of prisoners and soldiers. Nor has the Bingtuan been unique to Xinjiang: it was founded after Liberation in other provinces and autonomous regions as well – Heilongjiang, Inner Mongolia, Tibet and Hainan – its purpose to open up and industrialize China's more remote regions. Gistlaine's father had arrived on Hainan as one of its employees.

In the late seventies, the Bingtuan was disbanded everywhere except in Xinjiang, where it remained as an autonomous body organized along military lines. Through it the Party continued to open up and industrialize the region and to settle it with Han Chinese.

Along with the PLA, the Bingtuan is the basis of Han power in Xinjiang. One-sixth of the population is either an employee or a family dependant of someone who works for it. It provides an on-the-spot supply of armed militia when the locals start to riot, and as a business it effectively controls Xinjiang's economy. It continues to fulfil its original functions of controlling the frontier and establishing agricultural production and construction, but it also controls the province's infrastructure – canals, irrigation, power, communications, schools, railways, mineral extraction, hotels, foodstuffs, even airlines. In Urumchi I had seen hoardings along all the main roads advertising the products and services of its myriad corporate identities. There seemed no aspect of life in Xinjiang into which the Bingtuan did not intrude.

'Can Uighurs join the Bingtuan?' I asked in all seriousness. He looked at me as though I was a raving lunatic, then laughed out loud.

'Ha, haah! No, no, not possible! As I said, if you are a Uighur you must either accept a Chinese future for Xinjiang or remain sidelined. There is no political route you can take to represent interests that do not accord with the Party's views. You cannot even broach the subject or you are labelled a splittist. The only option for change is to support secession, but here there is no . . . possibility . . . of . . . success.' His hand slapped his knee to emphasize each word. 'Most Uighurs do not see themselves as part of a wider, Islamic struggle, so there is no groundswell of support. We are few, but the PLA has millions of armed men.'

'Do you think it would be a good thing if the Chinese left Xinjiang?' I asked.

He shook his head slowly. 'No. Imagine what would happen if China pulled out of Xinjiang because of terrorist attacks on its people. All our neighbours would want part of our land. India and Pakistan would pour across the mountains to seize the Taklamakan oilfields, Russia would take the oilfields in the north and the Kazakhs would fight them there, and the Kirghiz and the Tajiks would cross to Kashgar and Aksu. Even the poor Afghans might try to steal part of Xinjiang. We'd be no better off. Our only chance is to beg for more autonomy and hope that the Party listens. Take more meat.'

Though I disagreed with his apocalyptic view of Xinjiang's disintegration (the Karakoram, the Pamirs and the Tian Shan are forbidding ranges, enough to deter military incursions by all but the Kazakhs, the Russians and the Mongols who share its gentler northern border), yet he was right that the Party could never allow the region to secede. Russia – which in the nineteenth century had wrestled with Britain and China for control of this uncharted waste where their empires faded into one another – would hardly relish the destabilizing effect of an independent East Turkestan today, for then the states on her southern borders might dissolve into conflict over spheres of influence. India and Pakistan, both nuclear powers, might try to outflank each other over Kashmir, and America might feel compelled to flex its muscles to protect the region's oil. Besides, the loss of Xinjiang might be enough to trigger a collapse of China's economy and the end of the Communist Party.

So it seemed nobody would want an independent Islamic nation in East Turkestan, just as in the 1930s nobody had wanted one. Back then, like a brief snow flurry in the freezing winter of 1933–4, there had existed in southwestern Xinjiang a theocratic Muslim state. A reaction to both the succession of brutal Chinese republican governors of Xinjiang since 1911 and to the inroads made by atheistic communism in Central Asia, it called itself the Turkish-Islamic Republic of East Turkestan – TIRET – and it took Kashgar as its capital. For three months its assembly printed its own money, flew its own flag – a white crescent and star on a blue background – and looked about it for support. None came. The Russians were afraid that East Turkestan's rabid anti-communism would spread to their Soviet Socialist Republics in Central Asia; a weak, Kuomintang-led China saw it as a secessionist regime; and Britain, with her dominions in the Far East threatened by the advance of the Japanese, chose to bolster Nationalist China. On 14 February 1934, a Tungan general from the buffer province of Gansu led his forces in their own bloody homage to the St Valentine's Day Massacre and mercilessly put down the insurrection.

It is one of those strange ironies that, while the territory of the anti-communist TIRET was destined to become communist under the Chinese, if it had instead fallen to the Soviets it would by now probably be one of the Commonwealth of Independent States, having first served its time under Moscow as a Soviet Socialist Republic.

After we had finished breakfast, my teacher taught me phrases that he and the Uighur family had decided I might need in Kashgar: 'I am single' and 'Do you have a daughter?' We did not return to the subject of Xinjiang and secession, although I caught sight of him during the late morning staring at the floor of the carriage, silently shaking his head.

Outside, the desert varied its mood as the day wore on. It was by turns a calm, sandy beach; an angry procession of flood-scarred channels; and a patient bulwark between the anxious press of wind-carved hills to one side and the temptation of limitless space to the other. Oasis towns came into view as a sudden wall of dusty green, quenched themselves in a strip of meltwater from distant glaciers in the invisible Tian Shan, and then sank back into the grit. Gangs of Chinese labourers shovelled rocks from one pile to another. Guard towers and walls betrayed the positions of isolated mineral works and gulags.

After twenty-six hours of wasteland Kashgar was a delight. It had as many shades of green as the desert had had greys and browns. They shone in its groves of almond trees and on the leaves of its pomegranates, apricots and walnuts. The breeze tousled the wheat fields like fingers caressing soft velvet instead of wasting its effort on the unyielding faces of rock and stone. It rippled through the soaring leaves of white-trunked poplars and teased the foaming surface of the irrigation ditches. Adobe walls marked the edges of orchards or huddled in squares to form houses, their straight lines somehow inapt; almost alien so soon after the eroded anarchy of the desert's contours.

Kashgar

As THE QING dynasty drew to a close, Francis Younghusband, an army officer who had spent time in Kashgar in the service of British India, wrote of the city:

> the great gongs of the Chinese guardhouses beat the hours through the night, and at 9 a.m. a gun was fired and trumpets blown. The Chinese are always good at style even if they are no good at substance, but a great deal may be achieved by style alone. The noisy parade of watchfulness makes no small impression on the locals. The deep booming of gongs, the blaring of trumpets, the noise of the cannons are a reminder to the inhabitants of Turkestan that the Chinese are in charge and on watch.

There was no more booming of gongs to mark the day's passage, no more trumpets and cannons. The city walls, whose great gates were opened and closed to time signals from the guardhouses, had been hacked down by the PLA in 1950. They stood now in forlorn, isolated mounds, their parapets weathered into defenceless submission and their thick masses of mudbrick rent by deep scars.

One section of the walls ran alongside Seman Road, the route from my hotel into the centre of town. It had been barricaded from the tree-lined road by shabby restaurants, truck repair workshops, apartment blocks, compact general stores with their rank-and-file display cases of cigarette packs, the usual litany. Ugly, gaping voids had been excavated in its blank face by the local residents, for storage perhaps, but like graffiti on an irretrievably derelict building it did not seem to matter any more.

The day following my arrival in Kashgar I walked through the old town's tangle of streets in order to get my bearings. Each street smelt of the trade to which it was devoted: of coal dust in a street lined by the roaring furnaces and hammer-polished iron anvils of smithies; of sweet resin in an alley filled with the burr of spinning lathes and piled high with newly carved chairs, bowls and ladles. A white pall hung over Gypsum Street, where every stall and shop offered identical sacks of finely ground plaster. And over every scene, the barefoot children throwing stones, the beaten steel crescents of the wayside mosques, over the sacks of ground cumin, turmeric, coriander and plump chillies, and over the fat vendors of papery sunflower seeds, hung the background smell of Kashgar, a perfumed mix of warm dust, curling woodsmoke from *nan* shops, the charred mutton of the kebab vendors, the local aromatic tobacco and the omnipresent tang of freshly cut kidney.

Another section of wall survived on People's Road East, near where the old town edged its way down to the banks of the Tumen River. The sheer, compacted facing, on whose impregnability the ruling mullahs of the TIRET had mistakenly relied, had been undermined by decades of wind and rain. I kicked at it and unintentionally dislodged an avalanche of talcum-fine dust. It smelt like a urinal. People or animals had defecated under its precarious overhang. Already made hopelessly anachronistic by the removal of the wall adjoining it, its impotent bulk had suffered the added indignity of having a rusty Ferris wheel erected on top of its wide, defensive platform.

Joining the short queue of Chinese sightseers, I handed over my 10 *renminbi* and was bolted into a creaking gondola. The spindle scraped and pinked in its sheath as the wheel turned and the gondola ascended. At the point where we had both groaned our way past the height at which death, in the event of a spectacular failure of the fatigued metal, would be sure and swift, I stopped worrying and peered down through the dusty, palm-printed glass on to the old town.

That morning a warm, close mist had risen from the dust to shroud Kashgar. The sun hovered cold and pallid behind it in the south. The moist veil it had raised now dissipated its light, and the mud-brick houses of the old town lost the defining interplay of brightness and shade and formed a flat, pastel composition of diamonds and polygons. They abutted one another, their angles hinting at the existence of alleys and rat-runs unseen beneath them. Tattered cloth awnings drooped breathlessly over street stalls. Carved wooden shutters clung to the walls. On the single main street within sight, grander buildings with intricate, painted balconies in greens and blues broke the monotonous geometry of browns, and the odd, muffled voice broke free from the press and rose up through the mist. In the spaces between these and the pendulum creak of the spindle it was eerily silent. When the wheel had turned its full, lazy circle I was unbolted and scrambled down to the road.

My bird's-eye view had revealed Kashgar as two cities. They occupied the same physical space but were not in physical contact with one another. As a reminder to the inhabitants of Turkestan that the Chinese were in charge and on watch, a monumental crossroads had been hacked through the Uighur town. Proof of the supremacy of Han culture at the farthest edge of the Chinese nation, Liberation Road and People's Road ran in broad, straight lines that stretched symbolically to the four points of the compass from their central intersection. The Chinese city consisted of these crossed roads and of the adjoining People's Square with its colossal statue of Mao. The construction of each of the two thoroughfares had involved the demolition of an immense swathe of Uighur Kashgar, and had transformed the space they now occupied into one unrecognizable from that in any of the cities of eastern China. It was as though part of Beijing had been transplanted westward, which was precisely the intention. The work continued apace. On a low wall surrounding an acre of recently demolished buildings, a painted slogan read: 'Warmly welcome the Kashgar reconstruction project!' The justification here was not one of beautifying the tourist environment as it had been in Suzhou, yet the Chinese silkworm was still greedily nibbling away.

At street level, the same metal-shuttered booths sold CDs and video discs of Cantonese pop stars. I recognized some from Meiling's collection on Putuoshan. Their lyrics were blasted out into the road and their faces smiled out from posters. Signs pointed the way to restaurants opened by migrants to cater to the culinary nostalgia of their compatriots: Sichuanese hotpots; Shanghainese seafood; 'fragrant meat' for homesick north-easterners who missed the taste of dog. Boutiques sold Western clothing brands modelled by smiling Han girls. Stalls offered five-minute carving of *yinzhang*, the indispensable name-chops that serve for a signature in China. Hoardings listed the details of single men and women, all Han, all desperate for affluent marriage partners. Everything was in Chinese characters, the Uighurs' Arabic script conspicuous in its near absence from the two streets. The pavement was composed of the same red and white hexagonal tiles as I had trodden in Suzhou, Shanghai, Sanya and Chengdu. It stretched across to identical stainless steel barriers, and all around there were adverts for mobile phones and life insurance.

The faces were all Han. It was Friday, a day of prayer, yet the women made no allowance for the sensitivities of the locals. They were dressed in the usual short skirts and off-the-shoulder tops. They tugged at their blouses to reveal a little more cleavage, wrapped themselves around boyfriends or husbands, and tottered along on fashionable platform soles or stilettos. The Uighur women who strayed occasionally amongst them stood out in their frumpy layers of petticoats and overskirts, glittering sequined, bodices and headscarves.

The contrast between the two cities struck me most when I sat at the edge of People's Square. It was an unapologetically Chinese space, a communist space, and like all of eastern China's celebrated public spaces it felt empty. It neither needed nor sought the application of human scale to serve its purpose. This it achieved simply by being there, yet at the same time it seemed aware of the friendlessness of its situation. Stays drummed an occasional tattoo against their flagpoles, their plaintive noise lending the place a strange sadness.

The architecture of People's Square was a study of Chinese themes. Bridges with carved lotus-pod handrails arched over a winding river, just as in Beijing's Forbidden City or Shanghai's Chinese Renaissance plans. Enormous bright red Chinese lanterns hung from cold steel poles. A pair of carved stone columns, stiff with bamboo and writhing with dragons, soared from lotus-flower bases to capitals of imperial Chinese lions. Incised on both, in Chinese and in Uighur, were the words 'Long live the great unity of China's ethnic peoples!'

The columns framed a statue of Mao beyond who stood, his right arm outstretched in what hovered between greeting and threat, in a full-length trenchcoat despite the warmth of the late spring day. A slogan nearby encouraged all the peoples of China to join together their hearts. It was an exhortation that had the full backing of the law: in preparation for the western leg of my trip I had accessed the Amnesty International website from an

Internet café in Beihai, and had printed off reports on Uighurs who four years earlier had been publicly executed in Kashgar simply for hanging the banned flag of the TIRET on Mao's statue. The sheets had been stolen on the train, and would require a great deal of explanation if ever my assailants were caught with them. Small knots of tourists, dwarfed by the size of the square, took it in turns to photograph each other against the backdrop of the Great Helmsman. They were all Han, and now they had proof that they had visited Kashgar.

It was clearly not considered necessary for them to visit the Uighur city. Barely a single Han face was visible on the square outside the Id Gah Mosque when I reached it. Instead Uighurs, Kirghiz and Tungans milled around or sat talking and smoking. Each minority distinguished itself by its headgear: embroidered green pork-pie *doppas* or greasy *kapkas* – Russian-style flat caps – for the Uighurs, white skullcaps for the Tungans, China's native Muslims, and high crowns of heavy white felt for the Kirghiz. A weather-beaten old Kirghiz had attracted an audience. He sat plucking at his three-stringed *komuz*, the lute that had welcomed him into this world and would leave it alongside him, singing in a whisper from which, every few stanzas, he broke off for a mouthful of dry flatbread kept in the pocket of a voluminous overcoat. The sun broke through the last of the mist and a shaft of light spotlit his performance as if in celestial approval.

A burst of trees straining skyward at the western end of the square marked the precincts of the mosque itself. In front of them, thin minarets surmounted by crescents flanked the high arch of its gateway. The walls and the blind arcading were an earthy mustard, highlighted in thin whites, though here and there the paint was peeling to reveal the beige of baked mud beneath.

It was nearly 3 p.m. Beijing time but only one o'clock locally – Kashgar prefers to run on the unofficial time used throughout Xinjiang, two hours behind a capital that is 2,100 miles distant. A steady stream of men and youths poured from the leafy fringe of a street that ran alongside the mosque. Most carried prayer mats rolled up under one arm, some simple bolts of felt, others ornately embroidered rugs in silks and wool that bore verses from the Qur'an. The less pious of Kashgar's menfolk were busily fanning row upon row of mutton kebabs at the stalls lining the street, lunch for the worshippers when prayers were over. The smoke billowed from their braziers and hung amongst the branches of the trees.

I joined the men entering the mosque, and we shuffled into the first vestibule. Passing through it, we emerged into the sunlight and aligned ourselves to face a mihrab set into the far wall of the prayer hall. The crowd had already begun to overflow from the forest of wooden columns, and worshippers knelt in untidy rows between the trees of the courtyard, seeking out the patches of cool shade that they cast. I found a space beside a shallow water channel, unlaced my heavy walking boots and knelt.

The service had already started yet still people were arriving. A giant of a man in a heavy overcoat and the trademark hat of the Kirghiz smoothed out a faded rug to my left and lowered himself on to it with a grunt. He swept his cupped hands across his face and turned to look at his pale neighbour. I had expected to be stared at, as I had been throughout eastern China, but instead my neighbour simply acknowledged me with a nod and began to pray. By now I was hemmed in on all sides by worshippers. They stood, their hands cupped before them as if to catch the precious words of the imam, and then knelt to touch their heads to the floor.

The imam progressed through the service and the crowd rose and fell raggedly at its junctures. The language was classical Arabic, Islam's devotional lingua franca. The imam's voice revelled in its clipped consonants, emphasized the beauty of its long, smooth vowels, played with the cadence of its prayers. The voice was amplified through an unseen loudspeaker, its every texture made audible. I understood nothing but the Muslim declaration of faith and the occasional *Allahu Akbar* – God is Great. At one point, at the culmination of a long intonation, the voice breathed out a final *Allahu Akbar*. It started reedily, quavering and distant, but grew in power until it carried in a solemn echo from every surface of the courtyard. When it could no longer hold the note, it seemed to break with emotion and, trembling, emitted the final *akbar* as a pair of high, pinched syllables, savouring their truth almost to the point of tears.

The service had been pared down to its basics, eschewing anything that might encroach on the individual's communion with Allah. It was the essence of the Islamic belief that His will would be done, a world away from distant Putuoshan's soporific repetitions and petulant demands: may *my* will be done, if only I can offer enough incense and sweets. I had gone to the mosque to give thanks for my deliverance on the train, and now the grinning Amita Buddha seemed more insignificant than ever.

On the way out, we shuffled past the crippled and the widowed who had gathered to receive alms. They held out hands if they had any, or else mumbled prayers of thanks as coins chimed into the tin cans strapped around their necks. Outside, a trio of smirking Han migrants spotted me, nudged one another like awkward teenagers, and muttered *laowai*. I ignored them. For an hour at least, I had felt as if I were no stranger in China.

The desk sergeant at the Foreign Affairs Section of the Public Security Bureau wanted to know why I required an Alien Travel Permit for Ulugchat. The real answer was that I knew I would stand out like a sore thumb as the only Western face at the farthest edge of the Kirghiz Autonomous Prefecture, and I did not relish the thought of being arrested when the local Public Security Bureau discovered I had entered a restricted border zone illegally. On a more practical note, I had already approached a Uighur taxi-driver to ask the price of a ride to Ulugchat, and he had shaken his head and refused to take me without a permit.

'*Everybody* needs a permit to go there,' he had said. 'Even *Hanzular*.'

I told the officer of my plans to visit the four corners of China, and of how I had already seen Shengshan and Jinmujiao. I produced a map with my route so far marked in red highlighter ink, and Ulugchat and Mohe highlighted in yellow.

'There's nothing there,' he said, and then he disappeared through an open door into an office beyond. A large perspex plan of Xinjiang hung on the wall. It showed the outlines of the various counties, districts and prefectures, and coded them to indicate whether or not they were *kaifang* – opened up. If not, you required a permit or risked being arrested, fined or expelled, or all three if the police were in a bad mood. The system was complicated by the fact that, especially in restive Xinjiang, areas could be *kaifang* one day and *bu kaifang* the next, depending on the situation on the ground. Some areas were explicitly closed to all foreigners, and neither love nor money would buy a permit. Ulugchat was coded as *bu kaifang*. The sergeant returned.

'Foreigners aren't allowed into Ulugchat at the moment, I'm afraid.' He looked genuinely apologetic. I did not stay to argue. Once the Public Security Bureau has made a decision it rarely changes its mind. I would either have to forego Ulugchat and take Kashgar as the westernmost point of my trip or else continue westwards illicitly. I tried a few more taxi-drivers, but none was willing to accept my dollars if it meant having to explain at a checkpoint why the *Ingiliz* in his car had no travel permit. One spoke no Mandarin but eloquently acted out how as a Uighur he would be handcuffed and led away if I was found in his car further west.

If I could not manage the hundred miles to Ulugchat either legally or with a willing local driver, I would have to hitch an illicit ride on a westbound truck driven by a Han Chinese and presumably spend a couple of days getting there and back. Yet the episode on the train had unnerved me and the prospect of packing an overnight bag and disappearing off alone scared me. Suddenly visiting Ulugchat did not seem to matter as much as it had before. I was simply glad to have made it as far as I had, and the prospect of sitting drinking beer and playing pool with the Uighurs and the Pakistani cross-border tradesmen outside the hotel seemed infinitely preferable to a journey into the unknown.

'Ulugchat? Not good. There, there is nothing.' My Uighur partner at the table was typically dismissive of anywhere other than his home town, but I sensed none of the false modesty of the Han in his dismissal. He seemed genuinely bemused by my interest. He slammed the cue ball into the black, which rocketed into the far pocket. We had been playing for 10 *renminbi* a frame.

'You pay me, yes?'

His Mandarin was totally atonal and very shaky. I asked him what Ulugchat looked like, since I was curious as to what I was missing.

'Ulugchat *hun shiang jeli.*' Ulugchat was very like here. He passed me the cue and I broke the loose triangle of balls he had arranged. One leaped from the table and shattered my bottle of beer. I decided that the following day I would at least try to make it as far west as Kashgar would allow me.

In the popular imagination a desert oasis comprises two or three date palms arching over a sheet of blue water. The reality is quite different. The Kashgar oasis spreads for tens of miles and supports a population of a quarter of a million. To reach its edge I needed a bicycle.

The road led due west between double rows of tall poplars. Their slanting shadows stretched across the tarmac and over the rough brick of the car workshops and roadside eateries that lined the side of the road. The day was hot and I was thankful for the shade.

I cycled slowly, unused to the exertion after six weeks of buses, boats and trains. There was plenty of time for the call to go up ahead of me and for diners to leave their bowls of mutton and rice *pulo* and come to wave me on. Swarthy young men in flat *kapkas* paused mid-stroke in games of pool to shout. Some beckoned me to join them beneath striped awnings. *Nan* sellers pointed at me from behind the wooden trolleys they pushed and grinned at each other.

Slowly the town metamorphosed into a single settlement that straggled unbroken for mile after mile on both sides of the road. Hefty wooden doors with hammered brass fittings punctuated one long, seamless wall. Occasionally a doorway would stand ajar, and I would spy children squatting, mothers preparing food or chickens scratching in the yard. Now and then galleries projected above the line of the wall, their verandahs built of wood, their gaily painted balconies divided overhead into arched bays and carved into busy arabesques of flowers and birds. Dirty, freckle-faced children busied themselves with the dust and stones of the verges, or threw pebbles into the gurgling brown water in the channels between sentinel lines of trees. Otherwise the settlement looked inwards from its wall and kept itself to itself, though now and again it opened up to reveal fields and vineyards beyond. Soon these had pressed inwards to exert their presence, and gradually the wall acknowledged that beyond here they held sway.

With the arrival of the fields, those neat green trapezoids of wheat, barley and rice, I began to feel the wildlife of the oasis stir. Pied wagtails ran in tentative bursts across the road; gangs of sparrows and pigeons pecked at the wheat; pairs of powder-grey doves cooed in the branches; and at one point a hoopoe, startled by the clatter of my bicycle, flew up in a tumble of piebald and pink from a vegetable patch. I passed farmers making their way home from their work in the fields, their iron hoes hoisted over their shoulders. Donkeys pulling two-wheeled carts plodded back to their stalls.

Eventually the double lines of trees faltered as if unsure of the direction they should take, and the flat tarmac of the road gave way by degrees to a rough bridleway of stones. All around were fields. Now, the drooping frames of willows foiled the graceful height of the poplars. Soon, pedalling required too much effort against the unpredictable bumps and gullies of the track, and I dismounted and began to push the bicycle.

The fields grew gradually larger and stonier, the scrub marking their boundaries more stunted. Where the farmers' transforming hand had been light, the oasis floor retained some of its desert character, a tight matrix of loess and gravel gouged into bluffs and ledges, or heaped into promontories by ancient floods. Eventually the donkey track became too rough even to push a bicycle, and I propped it against a bush and continued on foot.

A ragged fringe of trees always promised to mark the edge of the oasis but, each time I reached it, it was replaced by another more distant one. Gradually the horizon of swaying, emerald needles grew lower on the skyline, until finally there were not trees enough to resolve themselves into this mirage border, and the bleached scree swept away to coalesce with the whitening late afternoon.

By now the sun had lost its heat, but its remaining light was reflected and magnified heavenwards by the desert that stretched westward in a crumpled blanket from the point where I had stopped walking. The ground shone with the same pale luminescence as the dusk sky. I stooped to choose a handful of small stones, and was surprised by their smoothness. They were glacial, carved from the Pamirs by the slow machinations of ice and water, and brought to the very edge of the Kashgar oasis by numberless inundations of a prehistoric Kizil River, caressed and polished by its summer flow. I had failed to reach China's western mountains, but I would take a minute part of them with me nonetheless.

Turpan

On the way east, the train now passed in daylight through what
I had missed in darkness on the trip west to Kashgar, and I regretted not having the old English teacher with me as I retraced the
line to Turpan. I felt he could have made the landscape speak
more clearly to me.

Around Korla, which we reached soon after a gunmetal dawn
had broken to reveal a featureless, stone-strewn plateau, the
desert bloomed, irrigated by meltwaters that surged down from
the Tian Shan. Rivers that had careered joyously, oblivious to
their eventual fate in the searing wastes of the Tarim Desert,
were for a while tamed as they tumbled through.

The desert bloomed with the perpendicular precision of the
draftsman. The Karaxahar and the Konqi were here sparkling
blue ribands, the irrigation ditches they fed laid out on the flat
desert floor like skeins of azure thread. Between them a seam-
stress's iron had smoothed elongated fields into bolts of pinstripe
cloth, their surfaces combed lines of polythene that radiated
from distant vanishing points amongst fringes of windbreak
trees. Here was the artificial world of the Bingtuan, the unvarying uniformity of industrial monoculture applied to the nomads'
desert. The postage-stamp fields of Kashgar had felt natural,
timeless, their existence unquestionable, grounded in the absolutes of an oasis's very identity – here the desert begins, so here
the cultivation must end. But these immense, rectangular
swathes were unnatural, their existence fragile. That they survived at all was only because of the constant labours of the
antlike workers who swarmed across the loom of their faces and
along their hems, tugging at their stitching and regulating the
blue threads that fed them.

The smothering darkness of the journey west had hidden
from view the town of Hejing – its name means Peace and
Quiet – the last settlement of any size that we were to pass

through before the line rose to negotiate the igneous convolutions of the Tian Shan.

Hejing looked to be wholly a Han town, its residential blocks built barracks-style as a reflection of the mindset in these parts, its name chosen as much out of hope as experience. Even in the nineteenth century, Francis Younghusband noted how almost all of the towns and villages on a journey from Turpan to Kashgar had consisted of a pair of distinct, walled settlements: one inhabited by the local Turkics, the other up to a mile distant by the Chinese. Near the Chinese town in each case – at Toksun, Kumux, Ushtala, Bugur, Kuqa and Aksu – he found a small garrison of Chinese soldiers, often poorly armed and generally feared and hated by the locals for their corruption and thieving.

The train halted alongside the stretch of dust that passed for a platform in Hejing. The accommodation blocks stretched away in garbage-strewn ranks and files from the tracks, each one surrounded by a mute brick wall pierced at intervals by gates, and consisting within of a single-storey building along one edge and a trellis-covered courtyard. A grid of alleyways divided each block from its immediate neighbours. Even at a distance they were unmistakeably Han dwellings: pasted on to the centre of every door was a large gold character – that of *fu*, good fortune – on a diamond of auspicious red paper. They had been stuck on upside-down, the phrase in Mandarin for 'good fortune is inverted' being a homophone of 'may good fortune arrive'. To the left and right of each door had been pasted at Chinese New Year eight-character couplets setting out the occupants' wish for peace and prosperity in the coming twelve months. The Muslim Uighurs do not follow these practices, and in Xinjiang they are the mark of the infidel immigrant.

The faces of the townspeople uniformly possessed the tanned skin and red cheeks that had engulfed the platform at Chengdu and had speckled the trackside spoil heaps of Guangxi. Only now their eyes had lost the look of awed incomprehension and they walked slow and erect rather than in a hunched scuttle. The same was true of the villagers in the mountain whistle halts that afternoon. As the engine pondered the endless rises between flat-bottomed valleys, the doors of houses and shops in the navvies' encampments would swing open to allow the workers some break from the tedium. Every face was Han, even those of the shepherds who drove their goats beside the tumbling streams. The daubed characters drumming up custom for a Sichuanese restaurant, or warning of the fines to be imposed on anybody caught defecating against the walls, were all in one language, Mandarin. The minarets and beaten steel crescents of Kashgar's neighbourhood mosques here were absent.

The mudbrick shelters of the men who had recently driven the Kashgar railway across the fringe of the Turpan basin had been sandblasted and reclaimed by the desert. All that was left, once their wooden rafters and tarpaulin roofs, their doors and their window frames had been pillaged and shipped on to the next resting-place, were the abraded blueprints of bare walls huddling amongst the dunes like so many Babylonian archaeological sites. Yet these buildings had been abandoned only a few years before. Farther out into the waterless wasteland entire cities, founded on the Silk Road as far back as the Han dynasty and abandoned when their glacial rivers had dried up, had been swallowed whole.

The annual inundation whose torrents tear at the moonscape floor of the Turpan Basin had washed away most of the tarmac that had led from Great Riverbank down to the town. The route the minibus now took on the long stretches between the surviving lengths was that of least resistance along the most recently excavated cliff faces and bluffs. On them the history of the basin's cataclysms could be read like a book. In places, tens of feet above the road, their meandering bands of grey scree and coral sand recorded decades of alternating floods and sandstorms. At some unmarked line of text the bus dropped below sea level.

Since my only words of Uighur were the useless phrases I had memorized on the way to Kashgar and the numbers from one to ten (apart from six and seven), I was compelled to speak to the locals in Mandarin, but I felt uncomfortable using what many considered to be the language of an occupying army.

'*Wo dasuan jintian wanshang qu Gaochang.*' I told the taxi-driver that I planned to go to Khocho that evening. 'How much to take me there and back?' He surveyed me, pushed his *doppa* to the back of his head, sucked on his home-made cigarette of newspaper and chopped tobacco stalks, and emitted a long, high note that did little to make me think I would be quoted a fair price.

'*Aiiieeee!* It is a long way to Khocho, especially in the evening. What are you? *Amerikiliq? Ingiliz?*' *Ingiliz*, I told him. 'If you are an *Ingiliz* then I will take you for nothing, but you must teach me how to speak in your *Ingiliztili*. What time do you plan to go?' I wanted to arrive at dusk, to see the moon rise over the ruins.

On the morning of his twenty-fourth birthday, in AD 240, Manes left the heterodox Christian sect in Persia where he had grown up, taking his pious father and two followers with him, and founded the religion whose dissemination he believed was his destiny.

Manes believed himself to be the Apostle of Light, the last in a line of prophets that had begun with Adam and that had continued through to Jesus. Granted permission from the Sassanids who then ruled Persia to preach his Manichaeism within their empire, Manes even organized missions to foreign countries, modelling them on the apostolic churches of the New Testament so that the entire world might hear his Word. Zoroastrianism's high priests, however, guardians of a state religion even then centuries old, feared Manes as a threat to their exalted position. He was driven into exile in India where, so it is said, at the age of sixty he was flayed alive and then crucified. To his followers, Manes' death was interpreted as proof of his divine status.

Manes had intended his foundation to be an ecumenical faith, drawing on the teachings of earlier prophets – Moses, Zoroaster, Christ and the Buddha – to create a universal, syncretistic religion that would transcend traditional boundaries. Its opponents saw it more as a religious Frankenstein's monster. Its basic premise was that the human condition was one of anguish at existing, and that man's capacity to feel a need for deliverance from the torment of existence meant that within man must reside some spiritual germ essentially superior to the evil of his physicality. If physical, tormented man is born of a good God, so Manes thought, then his torment must be due not to God but to some opposing principle.

Creation was brought about by the primordial interaction of light and dark, of good and evil, in a way easily understandable to anyone versed in the principles of *yin* and *yang* or in Zoroaster's dualism. The God-born particle of light residing within man needed to be reunited with God in order for man to be redeemed and freed from the earthly torment of physical being – a belief with which Buddhists, with their notions of karma, of escape from the eternal wheel of death and rebirth and of ultimate nirvana, could identify.

The everyday practice of Manichaeism was in essence gnostic, its aim being to employ Manes' complex cosmogony in the strict rituals of a church of the Elect so as to liberate the particles of light trapped within man from the dark that binds them, and so return them to oneness with God. Manes explained that the universe had been organized by God as a means of liberating His lost particles of light and of transmuting them back into Himself.

The Elect lived in monasteries doing – or not doing – everything within their power to avoid defiling the light that resided in them: they abstained from sex, which bound the light even more tightly to the dark; took vows of poverty; did not eat meat, drink alcohol or even partake in everyday tasks – sowing, reaping, hunting. At death, they hoped that this would be enough to guarantee them no further rebirths in tormented, human form.

By the Tang dynasty, four hundred years after Manes' death, adherents of Manichaeism had reached China, having made the long, overland trek on the caravans of the Silk Road. Less than sixty years later an edict was promulgated giving them leave to worship freely within the realms of the Son of Heaven. It was by these missionaries that the Uighur nation – its leaders having been allowed to remain in the Tang capital in recognition of their part in putting down General An Lushan's rebellion – was converted to Manichaeism. When in AD 840 the Kirghiz destroyed their capital in Mongolia, the Uighurs took their Manichaean beliefs with them to a new capital at Khocho.

My driver Abdusalam had wanted to learn English for a reason. Other young men in Turpan, he told me, could speak a little English or Japanese, and they drove the Buddhists who came to see the Thousand Buddha Grottoes at nearby Bezeklik. He wanted a slice of the action.

Abdusalam had brought his friend Sadik with him and, as his taxi negotiated the potholes in the road to Khocho, the three of us bounced around inside like some gay love triangle in Babel. Sadik sat beside me suggesting phrases in Uighur which Abdusalam would translate into Mandarin so that I could teach him the English equivalent. 'Where do you want to go?' 'I can take you to Grape Valley / a *karez* / the Friday mosque / the Flaming Mountains.' The old English teacher had been correct: the complicated phonetics of Uighur made its speakers far more comfortable pronouncing English than Chinese.

As we left the donkey carts and mud bricks of Turpan behind

us, Sadik leaned over and spoke to Abdusalam, who translated into a mixture of Mandarin and Uighur.

'*Ni xi bu xi hashish?*'

'*Yingwen shuo* "Do you smoke hashish?"' I answered, adding English to the linguistic mess. Abdusalam laughed and translated what I had said back to Sadik, who snorted.

'He doesn't want to know how to say it in English,' said Abdusalam. 'He wants to know if you smoke hashish.' Sadik, grinning, produced a fat joint from under his *kapka*.

The sun had not quite set when we rolled to a halt by the ruins of Khocho. The ticket-seller was nowhere to be seen although the sound of a television could be heard from his shack. Leaving Abdusalam and Sadik giggling to themselves in the cab, I walked through a hole in the wall where a gateway had once stood and into the city.

I was transfixed by its unearthly beauty. The sun, now sinking below the weathered outline of the earth wall to the west, cast the day's final, golden burst of light on to the eastern rampart. Its foot was submerged in shadow but the ragged parapet above shone like polished amber against a lapis-lazuli heaven. Where the sun's fingers had discovered odd cracks and holes in the western wall, spots of white glowed on the rising curtain of darkness like tufts of ermine on black velvet.

Laid out between the walls, which stretched away for a mile before turning at right angles to form the most distant bulwark, were the remains of the palaces, the monasteries and the houses of Khocho. In places they had been worn down until whole swathes were just a soft, undulating blanket. It was here that the Elect had sung, fasted and prayed, and here that the community of Hearers who supported them through alms had confessed their sins.

The ramparts along which Afanti had rolled his boulder back and forth had survived to a height of many yards and, in the shelter they afforded, some smaller walls were recognizable as buildings. The desert wind had rubbed at their weakest points, eroding holes where the Uighur builders had planned none and leaving gaping voids where once there had been a window or a door. For a few minutes before night fell, I found myself alone amongst a mute maze of Henry Moores.

The shadows scaled their way to the top of the eastern wall and the last speck of amber died away. Once the sun had gone, the oceanic expanse of Khocho was lit only by the twilight glow of the sky and by a bright moon. To the Manichaean Uighurs the moon had been a cosmic pump, a vital part of the universal machinations that reunited the light liberated from redeemed souls with God. As it waxed each month, the moon was seen to fill with light which, when it waned, would be transferred to the sun whence it started on its journey to Paradise. At that moment, it seemed to have stopped in the middle of an inhalation of souls.

When I got back to the car, Sadik was talking to himself in his sleep, but Abdusalam was facing Mecca, murmuring to himself the *shahadah* – There is no God but Allah, and Mohammed is His Prophet.

Sombre Warrior

'We say that water, cleansing through its yielding and weakness, likes to wash away man's evil.'

Guanzi

BEIJING

IT WAS UNSEASONABLY hot in Beijing. A dust storm had blown up from nowhere during the afternoon. A baking wind from the Gobi raised clouds of orange grit that forced the citizens off the streets, eyes watering, into the shelter of doorways or shops.

'We never used to suffer so many of these storms here,' the receptionist at my hostel remarked idly as I stood behind the rattling glass of its double doors, transfixed by the seething sand and its load of swirling litter. 'Beijing just seems to get drier and drier.'

Two hours later the storm had worn itself out and the hot sun reappeared. From what I had seen on the train from Turpan, it was not just Beijing that was getting drier and drier, but all of northern China.

The 2,000-mile journey, a longbow-shaped route skirting the southern fringes of the Gobi and crossing the carved loess plateau of the Yellow River, had been a procession of sepia slides framed by the carriage's rectangular windows: a thin brown ribbon meandered across a whitewashed riverbed between distant banks that it had long since ceased trying to span. A powdery brown village, inhabited by dusty, slouching horses, seemed to have grown from the baked earth. A grey bridge resounded over brown fields of crops way below where there should have been a river. I had seen this last slide time and again during the three-day journey. Every river seemed to have dried up.

In Beijing, stuck to the tilework beside every tap, was a reminder of the need to conserve water. An article in one of the city's evening newspapers listed the concerns of the Water Conservancy Bureau. The water table had dropped by forty-five feet since the fifties. Deforestation had increased both erosion and evaporation. Less and less water was entering north China's river system, and what water there was was being lost because the sluggish, silt-laden flow failed to carry it downstream. For years now, during the long, hot summer, the Yellow River had stopped flowing at all in the final 150 miles of its course. For large parts of the year, China's second river had become an inland waterway. At the same time, Beijing's population was increasing, demanding more and more from a dwindling supply. The article ended by lauding the Party's plans to construct a water pipeline from the Three Gorges project on the Yangtze all the way to the capital. I tried to picture Beijing as an abandoned desert ruin, a high-rise concrete Khocho, if this were to fail.

I took a taxi to the station, elbowing my way through the sweating scrum at the ticket gate and on to the platform where the Harbin train was waiting.

The gate faced the door to car 15. My ticket was for car 2, while the train stretched away in the opposite direction just as far. At last I collapsed on to my berth. A woman and her daughter, a sartorially incompetent teenager in a velvet puffball skirt and red baseball cap, struggled through the scrum in the corridor to my compartment. They deposited the woman's luggage on the rack and then struggled back the way they had come. From my bed I could see them hug each other goodbye on the platform. The woman sobbed her heart out on the girl's shoulder and then looked up, her red eyes streaming, into her daughter's face. I ought to have been moved by her display of affection, but her dark bob played around the curve of her ear and for an instant she resembled the woman who had robbed me. Instead of sympathy I felt a wave of cold nausea.

Another couple embraced just below my window, the girl stepping on to the train as the klaxon sounded and the guards' whistles blew. She too had been crying, and she waved tearfully as we drew out of the station. Her boyfriend walked perfunctorily alongside for a few paces, stopped to wave back, then turned to depart, hands in pockets. The Broadcasting Bureau of the

People's Railway played a morose tune called 'Saying Goodbye' over the loudspeakers as though trying to coax a few more tears from her.

Outside the station, on Beijing's boulevards and side streets, the stage had been set for what everybody was confident would be a successful bid to stage the 2008 Olympics. Slick hoardings had proclaimed the coming of 'A new Beijing, a new Olympic Games'. The five rings had been unsubtly woven into adverts and shop signs, and the glitzy hotels on the Avenue of Eternal Peace had borne banners pledging their support for Beijing's entry. Seven years earlier, when the bid to host the 2000 Games had failed, I had watched with disbelief and a grudging admiration as the Party wiped away all trace of its ever having applied. Hoardings had been painted over during the night, adverts had been dropped, and the pretty newscaster the next day had not so much as mentioned Sydney's success. Now, the city's streets were spotless. Entire neighbourhoods of dirty backstreet *hutongs* had been demolished and replaced by shiny department stores and joint-venture offices. Avenues had been widened and fronted by plate glass and steel, and the transport infrastructure was being renovated and improved in a way that only a dictatorship can manage.

In any city the slowest areas to change are the seamy corridors through which run its railways. Approached by train there is little to distinguish London from Beijing, or Chicago from Moscow. They all present the same impecunious face, lined with sagging power cables, powdered with rust, their eyes the gaunt, staring windows of obsolete housing projects. Beijing's hidden face was one that no visiting Olympic official would be required to check: crumbling apartment blocks, brick-built slums and the shanty towns of migrants, their roofs of corrugated iron and tarpaulins held in place by a mess of tyres, rubble, half-bricks and guyropes.

The black hatchwork of pylons and their swirling, inkdot

shoals of starlings were silhouetted against the sickly sun in a nicotine-yellow sky. The sun was so perfectly round – its corona having utterly vanished – its pallor so close to that of the cool of evening, that it looked as if a neat hole had punctured the firmament, and through it the light of dusk was ebbing away. Fields of wheat and enfilades of wayside trees briefly took the place of factories and suburbs before the pale crests of the Swallow Mountains pressed in on the track from the north. Now we were passing through farmsteads and woodland, but it was an ugly landscape, an awkward collage of elements uneasy in each other's proximity: a power station huddling beneath a billow of white steam, a herd of grazing sheep, the mirror of a fishpond, the concave scar of a quarry, peasants defecating by the trackside, shiny new foreign-funded factory complexes whose polished eyes glinted palely, graveyard hummocks, rubbish heaps.

As the last of the day seeped away, I thought I glimpsed the pounded earth rampart of the Great Wall at the point where the railway had been hacked through it. I was leaving the safety of eternal China and heading into the wilderness beyond the wall. Yet somehow I felt bored and restless. This was just another train journey, and I was now on the final leg of my trip, marking time until I reached Mohe where I could finally say I had done it, I had travelled to the four corners of this vast country, and could pack my bag and fly home to England.

So I had to pinch myself when, the next morning, soon after dawn, the attendant shook me awake to tidy away my bed-clothes, and I looked out on to the rolling landscape of Yorkshire as I remembered it in childhood. Greensward extended from the trackside ballast to the edge of loamy, deep brown fields where draught-horses strained in their harnesses to turn the rich sod with their ploughs. Villages of thatched, redbrick cottages nestled around ponds that mirrored the grey sky. Smoke curled from their chimneys. Herds of black-and-white Friesians grazed on pastures that shimmered with dew. Rooks, disturbed by our engine, flapped lazily into the treetops. The skyline was of deciduous woodland, species I recognized, the birch and the oak. I narrowed my eyes and pretended I was already home.

HARBIN

IN A COUNTRY where history has been shaped by a never-ending struggle to control the power of its great rivers, the land readily defines itself by its relation to the water that flows through it and that surrounds it. Many of China's provinces, their names exotic to a Western ear, are simply the names of her rivers, lakes and seas.

Hebei and Henan are named after their respective positions 'North of the Yellow River' and 'South of the Yellow River'; Hubei and Hunan similarly are 'North of Dongting Lake' and 'South of Dongting Lake'; Jiangxi is found 'West of the Yangtze'; Zhejiang is the 'Zigzag River', another name for the Fuchun that winds through the province; Sichuan is named after the 'Four Rivers' that flow through it; Liaoning is the 'Peaceful Lands on the Liao River'; Qinghai – Azure Sea – is a translation of Kokonor, the Mongolian word for the immense saltwater lake within Qinghai's borders; Jilin means 'By the Big River' in Manchu, the big river being the Sungari; and Hainan is to be found 'South of the Sea'.

Heilongjiang means Black Dragon River, the Chinese name for what the West, through the Russian fur-trappers who first reached eastern Siberia in the seventeenth century, called the Amur. This was in turn taken from the name used by Mongolian nomads – Kharamuren, the black waters – reflecting the dark tannins leached into the river from its forest slopes. For over 1,000 miles it coils and snakes over its sandbanks, marking the edge of the world for the Chinese and disowned behind coils of barbed wire by the Russians. Finally it turns north to disgorge 11,000 cubic metres of water every second, and 41,000 tons of sediment every day, into the fishing grounds off Sakhalin Island. With its tributaries, the Sungari and the Ussuri, the Argun and the Shilka, the Amur drains a diverse region the size of Western Europe, from the bleak steppe and nomadic grasslands of Mongolia to the Manchu homeland of the Ever White Mountains that overlook North Korea; from the fertile Manchurian Plain of Heilongjiang and Jilin to the great forest arc of the Hingan range and the Russian Far East. Into it is wrung, through its myriad rivers and numberless lakes, the vast sponge of the taiga.

The world of the river is a curious, looking-glass world, created as if in some act of determinism by the shamanistic spirits of the northern forests. Like the maps of medieval Europe, their imprecision provoking in us today a half-recognition of distended features, the geography of north-eastern Asia is a distorted ghost image, a skewed depiction of the lands to its south. Here, rising not in the Tibetan Plateau but from the Mongolian steppe, the Amur flows like a boreal Yangtze into the Sea of Okhotsk. The mountains of Russia's Primorye territory are the river's ice-bound substitute for China's graceful coastline; the river's cities, Blagoveshchensk, Khabarovsk and Nikolayevsk, echo the Yangtze's Wuhan, Nanjing and Shanghai, only here they are condemned to spend six months of each year in useless frozen torpor.

The Amur is the only one of Siberia's mighty rivers to flow not north into the Arctic Ocean but east into the Pacific. This geographical caprice was the spark that ignited Russia's interest in distant Manchuria and led eventually to the foundation of Harbin as a thoroughly Russian city.

European Russia's hunger for the wealth of Manchuria started with the activities of the Siberian trappers who provided its court and its furriers with exquisite pelts and skins to trade with the West. Following the mink, the arctic fox and the stoat as they scurried eastwards across the Urals, these hunters within a single human lifetime had reached the Pacific Ocean, covering on average one mile of forest every week for fifty-seven years. So rapid was their progress that, barely a decade after they reached the open ocean in 1639, the supply lines that kept their remote settlements habitable were at breaking-point. The scurvied trappers and the new Siberians they brought with them – European Russia's undesirables, its criminals and religious dissenters – looked on the Amur basin to the south as a lifeline, a near mythical region rich with grain and livestock, not to mention furs.

But when Peter the Great eyed the bounty of the Amur from beyond the Urals, the Manchu Qing dynasty was at its most vigorous, having recently consolidated its authority over all of China. The very idea of these hairy barbarians having a hand in what to the Manchu court was sacrosanct land was unthinkable. By the late seventeenth century, Manchu bannermen had besieged and burnt Russia's forts along the Amur, and the settlers had departed north-east to explore Siberia's farthest reaches in search of an alternative gateway to the North Pacific. For as long as the Qing were powerful, Russia would have to forego the one great artery that might ease its exploration and exploitation of eastern Siberia's wealth.

Things were to change. The Opium Wars with the British, and the carving-up of China by foreign powers that followed, tipped the balance of control away from the Manchus in northern Manchuria as elsewhere. When the expansionist Tsar Nicholas ascended the throne and sought a year-round, ice-free port on the Pacific, Russia turned its attention to the Amur's southern tributary, the Ussuri. In 1860 Russia forced the Qing to grant her control of the Sikhote-Alin, the mountain range whose bulk punctuates Siberia at its south-eastern edge, and of the harbour at its southern extremity that the Russian navy was to transform into the port of Vladivostok.

Content for the moment with their new port, which they discovered to their dismay did in fact freeze for a large part of the year, the Russians now looked on the erstwhile glittering prize of the Black Dragon River itself with some disdain. Far greater a prize, now that Russia held Vladivostok, would be the lands to the south of the Black Dragon, Manchuria itself, with all the wealth they offered and the possibility of a direct overland route from Russia to the Sea of Japan.

In 1896, the Russians compelled the moribund Qing to grant them the rights to build a direct link, the Chinese Eastern Railway, that would connect Vladivostok to the Lake Baikal region and thence Europe. Two years later, rights were granted to extend the line south to Russia's new ice-free facilities at Port Arthur in Liaoning. Where the two lines joined, at what had been an extemporized sturgeon-fishing village on the banks of the Sungari River, the city of Gorod Sungari, later renamed Harbin, arose.

Harbin was Russia's Shanghai, a foreign-founded city that grew fat on the cereals and beans it processed, the produce of the Manchurian backwaters that were opened up and changed forever by the advent of the railway. A refrigeration plant was established to export Mongolian lamb to London. Harbin's foreign community – a vibrant mix of Russians, Frenchmen, Jews, Germans, Italians, Poles, Ukrainians, Armenians, Britons, Americans and others – brought with it, as in Shanghai, European culture. Harbin was home to an early film industry; its citizens listened to European orchestras and prayed at Christian churches and Jewish synagogues; their children studied at the conservatory of music and attended ballet schools. There were organized boxing matches, football teams, skating and sailing clubs, horse-racing, and an annual Miss Harbin beauty pageant. On the coat-tails of civil society came the mob, bringing dance halls, drinking dens and prostitution, and controlling the darker side of China's Wild North through extortion and murder. Harbin's cosmopolitan heyday was more short-lived than that of Shanghai, however, lasting barely forty years from the opening of the Chinese Eastern Railway until the aftermath of the Japanese declaration of its puppet state of Manchuguo (as Manchuria was renamed) and, worse, the onset of war with the Allies. As Japan flexed its muscles Russia let slip its precarious hold on Manchuria.

By the time I stepped out of the station at Harbin the rain had started to fall. It was not heavy enough to merit struggling with both an umbrella and a rucksack, but it was still of the cold, insistent kind that seems to hang in invisible droplets in the air, effortlessly able to soak a person to the skin. I was wearing the same shorts and T-shirt that I had put on in Beijing the previous morning. The taxi touts took me for a hardy Russian and, when they spoke, betrayed the same unease with consonant clusters in that language as had the soldier on the bus to Hai'an in English. '*Zaduorasuotabuyiqi! Takuxi!*' '*Tafareeshi! Purasititutuka?*'

In my hotel room I pulled on long trousers for the first time since Canton. They felt awkward and stiff, and the woollen sweater made me strangely conscious of my arms, but at least they would keep out the damp. Then I set out to explore the city.

I wanted most of all to see the Sungari River. It sounded as though it had flowed out of some Siberian legend and strayed accidentally into Chinese territory. Its name reverberated like a distant echo, a reminder that at last I was within earshot of Russia, and so of that dot at the tip of the thread-vein road.

The Sungari was not so much a river as a series of wide, wind-swept puddles. It had yet to be swollen by the summer rains, and it slumped so low between its stone revetments that most of its surface was not water but swathes of rich, brown earth and the occasional green tussock. Nearby, the Chinese Eastern Railway crossed it on an Indian file of squat pillars and disappeared amongst the woods on its distant shore. A flotilla of rowing boats nuzzled the edge of one large sandbank, jostling for position, their hulls lapped by what ripples the breeze could muster from the Sungari's shallows.

Harbin lay behind me on the southern shore, leaving the horizon visible in every other direction. The cloud was so low I could almost reach out to touch it. From Stalin Park on the long sweep of the foreshore, I stood and watched its rain-pregnant belly as it raced north, beyond the tree-line of the far riverbank and out over an invisible expanse of plain and mountain toward Mohe.

For the rest of the day I walked the narrow, cobbled streets of Daoli, once the Russian heart of Harbin. Its broadleaf avenues were a Manchurian echo of a distant Moscow and St Petersburg; its streets, cradled between the bow of the river and the curve of the railway the Russians brought with them, an anthology of European architecture. It was as though Daoli were a piece of flotsam, a part of Europe that had been carried here by a high tide of Russian empire-building, and left stranded on this alien foreshore when the tide turned. The organic lines of art nouveau plasterwork played around plastic shop signs for burger chains and Italian clothing stores; wedding-cake pilasters adorned pastel façades that in turn supported the mansard roofs of the *rive gauche*, their architraves alive with cornucopias and swirling escutcheons. At the centre of this expatriate corner of Europe was the Russian Orthodox Church of St Sophia. It stood apart from the bustling shopping malls and department stores in the middle of a square, a cowled ascetic in brown serge. Orthodox crosses surmounted its spires and its onion dome. The interior was bare but for a sparse exhibition on Harbin's development from fishing village to cultural capital. The walls were of plain brick, and here and there rainwater trickled through velvety patches of moss. Its last Russian priests had long since departed, taking with them the icons and the censer, and Red Guards had finished the job of gutting the church.

The shops outside sold long chains of Russian sausages, russet in colour and pearly with fat, hung from nails above the windows. Behind them, shelves sagged beneath bottles of Hand Grenade, the Manchurians' equivalent of Fiery Jack Embrocation, which they take internally to ward off the cold. I bought a bottle. It was the same size and shape as a Mills bomb but in glass, with a plastic cap that perfectly mimicked a grenade's lever and pin. It boasted that its contents were one hundred per cent proof. Its name must have been a reference to its effect on the body of anyone fool-hardy enough to drink a whole one. I took a mouthful and pushed the remainder into the hands of the Chinese shopkeeper, who swigged from the neck and passed it back. '*Hurasho, tava-reesh!*' Good, comrade! He assumed I was Russian.

'*Nye hurasho,*' I corrected him and told him he could keep the rest. It had tasted filthy.

Most of modern Harbin had lost the postcard charm of Daoli, but still I felt a frisson of excitement when walking its streets, the same frisson I had felt as a child when I flicked through glossy coffee-table books on China. Then, in the late seventies, China was just waking up from the nightmare of the Cultural Revolution and such books were filled with photographs of ugly industrial cities peopled by blue-jacketed workers; of utilitarian shop fronts and packed trolleybuses and curious oriental faces under unvarying mops of black hair. At the time they had all seemed tinged with a grey-green haze. Communist China was to me a grainy world of decaying factories and olive mist.

Individual scenes reawoke these memories, as though I were flicking through a scrapbook of impressions of a China I had never experienced first-hand: a whiskery old man, smothered beneath the heavy padding of a green, army-issue greatcoat; the metal hatching of a railway bridge and the belch of salt-and-pepper smoke from an engine in its sidings; the battered, riveted steel of a hoarding and its hand-painted endorsement of Seagull

Brand welding-torches. The smells too were how as a child I had imagined they should be: oily steam rising from bowls of noodles; the pungent tang of coaldust; the smell of wet, cold air. For one whole day, when a northerly wind blew from beyond its tobacco-processing works, the city smelt of the sweet muskiness of an antique cigar humidor. Harbin's rustbelt backwardness assumed, through a childhood prism, an air of comforting innocence.

PINGFANG

A ONE-LEGGED MAN sold baked sweet potatoes from the firebrick-lined oildrum mounted on his tricycle. He lifted the dustbin lid and reached a hand inside. It emerged clutching a shrivelled tuber which he slit open with a penknife and wrapped in a sheet from the *Heilongjiang Daily*. On the sheet of newspaper was printed an article praising the local authorities for their renovation of what it called the Japanese Army Bacteriological Experimentation Base.

'What's this?' I pointed at the paper.

'A sweet potato.' He stared back at me.

'No, this article. What's the, er . . . *Rijun Xijun Shiyan Jidi?*' He beckoned me to pass him the steaming parcel, which he read. He nodded in recognition and handed it back.

'Ah, it's where the Japanese bandits killed many of us Chinese. They used all kinds of cruel methods: freezing patriotic martyrs to death, injecting them with diseases . . . ugh, they were very cruel.' He acted out the Japanese injecting patriotic martyrs with diseases, administering a shot to his forearm as though shooting up with heroin. I asked him where all this had happened. At Pingfang, a few miles to the south, he replied. Pingfang. Its jaunty name did not have the ring of an Auschwitz or a Dachau.

*

The new highway to Pingfang ran through a rolling English landscape of wheat fields, grassy meadows, woodland and quiet brooks. Later in the day I learned that it was the route along which Japan's secret police in Manchuguo had transported criminals and suspected insurgents to an Imperial Army camp. Not one of them had ever made the journey back to Harbin.

The bus dropped me on Xinjiang Road at the edge of Pingfang, opposite a building that resembled a Victorian prison in its mute bulk and fortress-like impregnability. The driver gesticulated towards it, repeating the same three figures until I had forced my way past the passengers in the corridor and slipped down from the doorway.

'*Qi san yao! Qi san yao! Qi san yao! Qu kan!*' 731, 731, 731! Go look!

The building was not the camp itself but a memorial museum, recently erected to house artefacts from what had been called Unit 731. The Japanese Kwantung Army that controlled Manchuguo had known Unit 731 by a euphemism, the Epidemic Prevention and Water Supply Unit, but in Harbin the three figures had become a shorthand for the atrocities that the unit had committed.

A mural in the entrance hall depicted men in rubber suits and gas masks amidst piles of skeletal bodies, and in two dimly lit rooms were displayed photographs, cabinets filled with artefacts, and ugly life-size dioramas. Beside each a dense panel of Chinese characters provided an explanation. I shared the rooms with a party of elderly tourists and a platoon of young soldiers brought by their officers to learn the lesson of what they were defending China from. Their guides swept them through the exhibits quickly, but I needed longer to absorb what I was reading.

The numbers themselves were not large. By the standards of the conflict in China, where after Japan's invasion in 1931 millions of Chinese soldiers and civilians were killed, 3,000 lives ended in a camp in the countryside near Harbin should have gone unnoticed. But, as I progressed through the exhibition, I became aware of the particular horror of what Japan had done here, of behaviour that reawoke a subconscious fear of white-coated doctors in surgical masks, of hypodermic syringes and an inescapable, clinical death.

Unit 731 had two aims: to research methods of germ warfare that could be put to use in Japan's conquest of East Asia, and to look into how the Japanese army might be made fitter for combat through research into extreme climates, the way in which wounds healed and so on. The unit was founded in 1931 in Tokyo, but was then transferred first to Harbin and in 1938 to the then remote site at Pingfang.

The camp took two years to complete, and when it was finished it comprised a complex of buildings surrounded by a dry moat and a three-mile-long earth wall surmounted by barbed wire and electric fencing. Like Auschwitz it was also equipped with railway sidings and an incinerator, and an airfield was constructed nearby.

I flicked back and forth in my dictionary to confirm that I had understood what I was reading. Many of the words were too specialized, and I had to ask the guide who hovered in the background to explain them. In this way, I slowly pieced together the story the museum presented.

In a large, square block of buildings at the camp's heart, young Japanese soldiers in rubber suits and masks produced enough bubonic plague bacteria to kill the entire population of the world. First, meat stock was rendered down and then sterilized and stored in aluminium flasks. Once the flasks had cooled, plague bacilli were added, and the infected flasks were transferred to an incubator where the humidity and temperature were maintained at the optimum for *Pasteurella pestis* to thrive. After a few days, the plague bacteria would be scraped off and put in cold storage.

This, however, was just the beginning of the nightmarish

work at the camp. One building specialized in breeding rats, another in breeding fleas on rats that had been infected with plague from the cold store. The use of fleas to spread plague amongst enemy troops and civilians had been decided on after it was found that the fragile bacteria would not survive dispatch from an aircraft without a host. Then it was discovered that the explosion required to break open a metal bomb-casing killed its load of infected fleas, so thin porcelain bombs were developed instead. Weighed down with ballast and filled with oxygen to enable their tiny passengers to survive the long, cold descent, the bombs were rigged to shatter above the ground, leaving no tell-tale signs for an enemy army to find. One porcelain bomb, left behind by the fleeing Japanese, sat on a wooden stand beside a dented aluminium flask in which bubonic plague had once been stored.

The bombs had to be tested. Prisoners were taken to a site in the countryside where they were exposed to the aftermath of detonations. Other diseases too were tested on live prisoners at the site: bomblets packed with gas gangrene bacteria and ball-bearings to cause the maximum number of infected wounds were exploded in the centre of concentric rings of Chinese tied to stakes. After suffering agonizing multiple shrapnel wounds, the prisoners were taken back to their cells at Pingfang where their deaths were observed and recorded by Japanese army doctors.

The effectiveness of mustard gas bombs was tested in the same way, as was the transmission of other diseases. Some of these I could not translate, and the guide found it impossible to explain them to me. It was not until I returned to Harbin and a large bookstore that I found a medical dictionary that did so. The pictorial and even poetic quality of some of their Chinese names had at the time hidden from me the full import of what they were: the Japanese had experimented on the transmission and effects of almost the entire known range of those organisms that civilization fears at a most basic level. Besides bubonic plague, gangrene, dysentery, botulism, tetanus, tuberculosis, salmonella and encephalitis, there were charcoal ulcers, sudden chaos, plum tree poison, speckled rash coldness and even the angelic-sounding 'heavenly flowers' – respectively anthrax, cholera, syphilis, typhus and the smallpox virus.

Once infected – whether through injection, through food, water or bomb blast, through fleabites or through contact with other prisoners in crowded cells – the victims were observed as the diseases took hold. Confessions from workers at Unit 731 described how men would writhe in agony, cough blood, stare at their blackened and rotting limbs or lie drenched in sweat from their fevers. All had previously been healthy, a prerequisite for their selection. Most were Chinese, some Russian, Mongolian or Korean. Some were women, and some of these were pregnant. Many of the victims were dissected while still alive so that doctors could follow the progress of their infection. A mock-up of one such human vivisection had been attempted. Masked surgeons rummaged in the wax torso of a naked man who had been tied to the operating-table, fake blood dripping on to the bare floor.

Equally disturbing were the experiments designed to improve the fighting ability of the Japanese army. The Japanese knew they might be required to wage a winter war against the Russians who were still eyeing Manchuria from across the Amur. Japan's military experience was limited to the temperate and tropical theatres of China and the Pacific, and it needed data on the effects of cold on the progress of wounds and disease, and on medical techniques that might give them an edge on their hardier foe.

In the dead of the Manchurian winter night, where the temperature regularly falls below −40 °C, prisoners were taken outside. Areas of skin were wetted and exposed to fans to produce a further windchill. When their flesh was so frozen that it rang out when struck, they were taken back to their cells and put in baths of varying temperatures to discover the optimum means for the Imperial Army to avoid frostbite. In a similar manner gunshot wounds were frozen and the progress of necrosis observed.

The effect of vacuums was also tested on prisoners, the intention being to understand what might happen during high-altitude depressurization. Prisoners were electrocuted, drowned, scalded, boiled alive, or slowly desiccated in ovens. They were shot, made to breathe smoke or poison gas, or exposed to massive doses of radiation. They were given full transfusions of horse blood to see if this could provide a plentiful supply for surgical units on the front line. Nerves and arteries were severed, air and urine injected into veins. The stiff-backed officers and smiling medical men in the parade-ground photographs of Unit 731's staff noted down the results of the experiments in grim detail. When they had finished, the day's quota of dead bodies was incinerated and they returned home to their submissive, kimonoed wives and uniformed children in the village built for them nearby.

As the war in the Pacific swung violently against Japan, Unit 731 looked at means of using biological weapons on the US Army, but on the day after the destruction of Hiroshima Soviet troops crossed into Manchuguo and the commanders at Pingfang ordered that the camp be razed. The buildings were dynamited, the surviving prisoners gassed, poisoned or shot and their bodies hurriedly burned in the incinerator or in shallow pits. The soldiers of Unit 731 fled as had the Nazis from Belsen and Treblinka. By the time Hirohito broadcast Japan's surrender to his people, the unit had been all but obliterated. The Soviet Army that occupied Manchuria until the PLA came to liberate it in 1948 demolished much of what was left. At the end of the exhibition, a panel noted that the Japanese government had always denied that Unit 731 had existed, in the same way that it still denied that Japanese troops had massacred Chinese civilians when they took Nanjing. It also charged the Allies with complicity in using the results of the experiments in their own weapons programmes after the war, in much the same way that data from the defeated Germans' V2 programme had helped put America on the moon.

The town of Pingfang had grown up on and around the remains of the camp. It was an averagely unlovely Chinese straggle of cheap noodle shops, minor-league investment banks and small manufactories belching smoke. They ran in a straight line where the southern perimeter wall of the camp had once stood. At what had been the only entrance, a squat sentry house built of white breeze blocks survived, sandwiched uncomplainingly between blocks of flats. Washing was hung out to dry on wooden poles from row upon row of windows, hanging down like funerary banners in the still, cold air. Gangs of labourers leaned on their pickaxes or brought their wheelbarrows to a stop as I picked my way across the rubble and entered the camp.

Men were laying a granite pathway from Xinjiang Road to the door of Unit 731's administrative building. A young boy wearing an orange hard hat several sizes too big for him was cementing a stone plaque into a wall. It outlined the history of the camp in a matter-of-fact way. The administrative building too bore a plaque, explaining how it was here that the Japanese had superintended the unit's work. It had been dynamited when they ran away, but its ruins had been restored and the workmanlike sound of hammering and sawing was audible from within. Demolition and reconstruction had done the task of cleansing, and, instead of sensing an air of evil about this building as I had anticipated, I found it looked like any one of thousands from China's Republican era, with its sloping, tiled roof-line and thin, white-mortared bricks. If it was hiding its past, it was doing so more as a taciturn youth than as a tight-lipped war criminal.

A few acres of land in a broad square had been cleared of post-war buildings, and a mesh fence had been erected at the perimeter where the rampart had once stood. The camp was being turned into a place of pilgrimage. Where Japanese and Russian demolition gangs had levelled the main buildings above ground, the rich soil had been excavated in deep, sloping pits to reveal their maze of surviving basements and foundations. Their banks had been returfed in soft greens, and landscaped paths snaked from one to the next. I stood and stared at one pit in particular. Red-brick walls rose waist-high from a floor of mortar and tiles. I could trace the passageways where prisoners were led after being infected, and the confined cells where they were watched in their death throes. At one end of the remains the wall turned in an amputated semicircle like the apse of a Norman church.

Other structures had survived above ground. One, the Consumptive Diseases Laboratory, was a spiteful little building that slunk behind a tall fence. A single iron door barred the only way in or out, and it was windowless save for two small grilles. Two tall chimneys had survived the destruction of the power plant and now adhered to an isolated slab of mustard-coloured masonry that soared arrogantly in defiance of gravity. Square, gaping holes yawned in its smooth surface, and twisted metal fittings stuck out at tortured, rusting angles where the demolition charges had ripped through them. For a while I could not place where I had seen something similar before, and then I remembered footage of torn factories after the atom bomb had been dropped on Hiroshima. Beyond it lay the Frostbite Research Building and the Animal Breeding Plant, and the remnants of the Poison Gas Production Plant were hidden in the backyard of an anonymous workshop.

I kicked through the weeds and debris that still clogged an unreconstructed corner of the camp and came out behind the administration block. One half of it had become a school. Children in white shirts and blue shorts ran laughing after one another in a boisterous playground exorcism.

Qiqiha'er

Back in Harbin that evening, every new turn in the road brought me face to face with a different aspect of Europe: now there were the fish-scale tiles of a Viennese apartment block, now the ramshackle factories and smokestacks of Industrial Revolution Coalbrookdale. The granite-faced old dowagers of London's Square Mile, the Mersey and the Huangpu looked disapprovingly down on teenage girls in revealing tops and miniskirts. Long-haired boys hung in knots around the entrances to underground discos, passing cigarettes back and forth with furtive cool.

What I wanted, however, was information on Mohe. The travel agent's office looked promising – it was well stocked with information on transport throughout Heilongjiang and farther afield, and its walls displayed gaudy posters of tourist attractions and details on how to reach them – but the teenage girl behind the desk was clueless.

'I want to go to Mohe.'

She was unsure where precisely Mohe was, so I pointed to it on a map on the wall behind her.

'You want to go all the way up *there*?' She put a hand to her mouth and giggled nervously. Figuring that, since I was there, I might as well see if she knew anything about travel permits, I asked about those too.

A travel permit? She decided to play for time rather than admit that she had not the first idea about travel permits to Mohe, whether I needed one, how I would apply, or from where. Swinging her shoulders to and fro, one finger between her front teeth and her eyes directed at the ceiling, like a school-girl who has been asked an uncomfortable question and hopes the teacher will give up before she does, she reached for the telephone and held it to her ear. She dialled, waited and then began to talk: '*Wei?* Do you know anything about travel permits for *waiguoren* to Mohe? No? Thanks anyway.' But I had seen her surreptitiously place a finger on the hook after dialling.

'Sorry but they don't know.' She held her hands together behind her back and looked pleased that it was now not her fault.

The Public Security Bureau officers flicked through my passport with interest and laughed at my photograph, but they found nothing in it that would tell them whether or not Mohe was *kaifang*. They recommended I try the military district office – the army was officially in charge of international borders. There I found a pleasant Mongolian restaurant and an Internet café whose thirty terminals were all occupied by teenage boys playing wargames, but nobody could tell me the status of their most northerly village. I decided to wait until I got to Qiqiha'er.

On my way back to my hotel, in a small square on Warp and Weft Street, I discovered the most fascinating statue in China. A larger-than-life model of a smiling woman in wellington boots, wearing a headscarf and proudly clutching her broom, had been erected by Harbin Municipal Council to commemorate all the city's cleaning workers. An inscription explained how 'each one of those who spend a lifetime in dirt so that ten thousand might enjoy a life of cleanliness' had been honoured: in Harbin, 26 October had been declared the day of the Hygiene Operative Festival.

The female washroom was across the corridor from my hotel room. The door had been left open, revealing a pair of pale Russian girls – human flotsam from the failed empire across the Amur – preparing for a night's work. One applied a thick cake of lipstick and unsubtle crescents of midnight-blue eye-shadow. The other stood before the mirror, her sleeveless top hitched up around her lovebitten neck, scrubbing at her bare breasts with a flannel. As I watched television I heard them proposition guests in a heavily accented, grammarless Mandarin. At around eleven I was woken by the phone and the inevitable invitation to take a massage. In the dead of night I was woken again by a vivid dream that a woman was at the foot of my bed, rummaging through my bag.

My room overlooked the long-distance bus station, and it was there the following day that I boarded a coach bound for the city of Qiqiha'er in the west of the province, near its border with Inner Mongolia. I had heard that from Qiqiha'er I could catch a train that would take me the final 600 miles north to the town of Xilinji, from where it was just 50 miles cross-country to Mohe and the Amur.

A light drizzle speckled the coach's windows as we crossed the Sungari. North of the river, the city struggled feebly to overcome the flat emptiness of the Manchurian plain and then vanished. From Harbin to Qiqiha'er the highway would cross from the floodplain of the Sungari to that of the Nonni, on which Qiqiha'er stood. The landscape might have been that of Poland or northern Germany, a carpet of rich, dark soil, the *chernozem* of European Russia, turned even blacker by the steady rain and the absence of the sun. The fields were large and practical, combed in tight lines for planting. Even in late May, here in the cold north of China the soil had only recently thawed sufficiently for ploughing and sowing to take place, and the first shoots of the crop were just showing.

'Wheat and soybeans,' the man sitting beside me remarked when he saw how intently I was watching the fields. Soybeans had always been the major crop of Manchuria. At the height of foreign involvement in Harbin, nearly all the world's soybean oil was produced in its mills, ending up as varnish on the hulls of ships from Shanghai to New York and as soap in baths from Beijing to Paris. 'It's been a very cold winter this year, everything is slower in the countryside.'

It looked lovely to me, this familiar earth. It was not the stunted pine-clad granite of the East China Sea, nor the precarious lushness of the tropics, nor the desert scree of Xinjiang. It was honest, hardworking, unchanging farmland. I daydreamed that the murky figures leading their teams of draught-horses spoke with Yorkshire accents. As the drizzle hardened into a steady rain, their thatched villages shimmered and disappeared behind the wet glass.

I awoke as we were leaving the town of Lindian, Forested Domain, brought round by the crump of our suspension on the rock-strewn road. The rain had moved north to leave a blue sky overhead. Lit by the midday sun, the retreating black storm-clouds towered over the grassland like a range of mountains. Herds of sheep grazed at their feet. Nearer to Qiqiha'er the land began to ripple, and crystal-clear water threw splashes of light on to blankets of tall, yellow reeds. Cranes and ducks flew off as we neared their hideaways. But as we approached the city the landscape became drier and the rich depth of the soil faded to a washed-out beige.

In the language of the Daur, the natives of this corner of Heilongjiang, Qiqiha'er means natural pasture. It was easy to see why. Now the fringes of nomadic Inner Mongolia began to make their presence felt as the horizon broadened and the few remaining trees drew back to reveal an arid grassland extending all the way to a circle of blue sky.

Qiqiha'er came as a surprise. I had expected to find a grim, rust-belt museum-piece of Soviet housing blocks and despairing people. Instead I discovered an ostensibly well-dressed, bustling city. Its railway station was a classic of art deco appropriated by communism: lines of characters above its crenellations read 'Long live the Chinese Communist Party!' and 'Long live Mao Zedong thought!' Such physical reminders of the time before China's opening-up are rare nowadays. In the plot of landscaped gardens facing them, the late Deng Xiaoping looked down from an enormous, chrome-edged billboard, the unlikely successor to the big-character posters of the sixties, declaring his maxim that 'Development is the sole hard rationality'. Between ranks of department stores and privately owned shops a six-lane highway led to the centre of town. A few buses and taxis slid down its broad expanse of tarmac. Along the pavement, people had set up stalls selling fruit and vegetables, clothes and electrical hardware.

Every aspect of China's consumer boom was on show here, from a Kentucky Fried Chicken franchise to advertisements for Volkswagen cars and Italian clothing brands, and of course the now ubiquitous *wangbas* or Internet cafés, dance halls and karaoke lounges. A harlequin's coat of mobile phone and life insurance logos was draped over every storefront and footbridge. Qiqiha'er's middle classes were tempted into buying home furnishings by pretty girls with wasp waists and airbrushed smiles. Its teenagers wore the same blue jeans pictured on the enormous, neon-framed hoardings above their heads. Young men in Hawaiian shirts had grown their hair long and had tied it back in pendulous ponytails. Their girlfriends peered at the one foreign male in town over the rims of their orange-tinted spectacles and toyed flirtaciously with their pigtails. Other girls sat on roadside benches, their high-heeled legs crossed, and pretended to flick through their style magazines as they watched him struggle with his rucksack. They read the same titles as had Gistlaine in Sanya. On the fringes of the Inner Mongolian desert the youth of Qiqiha'er were outwardly exactly like the youth of Beijing, Hainan or Shanghai.

Heilongjiang has a lower population density than most parts of eastern China – just 80 people per square kilometre compared with Shanghai's 2,300 or more – and perhaps it was for that reason that the inhabitants of Qiqiha'er seemed more respectful of others' privacy. I had become used to the unremitting stares of the big city that strip away your individuality and reduce you to a pair of blue eyes and a big nose. Here, however, the locals confined themselves to mumbled misidentifications, the anachronistic *Sulianren* – a Soviet – voiced amongst the universal assumption that I was an *Eluosiren*, a Russian.

The woman in the run-down café took her only customer in her stride, placing before me a small dish of pickled, shredded cabbage and a pair of disposable chopsticks before disappearing to fetch a plate of steamed pork dumplings and a bowl of pig's blood soup.

'So where are you from? *Sulianren?* What are you doing in Qiqiha'er?' I explained that I was on my way to Mohe, and her eyes widened slightly.

'Why do you want to go to Mohe? There's nothing there. You'd be better off going to Harbin.'

I polished off a dumpling moistened in the oily surface of the soup. 'I've just come from Harbin. What about Qiqiha'er – what is there to see here?'

'There's nothing in Qiqiha'er either.'

'There must be something – a museum, a park?'

'If you're desperate there's Dragon Sands. It has a zoo, or you can hire a rowing-boat and land on one of the islands in the lake. You tend to get a lot of couples there in the summer, but it's still a little cold right now.' She stopped and thought. 'Mohe? But it's so remote . . .', as if Qiqiha'er was the hub of the universe.

The soldier guarding the door to the Public Security Bureau building fingered the muzzle of an ancient-looking rifle. He snapped his free arm out horizontally in the direction of a stairwell and barked a room number. The room was warm, heated by a paraffin stove in its centre, but otherwise contained only a leather sofa hardened and flaking from years of use and a wooden desk. Behind this sat a woman in her forties whose job it was to allot travel permits to foreigners. I didn't imagine she had much to do. She beckoned to me to sit, and the sofa creaked and complained under my unexpected weight.

'Why do you want to go to Mohe?' she asked coldly. She opened a drawer as I began to babble out the justification that I had been rehearsing, and pulled out a file. Down one side of it were listed place-names.

'It's . . . it's the most northerly village in China. I've already been to Shengshan – it's an island . . . in Zhejiang – and then I went to Jinmujiao. You probably don't know the name, but it's actually the southernmost point of your honourable country. Apart from the Zengmu Shoals. Oh, oh . . . and Shengshan is the easternmost . . .' Thankfully she cut me short.

'Mohe county is actually *bu kaifang*, but we are currently issuing border permits to aliens for short visits. Fill in this form.' She handed me a sheet of paper and a pen and left the room. When she returned she took the form, asked for a 50 *renminbi* fee and gave me in exchange a small booklet of insubstantial green card that read Aliens' Travel Permit. Inside, the circular red inkstamp of the Qiqiha'er City Public Security Bureau Alien Affairs Office hovered in non-negotiable confirmation of my itinerary above two cursive, handwritten characters – *mò hé* – Silent River. Both of them possessed the three tiny strokes that together symbolize 'water' in Chinese script. Water, residing in the north, governed the breath of winter. The Amur. I had been given four days to cover the final 650 miles.

The air of decay that I had expected to sense in the city of Qiqiha'er hung thickly over Dragon Sands Park. The stallholders selling ice cream and soft drinks outnumbered the visitors, and they sat huddled inside quilted jackets from which poked puffy fingers and rank cigarettes. Physical Labour Lake, a dammed section of the Nonni River, was being dredged, its water drained to leave only a black, stinking slime speckled with patches of green algae. The half dozen islands where, come the warmer weather, courting couples would row ashore to mate, were left marooned in the mud. The boats were turned turtle on the stony shore, lined up and shrouded in tarpaulins that at a distance made them resemble flag-draped coffins.

I climbed the artificial hill at the heart of the park. Perhaps it was the cold wind or the clouds threatening rain that made the park seem so sombre that afternoon. It must have been something external, because my stomach still turned cartwheels every time I slid a hand into my coat pocket to finger my travel permit. I had been unable to buy a ticket north to Xilinji on the day the permit was issued – the only train had already left – and now, the following day, I was still stranded in Qiqiha'er because that day's train was full. However, I had managed a ticket for noon the next day. If I spent one night in Xilinji I should still be able to reach Mohe before the permit ran out, I reasoned. And if I was still there when it became invalid, the worst the army could do was fine me and send me back to Qiqiha'er. I felt the permit again to reassure myself.

In the middle distance, the Nonni River was visible in short, silvery bursts between low-rise apartment blocks and factories as it straggled across its floodplain. The Daur, inhabitants of the plain formed by the Nonni and its tributaries, once believed that Birge, the river goddess, resided in its depths and guaranteed plentiful fish. The river used to breach its banks regularly and catastrophically once every thirteen years. In 1932, in a petulant dismissal of the power of the newly established puppet state of Manchuguo, it inundated thousands of square miles of farmland and drowned countless villages. When the communists arrived they proved a point by building defences against further inundations. As the land had been conquered, so had the river.

Now the Nonni had shied into its flat landscape, and from ground level it was almost invisible. I picked my way over hummocks of soft grass, through stands of birch saplings, past the tarpaulin bivouacs and smouldering fires of vagrants' encampments. The clayey hummocks gave way to sandy dunes held together by rhizomes of tough grass. A herd of goats grazed on paper bags trapped by their dense stems. Couples kissed in tight, emotionless embraces in the lee of the larger dunes, but I failed to notice the pair I almost trod on. The woman let out an embarrassed squeal, hitched up her stockings, and ran off behind her unchivalrous lover who had bolted as soon as he saw me. The Nonni itself was in subdued mood that day, slowly meandering over its sandbanks, bringing the distant headwaters of the Hingan Mountains to lay them as a glittering tribute there at my feet.

Missionaries were amongst the earliest Europeans to set foot in the nomadic fringes of Heilongjiang. In 1876, Dr Hunter of the Irish Presbyterian Church spent three months making the arduous 2,000-mile overland journey from the Church's Manchurian foothold at Yingkou in Liaoning to the banks of the Amur in Heilongjiang's far north. There he spent a night with a Chinese whom he was overjoyed to discover was already well versed in Christian doctrine, the Orthodox Church having reached the far bank of the Amur across Siberia on the backs of trappers and explorers.

St Michael's Cathedral sat isolated amidst Qiqiha'er's crumbling backstreets, at the end of a row of Muslim restaurants run by Tungans from Lanzhou. It had been proudly constructed by a Swedish missionary in 1931 in that interwar style thought modern at the time, but its reinforced concrete had aged into ugly utilitarianism. Since the laws on religious worship in China require that churches be locked other than on Sundays lest Christians cease to regard the Party as omnipotent, its front gate had been padlocked. However, somebody had forgotten to push the bolt home, and when I touched the gate it swung ajar and I entered the grounds.

A side entrance to the cathedral had also been left open, and from behind the vestry door came the muffled sound of voices. Outside it had begun to drizzle, but the glass in the long, narrow windows was blue, and here indoors the effect was of crystalline, airy clarity.

The interior was stark, its lofty nave accompanied on either hand by tall aisles in which all lines met at the comfortless right angles that their building materials dictated. The light fittings were brass-framed panels of frosted glass, and the white, coffered ceiling had been painted in dirty pastels – pink, yellow and lime green, the tatty luxuries of a soft-class waiting-room. The floor of the nave was of polished wood, stained blood red, the pews green. On the altar-cloth were embroidered a golden alpha and omega. From the ceiling to either side hung long silk banners like those in the temples of Putuoshan, only here they proclaimed Christian truths. On the walls the Stations of the Cross were depicted in a naïve hand. A chime of footsteps on stone carried lightly from the far end of the cathedral. They approached me as I pretended to study a painting of Simon the Cyrenean helping Jesus to bear the cross, and I turned around to face them, expecting to be ejected. A young man with closely shaven hair looked into my eyes.

'Are you a believer?' he asked. I nodded.

'I'm afraid I'm not a practising Catholic,' I added.

He smiled. 'There are many denominations, but only one Yesu Jidu, is that not right?' His words came unnaturally, as though he were repeating a phrase learned by heart. His eyes shone with the enthusiasm of the convert, eager to believe and to communicate his new-found faith. Although he looked to be in his mid-thirties, he wore the clothes of an older man: a white shirt, pinstriped in thin brown lines and yellowed through years of wear, its collar a little frayed where it had rubbed against his pasty neck, a sleeveless pullover of mottled browns and polyester slacks. He had been making do while the rest of Qiqiha'er had been buying new outfits for itself.

'Are you a priest here?' I asked.

'No, no – a member of the congregation.' He turned to indicate the door through which he had entered the nave. 'I help to maintain the church, clean up, things like that.' He looked at the floor and the conversation stalled.

'So, is the congregation here large? There are lots of seats,' I commented. He looked up and spread his hands wide, conjuring up a throng of believers.

'Every Sunday the pews are full, and on feast days people stand in the aisles to hear the Word. We recently celebrated the Annunciation of the Blessed Virgin. On Fridays our priest hears confession.' He could probably have recited the entire church calendar to me had I asked him, but I wanted to know how he had come to be here.

'How does the church find its members? On the streets?' He shook his head roughly.

'We would feel too embarrassed. Chinese people would laugh if you just walked up to them and said "Excuse me, there is no such god as Buddha – there is only one God, and he died on the cross for you." Our society is not ready to accept such a straightforward declaration as that. We attract new believers mainly through friends and family who already believe. You cannot make people believe, it must come from within them. It's a long process.' I edged along the pews and stopped in front of a painting of Veronica wiping Yesu Jidu's face.

'Are you allowed to go out on the streets to attract new members?' I asked. He faltered and avoided the question.

'I . . . would feel too embarrassed. The people who worship here are of all ages. Children generally come through their parents. Some older people come because they have heard from members what our church can offer spiritually. Many of them are in despair.' I turned from the painting to face him.

'In despair?'

'Our social situation here in Qiqiha'er is very bleak, you understand. We all say that the government is good, but we all know that it's not true. The adult unemployment rate is sixty per cent in the city.'

'Sixty?!' It seemed impossibly high. Was he sure? He formed his right hand into the sign for six – thumb and little finger spread wide apart, the remaining three fingers tucked against his palm – and then clenched his hand into a fist to indicate ten. Six tens. Sixty. Despite the unmistakable clarity of his gesture, I still found it hard to believe. Surely no society could operate with so much unemployment?

'There's no social security net anymore, no iron rice bowl for workers. Qiqiha'er is an industrial city. The Party established heavy industry here after Liberation – vehicle plants, machine-tool factories, steelworks – but the reforms made them uneconomic. The workers were laid off, and now they rely on family or on odd jobs. You must have seen them on the streets, selling whatever they can. They have to make money somehow.'

'Work hard today, or work even harder finding work tomorrow?' I suggested, echoing the slogan I had seen everywhere.

He shook his head. 'These are men who, no matter how hard they might have worked, would still have been laid off. We're told that we're now free to move around to find our own work, but we're not free to say we don't like things the way they are. What kind of freedom is that?' I did not ask, but presumed that he himself was one who had come in despair.

China abhors a vacuum. Once you walk off the main streets of Qiqiha'er you find yourself in a low-rise grid of block housing, constructed after Liberation for the heavy industrial workers allotted jobs in the city's new factories. The questionable freedom to be one's own *laoban* has filled the blocks at street level with every sort of enterprise: kindergartens, travel agents, restaurants, snack shops, door after door bearing the fluorescent *wangba* characters of an Internet café, beauty parlours filled with lounging girls in miniskirts and stockings. The pavements are dotted with extemporized stalls: the flat backs of tricycle carts that serve as mobile shop windows for vegetable sellers and

hawkers of socks, combs and old ladies' bloomers; the un-
employed housewives who will throw together an egg pancake
for a few *mao* or the hunched old man who mumbles through
his whiskers and guards his saucepan of soy-braised eggs and glu-
tinous rice dumplings as though their sale is all that keeps him
from destitution. One up from the limbless beggar, balanced on
his bamboo highchair, are the vagrants who have spread their
wares out in neat rows on a square of blanket. They will mercilessly overcharge you. A reel of sticky tape will cost 5 *mao*, new
batteries for your shortwave radio a few *kuai*. They notice your
watchstrap is close to breaking and offer to replace it. They sell
you a recycled coffee jar with string tied around the neck for a
kuai – you can drink from it on your train journey. You have your
fortune told by the physiognomist who sits with a palm sketched
on a piece of torn card before his feet. You weigh yourself for 2
mao on a boy's bathroom scales, and he pockets the flimsy note
with its smiling portraits of costumed minorities and carries on
staring up at you.

Back on the main road you pass a shovel gang on a building
site. They are not the whiskery, migrant peasants of the coastal
cities but clean-shaven, pale-skinned, middle-aged men. Ex-
factory workers. You feel ashamed that you had not noticed
them there before.

XILINJI

THE NONNI HAD bled out across its floodplain into a lazy tangle
of channels and streams that reflected the vast white canopy of
the sky. It seemed that the river had inhaled from the fields as it
rolled south from the mountains, taking from them a little of
their earth-bound solidity and breathing back into them something of its own nature, until land and water appeared to meld
into each other and the river seemed less to flow over the earth

than to be indivisible from it. The railway shied away from the bleak foothills of the Mongolian grassland on the western horizon and struck out instead over the rivulets of the Nemor and the Laolai. There were few trees, the only splashes of colour on the landscape's watery palette that afternoon the plants that accompanied the train north: the purple of willow-herb, buddleia's lilac spurs, the delicate white of jasmines and honeysuckles, stands of white and pink dog-rose and yellow bursts of what looked like furze. Kestrels hovered high above the trackside, the only human figures the hunched forms of the distant chain gang that swung their picks in a forlorn percussion.

The train was elderly, living out the remainder of its days plying the lumber trail between Xilinji and Qiqiha'er. Its carriages were of the vintage once found on all China's routes, their wooden surfaces darkened through decades of dirt and grease into a shiny black, their mite-ridden bunks suspended on crumbling leather straps and their toilets just faeces-smeared holes in the floor. When at dusk the lights were switched on they emitted only a pallid glow beneath which the passengers craned over their newspapers.

The plain narrowed and rose perceptibly as the Lesser and Greater Hingan ranges pressed in from both sides. I was disappointed not to see for myself the villages of the Daur, those stocky Altaic hunters who had turned away from Birge the river goddess, from Bainabi the spirit of the forest and from Bonacha who would grant them success in their hunting, and who had taken to planting beans and tending fields of millet. At Nenjiang, Delicate River, the tracks made a decisive thrust westward towards the rail junction of Jagdachi. We crossed the middle reaches of the Nonni one final time, its writhing water briefly visible in the patch of dim light cast from our windows, and thereby passed from the historic homeland of the Manchus to that of the Mongols. At Dayangshu, Big Poplar Tree, heartland of the Oroqen people, the last of the cold day faded into night.

*

The Records of the Grand Historian, a work completed in the first century BC and covering the period from high antiquity down to 95 BC, includes in its biography of Confucius the legend of the Sushen arrow.

In 496 BC, Duke Min of the feudal state of Chen was in his palace when an osprey, run clean through by an arrow, dropped dead at his feet. The shaft of the arrow, whittled from a thorn bush, was red, while the head was of blue flint. The Duke sent for Confucius and consulted him on the arrow's provenance. Confucius said that the osprey must have come from far off, for the arrow was crafted by the Sushen who lived on the Sungari River.

'In ancient times,' he explained, 'when King Wu had defeated the Shang, he opened up channels to the barbarians on all sides of his realm. Of each he ordered that they send as tribute a treasure native to their region. With this, the Sushen presented King Wu with such an arrow as this, its shaft eighteen inches long and with a head of hard, blue Sungari stone.'

The Sushen were the ancestors of the Jurchen, a nomadic tribe of the Ever White Mountains who remained unsinicized on the remote upper reaches of the Yalu River. As the Ming dynasty's control of China dwindled in the twilight of the sixteenth century, a man named Aisin Goro Nurhaci came to prominence in this tribal border region as head of a political union called the Jianzhou Federation, a grouping of not just Jurchen but also Mongols and Han. He created the myth of Manchu identity, placing himself firmly at the head of a military force into which anybody could buy entry, and in doing so title himself a Manchu, as long as he promised Nurhaci and his federation unquestioning allegiance. Nurhaci granted the Manchus' spoken language official status and gave it an alphabetic script. Based on that of the closely related Mongolian tongue, the Manchu script derived ultimately from the writing systems of Aramaic and Semitic three millennia earlier. The Manchus' vertical squiggles were by design very different to the written characters of the Chinese subjects whom they were shortly to conquer.

In 1616 Nurhaci declared himself Great Ancestor – first emperor – of a new dynasty he called the Later Jin, borrowing the name from the Jin dynasty that had been founded by a branch of sinicized Jurchen some five centuries earlier. Nurhaci's dynasty, structured on the bureaucratic model which had proved so enduringly successful for the Chinese to the south, based itself on the paramountcy of the Aisin Goro clan and on the *realpolitik* that any political partnership would be acceptable if it helped the Later Jin to win control over China as a whole. The transfer of power in 1626 to Nurhaci's eighth son, Aisin Goro Abahai, set the pattern for the next 300 years: all ten rulers of Abahai's Manchurian dynasty were from the same clan. When the last Manchu emperor Henry Puyi abdicated the imperial Chinese throne in 1912, he would end an uninterrupted period of rule in which the Aisin Goro clan had been the embodiment of Manchu identity.

In 1636, Abahai renamed Nurhaci's Later Jin dynasty, giving it the dynastic title Qing. He well understood the political significance of the change: according to the Five Elements Theory, metal produces water. *Jin* means 'metal', while the written character *qing* – 'purity' – has as its signifying component the three short strokes of 'water': so the Later Jin produced the Qing. The written character *ming* – 'brightness' – the name of the ruling Chinese dynasty at the time, possessed the signifying component for 'sun': as fire was conquered by water, so the Ming were to be conquered by the Qing. Within a decade of changing their dynastic name from Jin to Qing, the Manchus had declared themselves the Heaven-appointed rulers of China. Remnants of the Ming held out in the south, but by 1661 the embers of China's last native Chinese dynasty had been extinguished.

But if the Qing Manchus' northern identity and the idea of

an ethnically unique Manchuria was a politically inspired fiction, it was to be a remarkably resilient one. It entered Western consciousness most notably in the guise of Fu Manchu, a scheming Manchurian plotting world domination, who became the embodiment of the Yellow Peril. Long before the fictional Fu Manchu, however, the Qing had manufactured a Manchu cultural identity where none existed. The Manchu nation traced its genesis to the shores of the Lake of Heaven in the Ever White Mountains. There, a fairy maiden descended from the sky and ate a red berry brought to her by a golden bird. She became pregnant and bore a boy who could speak from the moment he entered the world. She named him Aisin Goro.

As it became increasingly distanced from its roots in the Ever White Mountains, the Qing court reached a crisis of legitimacy: if its élite was to insist on the uniqueness of the Manchu right to rule the Chinese people, requiring that the succession be through the Manchurian Aisin Goro clan alone, it had to show that its ethnic inheritance was both thriving and genuinely different from that of the Han. As a result a hotchpotch of traits associated with the nomadic roots of the Aisin Goro clan were given the status of cultural markers.

To begin with, the north-eastern provinces were declared to be a pure Manchurian homeland and were sealed off by a wooden pale to prevent contamination from China proper. Shamanism, the socially acceptable face of losing one's mind in the icy wastes of the taiga, was given a formal structure and canonical books, and the Emperor took part in its stage-managed religious ceremonies. Everyday practices amongst the people of the north-east took on a defining significance. The Chinese joked about the Manchurians' inveterate love of tobacco, which extended to all ages and both sexes, and about their babies' cradles, always suspended in mid-air from a rafter in the house as a reminder of how nomads would keep new-born babies out of the reach of hungry wolves. A legend telling how Nurhaci had, while fighting the Ming, been rescued by a dog from a burning reed bed was cited to explain the Manchu's irrational objection to eating dogmeat, a culinary favourite amongst the Han. According to the legend, the dog had wetted its fur and rolled over and over on the burning reeds to extinguish them, dying in the process.

The Manchus' insistence that they were culturally distinct from their subjects was used against them when the Qing were called to account for the turmoil of the closing decades of their reign. In the atmosphere of impotent stagnation and popular revolution that characterized the late nineteenth century, the Chinese took up the Manchus' banner of Manchu otherness to justify their overthrow, and their dynasty was made the scapegoat for the ills that afflicted all of China. (Interestingly, less than twenty years after the establishment of the Republic of China by the Cantonese Sun Yat-sen, the cry had changed: Japan's annexation of Manchuria in 1932 demanded that the region be regarded not as the ethnically distinct homeland of a foreign dynasty but as an inalienable part of Chinese territory that had been stolen.)

During the final years of the Qing, Manchuria fell under the influence of Russia. Yet though the Russians built the Chinese Eastern Railway they contrived to keep the region economically backward, as had the Qing before them. The Russians wanted Manchuria to remain in a colonial relationship to them, a market for their manufactures – ironmongery, industrial plant, medicines, cloth, paper – and a producer of the raw materials – primarily coal, oil and grain – which Russia required in exchange.

Russia's sphere of influence in Manchuria was to prove short-lived. The Great War and the October Revolution left Russia's economy hamstrung, and as its star waned in the east so Japan's rose to take its place. Japan similarly had little interest in colonizing Manchuria with Japanese civilians, but it did rely on Manchuria's otherness for the legitimacy of its rule there. Its establishment of the puppet state of Manchuguo in 1932, with the resurrected Qing emperor Henry Puyi at its head but with real power resting with the Japanese army, made of Manchuria a colonial producer, providing Japan with raw materials as it had Russia. Here in China's great north-east it seemed that, to justify their various ends, whoever controlled Manchuria was reliant on the fiction, conceived centuries earlier in the Ever White Mountains of Jilin, of an autochthonous homeland for the Manchu people. Everybody had an agenda requiring Manchuria's independence from the rest of China.

Only with Liberation was the spell of Manchuria's otherness broken, and Manchus became just another of China's fifty-five ethnic minorities. Today the Manchu language survives only amongst the few thousand Xibo people of Xinjiang, said to be the descendants of Manchu troops sent to the New Frontier under the Qing. Nurhaci's alphabetic script, in which the Middle Kingdom's official documents were for centuries written, can now be found only amongst the dusty strings of Chinese cash sometimes sold in junk shops. How the mighty have fallen.

The man in the opposite bunk blinked the sleep from his eyes, raised his weight on one elbow, cleared his throat noisily and leaned out over the scarlet linoleum of the floor to expectorate a long strand of mucus. Then he lit a cigarette and drew deeply on it before noticing that I too was awake. He held the pack out to me.

'Harbin cigarettes – the best tobacco in China,' he enthused, pointing to his chest and adding 'I'm *Manzu* – Manchu – where are you from? Xinjiang?'

In the darkness we had crossed an invisible watershed. At the height of the Yilehuli Mountains, at a settlement named Taiyanggou, Sun's Furrow, the tracks had performed a brief oxbow loop and the train had passed back into Manchuria. From now on we would be descending toward the Amur.

It was barely 4 a.m. but the sky was already light. The glass of the windows had frosted over during the night, and icy ferns now grew in delicate bracts from the wooden frame. Clearing a peep-hole with a sleeve I looked out on a world unrecognizable from that which we had left at nightfall. The Pagoda River danced along at our heels, now to our right, now to our left, a joyous stream bubbling and chuckling above the soft click-clack of the wheels as though eager to show us the way to the Black Dragon. The forest floor was light brown, shards of shale cracked and splin-tered by an eternity of freezes and thaws. Above it the colours of new growth were velvet greens, and above these the sky was the most beautiful of blues. Bushes burning with purple flowers car-peted the riverbanks. Now and again the forest parted to reveal clearings whose hollows trapped the pure white of a snowdrift, or was sliced deeply by a sudden turn in the river to reveal the club-feet of its ice-bound roots, or slumped down exhausted and receded into the distance where a mountain top would be crowned by grasses. I sat, my hands clasped around my coffee jar of hot tea for warmth, as the whistle-stop names of the logging stations counted down the remaining miles to Xilinji: Sea of Trees, New Forest, Sing Loud Working Area, Beautiful Countenance Working Area, Wealth and Happiness. Each was nothing more than a handful of shacks constructed from oddments of planking, like the abandoned Wild West towns of the movies, only much shabbier and dirtier. The ground around them was bare earth, patches of mange eating into the thick mane of the taiga. Makeshift corrals held a sorry-looking donkey or a few chickens.

I told the Manchu I was English. Was he headed for Xilinji?

'We're getting off at Powerful Wave Township. We're assigned to a logging station up north, but we're stopping off to do some work first.' He pointed to the berths above our heads, where two mounds of duvet snored contentedly. Finishing his cigarette he joined them, and presently I pulled the tattered curtain to and lay back down to sleep.

I woke again in the late morning. The blue sky had been replaced by a blanket of damp mist that swirled amongst the trackside larches. My companions were awake and sat slurping noodles from steel billycans. The train was stationary, motionless on the edge of some nameless halt. The shriek of a whistle, and the diesel engine of a lumber train slid past, followed by a procession of open wagons on which were piled the straight, brown trunks of trees, each two feet thick, their few side branches closely cropped and their bark stripped away.

'Larch,' one commented.

'And birch,' added the Manchu.

The wagons trundled by the window for a few minutes until finally the guard's van disappeared behind us and our train heaved back into life.

'How much forest was there on that train just then?' I asked the Manchu. He looked to his colleagues.

'About . . . 2,000 *mu*, wouldn't you say?' They nodded silently in agreement. Three hundred acres on the back of a single train. For the final sixty miles until we reached Xilinji we passed half a dozen such trains, each one as long as the first. How many had we passed in the night?

'How long did they take to grow?' I asked. He held his hands out as if to grasp a two-foot trunk.

'So big? Say . . . a century? Not less than seventy or eighty years. The cold around here means you only get good growth in late spring and summer, but you also get good, strong timber, with tight rings.' He seemed pleased by the quality of the timber we had seen. One of his companions had remained taciturn, staring from the window as we crept down the wooded slope. Now he addressed me.

'What thoughts go through your head when you see all that timber on those trains?' I was unsure how to answer. They were all three of them professional lumberjacks.

'It's a shame to see all this forest being chopped down, but presumably the trees are replanted.' I had decided to hedge my bets. 'What do they use them for?'

'That depends on the species: paper, telegraph poles, disposable chopsticks . . . It's all Russian timber.'

'Russian?'

'We work for a Sino-Russian company. We cross the Amur up where the Argun and the Shilka meet, drive fifty miles into the forest, chop the trees down and send them back to China. I don't like doing it. You should see the mess we leave. These trees take decades to grow; you can't just replant them and expect everything to be all right. I feel we're taking advantage of the Russians: they need the money and they're less strict about uncontrolled logging. They don't agree with me, do you?' He smiled sheepishly at his colleagues.

'I've a family to support. I'm glad of the income,' said the Manchu.

West of Changyingzhen – Long Tassel Township – the forest thinned. Though there was much new growth, the embankments that had been held together by the forest's roots higher up the valley here had eroded and collapsed. Stumps of trees were scattered amongst the saplings, charred root balls protruding from the beige scree. The shy man pointed.

'In 1987 there was a forest fire – it incinerated everything from Mohe all the way up the valley to Long Tassel. The forest regenerates, but even now you can see the dead trees.' Outside, the fragile white skeletons and corrugated iron roofs of lookout towers pierced the canopy. Signs had been erected at intervals along the trackside. 'Fire is the enemy of the forest!' 'Struggle to make Mohe County a place alien to the tragedy of forest fire!'

'Did people die?' I asked. He shrugged.

'Yes. How many, I don't know. At least two hundred. Xilinji was razed to the ground, and all these small working areas. It took weeks to burn itself out.'

*

273

'Months,' corrected the Manchu.

At Xilinji a Lanzhou bus ferried me from the station to the town centre. Xilinji – its name in Chinese means Auspicious Western Woods – lies in a now treeless bowl at the indecisive confluence of half a dozen rivers and streams that coalesce to press on northward to the Amur. It was easy to imagine how a forest fire would have raged through this wide valley. My driver had been in town when the fire reached it. He had gone down to the largest river, the Emu'er, where he had hidden, terrified, until rescued. He had returned to find that his home had been destroyed, as had everything else. It had been *kepa*, frightful. The town had been rebuilt, and though it was now ugly it would at least survive the next fire, he said. He went on to talk about the winter here, referring to temperatures below freezing with the same fluency as I would have used to refer to those above. 'It was twenty degrees only a couple of months ago, but in January it was truly cold – over forty.'

There was only one bus each day to Mohe. It waited as its seats gradually filled up. Just as in Qiqiha'er, a lone foreigner attracted few stares, the Heilongjiangese hereabouts having, and so granting each other, far more personal space than their cousins in eastern China. Bit by bit the gangway filled up with freight: a television wrapped in a horse blanket, two plastic bags of wobbling belly pork, a case of Famous Aged Vinegar from Shanxi province, a box of shoes, a nylon sack of potatoes, one mesh sack of cabbages, one large bag of beancurd dumpling skins, assorted cardboard boxes (contents unknown) tied with twine, and two plastic drums of an unidentified liquid that sloshed on to the floor and through jagged cracks down on to the road.

The cloud came down to meet us as we ascended by alternate lurches and shudders into the Hingan. In the vast timberyards that skirted Xilinji's brick slum sprawl the mist hung in eddies about the wood stacks. Species were piled neatly in great triangular heaps, like a titanic tobacconist's window. Through the drizzle, silver birches with their white bark were his cigarettes, the thick brown trunks of larches and pines enormous Havana cigars, the thinner stems piles of cheroots. Cranes waited to load them on to railway wagons. The sweet smell of wet wood shavings and sawdust rose from the tyre-pounded earth.

The clutch growled its displeasure as the driver urged it across the first watershed, then the pitch changed and it sighed and relaxed as the engine was switched off and the bus freewheeled. When the inertia gained on these downhill runs was insufficient to carry us over the next rise, the engine would be refired for no longer than was absolutely necessary.

The road was unsurfaced, existing only by virtue of the fact that many vehicles had passed that way before. Signs of the fire that had razed Xilinji were everywhere. For miles outside the town the forest had simply disappeared, as if a hurricane had torn each tree off at its stump like so much matchwood and tossed away the trunks. Grasses had colonized the blackened floor, which extended away on either side to the stickleback ridges of hills. In the Hingan's secluded valleys a climax vegetation of spindly saplings surrounded the burnt stumps of dead trees. Through the misty half-light they stood out like frail spectres, tall as a man yet thin as a man's thumb, consorting in a ghoulish séance with the charred remains of their predecessors. I was relieved when the bus heaved over a final rise in the road and into pristine taiga, its trees broad, straight and ancient. After two hours the engine died on the flat and we coasted to a halt before a checkpoint. Three soldiers of the Frontier Defence Bureau emerged from a hut and one of them boarded the bus. Our *shenfenzhengs* and travel permits were checked, their numbers and validity noted down, and one man was led away. The barrier was raised and I entered Mohe.

MOHE

MOHE WAS A small settlement, consisting of little more than a single main street, unpaved, and a few muddy tracks that led down to the Amur. Its houses were mainly wooden, their roofs of thatch or planks and their timbers daubed in mud and straw to caulk the gaps, but it had an Agricultural Bank in brick, a clutch of half-finished hotels for the Chinese tourists who would visit on the longest day when the sun would not set, and a general store that stocked everything one might need, living at the end of a forest track at the northern tip of Manchuria.

The houses each sat in their own plot of earth surrounded by a wooden pale. The gardens were tilled, and the first growth of vegetables had pushed green filaments through the black soil. Piles of firewood lined the alleys between the dwellings, their buff mosaic draped with beaded necklaces, the dew-laden silk of fat spiders. Shallow ditches lined the main street, ankle-deep in wet leaf litter, so that people reached their homes across duck-boards. Dogs followed at my heels, boys played football, the elderly sat on their porches to watch another day fade to dusk. A tangle of electricity lines and telegraph wires wove its way overhead through the shabby crowns of the roadside larches, their lazy sag punctuated by the black commas of swallows. The drizzle had drawn into the air an earthy aroma that merged with the sickly sweet scent of elderflower and hawthorn. Above the forest of makeshift television aerials, through the wisps of smoke that curled from beneath the eaves, the Russian shore rose vertically from the far side of the Amur.

The *zhaodaisuo* smelt of damp rags. I had not yet eaten that day and when the *laoban*, a sunken-cheeked woman in late middle age, offered to prepare a plate of braised aubergine and a bowl of rice, I decided to wait a little longer before walking to the river.

While she cooked in the adjoining room, I threw my rucksack down on the wooden floor of the bedroom and rested on the *kang* – a brick sleeping platform, warmed from within by the heat of the kitchen stove. The bedroom walls were bare save for a curling poster, its whites stained by years of nicotine, its flesh tones bleached out until it was uniformly shades of yellow in which were set four dark pupils, like a row of currants in a bowl of custard. All four pupils belonged to one baby, his chubby face having been reproduced in a close-up mirror image so that in stereo he now appeared to be a pair of male twins – some woman's heart's desire in a village where she might only give birth once.

The *laoban* called out and I rose to sit at the table in the communal hallway. The aubergine was not at its best, it was not yet the season. She apologized on its behalf. It had been finely chopped and then half-fried, half-boiled, a handful of chopped garlic and coriander spread over its oily surface. The rice came in a great steaming mound. She stood across the hall as I ate, her arms folded defensively over a greasy green quilted waistcoat and short pinafore. Her mouth was permanently half-open, her chapped lips drawn back into an elongated snarl to reveal yellowing teeth. One was prominently absent. She watched me as I ate, only allowing her face the luxury of the slightest satisfaction when I assured her the food was good. Then again it might have been a sarcastic smile.

She stretched up to turn on the television perched on a high shelf, and it crackled into a programme on the wildlife of Heilongjiang. Turning back, she tightened her arms around her middle, muttered under her breath and seemed to weigh her words before she spoke.

'Where you come from, your cadres . . . if you want to get something done, do they say you must pay money?' Where I came from we did not have political cadres as they did in China, I told her. Why had she asked? Her lips formed petulantly about her words, as though the very taste of them disgusted her.

'These ones today, all they want is money. They're all corrupt, and if you don't have money to give them they won't do anything for you. They won't give you the right bits of paper you need to get things done. It doesn't matter how much you *koutou*, it's "no cash, no can do". We all *hate* them.' She spat out the word in a venomous whisper. I had never heard a Chinese use the word to refer to another Chinese before and was taken aback. Her eyes had begun to fill with the same tearful, impotent desperation as I had seen in the newspaper vendor on that platform in Hangzhou weeks before.

'Do you know of Mao?' she asked. 'When Mao was alive it was always *wei renmin fuwu* – serve the people. Now the cadres live by *wei renminbi fuwu* – serve the *renminbi*. I'm still owed that money from before the plant closed down, but *he* says he'll only "find" my back pay if I pay him a service fee to look for it. It's not hard to find – it's in his bloody pockets! I *hate* them!' She had passed an invisible line and the hatred poured out. She became more animated, white spittle gathering at the corners of her mouth.

'My brother, he still hasn't received the money he was promised from when his house in Xilinji burned down. It's gone straight into their thieving hands. Teachers are the same. If you don't pay their extra fees – oh, who am I kidding? – *bribes*, then your child doesn't get the grades. It makes me furious, but you don't want a child to end up jobless around here, do you?' She looked out through the half-open door to the men who stood idly on the dirt roadway. 'So you have to pay.'

Her eyes were by now small red slits. She pursed her lips together and looked away, sniffing, pretending to watch the television but visibly seething with frustration. At the far end of the hallway her daughter sat at a second table, toying with a pair of disposable chopsticks and fidgeting nervously. She looked down when I caught her eye.

In the communal bedroom I switched on my shortwave radio

and tried to find an English station, but instead the room was filled with a whining white noise that coalesced into first Mandarin and then Russian. The announcer was a woman, her voice dripping with the throaty lushness of the Slavic tongues. She mentioned the words *Ostrov Hainan* and *shpionski samolyot* – spy plane – several times, but I caught none of the detail. She might have been broadcasting from Ignashino, a few miles distant, or from Moscow on another continent.

I scooped a handful of pebbles from the sluggish, tannin-brown water of the shallows of the Amur. On the Russian bank, one of the newscaster's countrymen stood motionless in the mist. He was angling, his rod and line now and then whipping silently over his head to land his float with a faint plop a short way out. The circles that grew from its orange speck slowed until they lost themselves amongst the rainspots that teased the river's black surface.

To him, this was just another bend in the river, another place to fish for silver carp or dog salmon. On his fishing trips he might have grown used to the barking of the dogs in Mohe and the sound of Radio Beijing being broadcast from loudspeakers hidden in the treetops. Perhaps he recognized his own town in the thatch of its cottages and the smoke that rose vertically from them. If he had grown up surrounded by Soviet slogans he might have guessed at those on Mohe's streets: 'Love our China, love our Mohe!' 'Preventing forest fires is the responsibility of us all!' He must have noticed the old woman who fished with a net cast into the shallows near the Chinese shore. From his side of the Amur, Mohe must have looked so familiar.

Yet the detail of the People's Republic, those comforting constants that had followed me, would have been alien; unvarying from the islands of the East China Sea to the barracks towns of Turkestan; from the Southern Pillar of Heaven to the Manchurian taiga, yet invisible from Russia just a two-minute boat trip away. The fisherman could not have smelt the pork and onion buns steaming over the log stove in the *zhaodaisuo*, their smell the same as on Suzhou's streets the morning I had begun my journey. After three months in China it was strange to think that on that far bank they neither cooked with a *wok* nor ate rice and noodles as their staples. And the written Chinese character, understood from the fishermen's huts on the Zengmu Shoals to the forests of the Hingan, would have as little currency three hundred yards north as it would west of the Urals.

The world beyond the Amur was unaware of the poor woman who, when I returned from the riverbank, dried her eyes with the back of a hand and pretended to her daughter that she had not been crying. I passed her in silence and walked back into the bedroom. There I lay on the *kang* and cast an eye over the room's sparse contents: a poster of male twins; an inverted gold character pasted to the door on its red paper diamond; empty crates of beer stacked in one corner; a battered thermos flask with its cheerful stencilled roses and Double Happiness motif – the grubby, homely emblems of every room, every sleeper carriage I had lain down in for ten thousand miles.

Appendix

Glossary of Terms

Amituofo
: The Amita Buddha. Amituofo taught that nirvana was attainable by faith – not just by meditation as Sakhyamuni, the founder of Buddhism, had preached – and so was available to all

assahlahmu alaykum
: (Uighur) 'peace be with you' (answered with the words *wa'alaykum assahlahmu*, 'and with you, peace')

Avalokitesvara
: see Guanyin

baba
: dad

baijiu
: 'white alcohol', distilled sorghum spirit

Bingtuan
: 'military corps', the abbreviated name of the Shengchan Jianshe Bingtuan, the Production and Construction Corps, a paramilitary organization founded to open up, develop and defend China's distant regions. The Bingtuan remains as an economic and paramilitary force in Xinjiang

binguan
: guesthouse or hotel

bodhisattva
: Buddhist saint who has postponed entry into nirvana so as to help those on earth

bu
: no, not

bu kaifang
: not opened up (for example, a region or city)

caipiao
: 'choose ticket', a lottery

chao mian
: fried noodles (often anglicized to *chow mein*)

danwei
: work unit, the basic level of economic organization in communist China

Daojiao
: Daoism, Daoist

doppa
: (Uighur) round skullcap

doujiang
: soybean milk, normally served sweetened and warm as a breakfast drink

ganzhe
: sugarcane

Guangdonghua
: the Cantonese language

guanxi
: 'connections', a network of social contacts

Guanyin
: '(the one who) hears the sound (of suffering)', the Chinese translation of the Sanskrit name

	Avalokitesvara. Guanyin is a manifestation of the Buddha who offers comfort to man
Han	China's dominant ethnic group
Hanzular	(Uighur) the Han Chinese
hutong	alleyway (especially in the backstreets of Beijing)
I-Ching	*The Canon of Changes*, a mystical divinatory text of the Zhou dynasty, noted for its elucidation of sets of trigrams and hexagrams and their use in prediction
Ingiliz	(Uighur) Englishman
jiangnan	(of) the region south of the Yangtze, especially southern Jiangsu province
jiayu	'armoured fish', the horseshoe crab
kaifang	opened up (for example, a region or city)
kang	hollow, brick-built sleeping platform, warmed by hot air from an attached stove
kapka	(Uighur, from the Russian) flat cap
karez	(Uighur) underground irrigation channel that takes water from the mountains to where it is needed in the fields. Every so often a vertical shaft is dug from which water can be drawn off
kepa	awful, frightful
koutou	'knock the head', to kowtow
laghman	(Uighur) hand-pulled noodles
laobaixing	'old hundred surnames', the masses
laoban	one's superior or boss; the person in charge of a business
laowai	'old foreign', the informal Chinese term for a foreigner
li	a unit of distance, around one-third of an English mile
mafan	trouble, hassle, bother
mantou	steamed bread bun
mingyun	fate
minzu	ethnic nationality
mu	a unit of land area, around one-seventh of an acre
naguoren?	which country are you from?

nan	(Uighur) baked flatbread
PLA	People's Liberation Army
pulo	(Uighur) rice and mutton, eaten with the fingers
Putonghua	'Standard speech', in other words, Mandarin Chinese
qi	'breath', life force
Qingming	'Clear and Bright', one of the solar terms which make up the farming year and also the name given to the Festival of Tomb Sweeping
renkou	'people mouths', population
samsa	(Uighur) savoury pastry filled with minced lamb
shan	mountain (a suffix commonly used in the names of islands)
shenfenzheng	citizen's identity card
suoman	(Uighur) pasta slices, often served with a tomato and mutton sauce
TIRET	Turkish-Islamic Republic of East Turkestan
tongzhi	comrade
Tungan	(a member of) the Hui nationality, a non-Turkic Chinese Muslim
waiguoren	'foreign country person', a foreigner (formal)
wan'an	good evening, goodnight
wangba	'net bar', Internet café
yakshimusis?	(Uighur) how are you?
yang	the positive, male principle in Chinese philosophy
Yesu Jidu	Jesus Christ
yin	the negative, female principle in Chinese philosophy
Yingguo	'Heroic Kingdom', the Chinese phonetic translation of the word England
yinzhang	name-chop
youtiao	'oil stick', a Chinese breakfast staple
zaijian	goodbye
zhacai	pickled mustard greens
zhaodaisuo	hostel (generally permitted to accept only Chinese guests)
zhou	rice porridge

MONEY

The currency of the PRC is officially the *renminbi*, literally 'the people's currency'. Its standard unit is the *yuan*, which is divided into ten *jiao*. Each *jiao* is further divided into ten *fen*, but the near-worthless *fen* is growing increasingly obsolete for everyday transactions outside the most rural of areas. The *yuan* is almost always referred to in spoken Chinese as the *kuai*, while the *jiao* is almost always referred to as the *mao*. One *yuan* was worth around eight English pence at the time of writing.

SPELLING AND PRONUNCIATION

I have used the mainland's pinyin romanization for most Chinese words and place-names, occasionally lapsing into variants if I felt that an alternative spelling would be more familiar or less convoluted. For example, I have used Canton instead of what look to me the uglier, if more correct, Guangzhou (the city) and Guangdong (the province). Similarly, I have used widely recognized forms of certain personal names, preferring for example Chiang Kai-shek to the (pinyin) Jiang Jieshi.

For the purposes of reading to oneself (rather than being actively understood), most letters, and pairs of letters, are pronounced along roughly similar lines to English, with some exceptions.

a	before the single letter n, as the *a* in *dad*; otherwise as the *a* in *father*
ai	as the English pronoun *I*
ao	as the *ow* in *how*
c–	pronounced as the *ts* in *hats*
e	as the *er* in *her*
ei	as the *ay* in *hay*
en	as the *un* in *fun*
i	after the consonants c, z, ch, zh, r, s and sh, the vowel i is 'swallowed', resulting in a kind of *uh!* sound. It is one of

	the harder pronunciations of Mandarin to master. Otherwise, i is pronounced as the *e* in *he*
ian	as the alphabetical pronunciations of the two English letters e and n in succession; similar to the English word *yen*
ie	similar to the *ye* in *yet*
j–	as the *g* in *gin*
o	halfway between the English words *or* and *war*
ong	similar to the *ung* in *sung*
ou	similar to the *oa* in *coat* or the *oe* in *Joe*
q/ch–	there is a small difference between the two, but for the purposes of this book both can be pronounced as the *ch* in *cheese*
u	after the consonants j, q, x and y, pronounced as the German letter ü. Otherwise, as the *u* in *flute*
ü	as the German letter ü
ui	as the *way* in *sway*
x–	a halfway house between the *sh* in *ship* and the *s* in *sip*
yu	as the German letter ü
z–	as the *ds* in *beds*
zh–	similar to an English j but with the tongue curled back into the roof of the mouth

An apostrophe is sometimes used to clarify that two characters are being romanized, if a pinyin spelling might otherwise be interpreted as a single character. For example, Xi'an (the name of a city) is two characters, pronounced 'see Anne', while *xian* (fresh) is a single word, pronounced 'syen'.

It should be noted that the names of many peoples and places in this book – mostly in the provinces of Xinjiang and Heilongjiang – are rendered in languages other than Mandarin, examples being the towns of Kashgar, Turpan and Jagdachi; the Kirghiz, Ewenki and Daur ethnic minorities; and the Kizil, Sungari and Nonni rivers. Such words generally look very unChinese, and it is normally apparent that the above rules do not apply to them.

Appendix

Chronology

The following list of the major Chinese dynasties is simplified for the purposes of this book. For long periods of China's history, more than one dynasty ruled concurrently in different regions, and the dates shown sometimes overlap for this reason.

Western Zhou	1045? BC–771 BC
Eastern Zhou	770 BC–256 BC
Spring and Autumn period	770 BC–476 BC
Warring States period	475 BC–221 BC
Qin	221 BC–206 BC
Western Han	202 BC–AD 23
Eastern Han	AD 25–220
Six Dynasties era	220–589
Sui	581–618
Tang	618–907
Five Dynasties and	
Ten Kingdoms era	902–979
Song	960–1279
Northern Song	960–1127
Southern Song	1127–1279
Liao (Khitan)	916–1125
Jin (Jurchen)	1115–1234
Yuan (Mongol)	1279–1368
Ming	1368–1644
Qing (Manchu)	1644–1911
Republic of China	1912–1949 (thereafter on Taiwan only)
People's Republic of China	1949–present

Acknowledgements

Without the love and support of my mother, my father, my sister Sarah and my girlfriend Becky I would never have had the confidence to pack my bags and set out on my journey, and my notes would never have been written up into a typescript. I am eternally grateful to all of them. Without Chris G. and Annette B. the chapters on eastern China would have been far duller to research; and without Dave I would have spent far fewer mornings in the British Library nursing a hangover. My thanks to them, to all my friends in York, and to Dr Chard *et al.* at the Oriental Institute for filling my head with enough Chinese to see me through it all.